D0083607

Retailing in the European U

As retailing becomes an increasingly important part of economies worldwide, the similarities and differences in retailing from country to country are more evident. *Retailing in the European Union* is a unique and timely study of the different National retail structures across Europe, offering an insightful overview of the internalization of retailing and asking important questions about the effectiveness of different retailing sectors.

With chapters on Denmark, France, Germany, Greece, Italy, Spain and the United Kingdom, this contemporary examination of the structural, economic and legislative differences in retailing across the European Union examines the extent to which Europe's increasingly homogeneous environment applies to retailing. By considering the overall structural and socio-economic variables of country-to-country retailing, this book draws fascinating conclusions on the efficiency and competition of retailing across the European Union.

A major contribution to the field of European retail studies, this is a significant work in comparative legislation that is essential reading for anyone studying retailing at postgraduate or undergraduate level or with an interest in comparative economics.

Stewart Howe is Director of DBA programme, Dundee Business School, University of Abertay Dundee.

Retailing in the European Union
Structures, competition and performance

**Edited by
Stewart Howe**

Routledge
Taylor & Francis Group

LONDON AND NEW YORK

First published 2003
by Routledge
11 New Fetter Lane, London EC4P 4EE

Simultaneously published in the USA and Canada
by Routledge
29 West 35th Street, New York, NY 10001

Routledge is an imprint of the Taylor & Francis Group

Typeset in Times New Roman by
Newgen Imaging Systems (P) Ltd, Chennai, India
Printed and bound in Great Britain by
MPG Books Ltd, Bodmin

British Library Cataloguing in Publication Data
A catalogue record for this book is available from the British Library

Library of Congress Cataloging in Publication Data
Retailing in the European Union/edited by Stewart Howe.
    p. cm.
  Includes bibliographical references
  1. Retail trade – European Union countries. I. Howe, Stewart, 1945–

HF5429.6.E9 R483 2002
381′.1′094–dc21   2002026935

ISBN 0-415-25741-7 (hbk)
ISBN 0-415-25742-5 (pbk)

Contents

Figures

Tables

Contributors

Klaus Barth is professor at the Gerhard Mercator Universität Gesamthochschule, Duisburg, Germany

David Bennison – Department of Retailing and Marketing, The Manchester Metropolitan University, Manchester, United Kingdom

Enrico Colla is Professor at the Centre International de Formation a la Vente et a la Negociation Commerciale (NEGOCIA), Paris, France

Marta Frasquet – Departament de Direcció d'Empreses, Universitat de València, Valencia, Spain

Hanne Gardner – Department of Retailing and Marketing, The Manchester Metropolitan University, Manchester, United Kingdom

Irene Gil – Departament de Direcció d'Empreses, Universitat de València, Valencia, Spain

Michaela Hartmann – Gerhard Mercator Universität Gesamthochschule, Duisburg, Germany

Stewart Howe – The Dundee Business School, University of Abertay Dundee, Dundee Scotland

Alejandro Mollá – Departament de Direcció d'Empreses, Universitat de València, Valencia, Spain

Luca Zanderighi is professor at the Dipartimento di Economia Politica E Aziendale, University of Milan, Milan, Italy

Acknowledgements

My greatest debt as the coordinating author of this study is to my fellow contributors of the individual-country chapters. These are collaborators who, with the exception of Dr Bennison and Ms Gardner based at Manchester Metropolitan University in the United Kingdom, I have not met other than through correspondence of one form or another. In a number of cases their invitation to become involved in this work was the result of a second-hand recommendation to me, and thus on the part of potential collaborators I was initially at least very much an unknown quantity.

These fellow authors, details of whom appear elsewhere in the publication, have, however, borne with myself and the publisher over a fairly lengthy period of time in bringing this study together. In particular, the writing of the chapters, albeit within a common template provided by me, has involved a number of repeated drafts of the material; and in this process, the individual-country authors have both stoically and cooperatively responded to my requests for more information, further analysis and recasting of their ideas in more elegant English. This last requirement has to be taken in the context of the fact that for the most part the individual-country chapters have been contributed by members of the particular economies and for whom English is not their native language, although one of the contributors appears to write academic articles in three languages. I am particularly grateful in this respect for the patience of these fellow authors in their correspondence with a typically monolingual Briton.

Although I have not had the opportunity to benefit from a reading of my own UK material by any colleagues, nor for collaborating authors to consider the content of the final chapter, the publisher arranged for a number of the individual chapters to be read by an anonymous assessor. This person provided me with quite detailed and very constructive feedback, and this contribution is much appreciated by me and should not go unacknowledged. I am also grateful to a number of Dundee Business School colleagues for their assistance in processing some of my own material.

Finally, I should also mention the patience and support of the various personnel at the publishers Routledge with whom I have been in contact, and I acknowledge this contribution to the appearance of the study. It is only as a reflection of my age and stage in my career that I confirm that, after a number of such endeavours, this is the last book that I shall be involved in writing!

Stewart Howe
Dundee Business School
University of Abertay Dundee
Dundee
April 2002

Introduction

Background

Retailing is a significant part of the total economic activity of developed economies, with wholesaling and retailing value-added accounting together for around 13 per cent of the gross domestic product (GDP) of the European Union (Commission of the European Communities, 1993).

Moreover, retailing is of concern both to governments and consumers not only because of the proportion of GDP for which it accounts in developed economies but also because of the size and market power of individual retailers and the evidence that suggests that retail markets do not necessarily work in a 'perfectly competitive' manner. With regard to their absolute size, for example, Belgium's largest business in terms of sales revenue is the retailer Delhaize 'Le Lion'; in the United Kingdom Tesco and Sainsbury, who are respectively the market leader and the second company in the grocery supermarket sector, are among the top ten companies in the economy, and their counterpart in Germany, Metro group, is also among the largest firms in that economy (see data in Dobson and Waterson, 1999). Not only are retailing organizations large businesses within their own economies, but they also enjoy considerable market power in terms of familiar concentration ratios. In the mid-1990s, the top five grocery retailers in a range of EU economies enjoyed market shares which, while they were only 25 per cent in Spain, rose to double that proportion in Belgium and France, and to 61 and 64 per cent in the Netherlands and the United Kingdom, respectively. This situation is the outcome of a significant trend that is evident across the whole of the European Union. In the United Kingdom, supermarkets increased their market share of fast-moving consumer goods (FMCG) from 20 per cent in 1960 to 85 per cent in 1997, and across the European Union there have been significant reductions in the number of grocery retail outlets. In northern Europe, the typical porportionate reduction over the 1960s to 1990s was 70 per cent, while rather smaller proportionate reductions, albeit over a shorter period up to the early 1990s, were experienced in Portugal and Italy.

Finally, in terms of these indices of retailing and retailer importance and causes for interest or concern, there is evidence of quite significant differences in prices and profitability among retailers within the European Union. Of particular concern to UK consumers, there are, for example, data which show that, taking the cost of a representative basket of groceries in the United Kingdom as a base, the comparative indices in France, Germany, Belgium and the Netherlands were 74, 65, 62 and 61 respectively, showing that shoppers in the United Kingdom were paying more than half as much again for such items as consumers in the last three EU countries. International comparative data, although not without their flaws, show that UK retailer profitability is clearly above that of other EU competitors – highlighted in the case of grocery supermarkets by Corstjens *et al.* (1995). And Dobson *et al.* (1998: 42) associate UK trends in this respect with the rise in retailer market concentration over the decade to 1994, when five-firm sales concentration ratios rose from 15.6 to 23.4 per cent for All Retailers and from 28.2 to 43.5 percent (to 1992) for Food Retailers, accompanied by increases in net profit margins from 5.77 to 7.79 per cent and from 4.07 to 6.22 per cent respectively.

Thus, in terms of their national size, market dominance and competitive behaviour and performance, retail organizations and the various retail markets are a significant part of individual domestic economies, and in this context alone can benefit from a study offering international comparisons.

The internationalization of retailing

In addition to its significance in a number of domestic contexts, retailing is, moreover, a surprisingly international activity when all dimensions of this are recognized. This 'internationality' can be seen at three levels. First, there is the internationalization of retailing as a business strategy, comprising retailer management decisions on exporting, direct investment abroad, participation in international alliances and merchandise imports. However, although this is a growing activity, international sales even by leading European retailers typically account for only some 25 per cent of their total, and this 'is still the minority activity for the majority of retailers' (McGoldrick and Davies, 1995: 1–3). Thus, despite what some writers have described as the 'globalization' of retailing (Alexander, 1997: chapter 5), most retailing in terms of firms' activities is still essentially domestic in its nature; and with reference to the United Kingdom as a particular example, Burt summarized in the early 1990s that 'The vast majority of British retailers have made few incursions into foreign markets' (Burt, 1993: 408).

A second strand in the literature regarding the 'internationality' of retailing is concerned with the internationalization of retailing phenomena. Kaynak (1988) provides an example of this, with his emphasis upon larger scale common trends in retailing, such as the increase in the popularity of convenience stores, and the passing on of such trends from developed to less-developed economies. With particular regard to retailing in Europe, Sternquist and Kacker (1994) consider that retailing has become 'commoditised' as a result of increasingly homogeneous standards of living and parallel consumer profiles; internationalization of retailing formats, often as a result of the corporate strategies of their owners such as IKEA, Benetton and Body Shop, or retail concepts such as 'sheds' or 'category killers'; and common retail technologies such as e-commerce or e-tailing. In this scenario, 'Retailing ideas have flown from one country to another' (Sternquist and Kacker, 1994: 2), and the focus in this literature is upon what is common or tending to become common among countries, with retail organizations themselves playing a role in spreading new retailing formulae across a world that exhibits relatively few barriers to the importing of these.

By contrast, this study, in contributing to a third international dimension of retailing, focuses very largely upon what is particular to the separate economies: what is different among them with respect to retail structures, behaviour, government legislation etc. In particular, it seeks to answer questions regarding the efficiency of retailing by reference to individual-country differences in, for example, government legislation in this field.

A concern with efficiency

One of the principal emphases in this study is the 'efficiency' of retailing in each of the economies covered: how well served consumers are in terms of their 'welfare', and how this is contributed to by competition in retail markets themselves, the relationships between retailers and their suppliers, and the role of governments in influencing retailer competition and efficiency through competition policy, spacial or land-use planning legislation etc. A broad basic premise is that it is through the operation of the market forces of supply and demand that retail consumers are satisfied in the most 'efficient' manner – that is, at the lowest resource cost. Thus the question we want to be able to ask of any economic system, or part of a system such as retailing, is 'are goods being supplied to consumers in the economy at the lowest possible resource cost consistent with the quality of service that shoppers want?' The matter of 'what consumers want' is, however, an unclear one in a number of respects. Not least are the issues which it raises for the measurement of retail productivity, where a small number of transactions per retail employee may reflect shoppers' desire for a high level of customer service rather than the inefficient use of labour in retailing (Howe, 1992: chapter 3). This also raises particular difficulties in the use and interpretation of retailer sales-margin profitability as a measure of retailer efficiency and market performance (Howe, 1998), and this issue is returned to in the final chapter of this study.

As a particular approach to these issues, in the case of each of the economies covered in this study, the focus is largely upon the structure of retailing and changes in this over the past ten to fifteen years in particular. This is linked to the initial structure of retail markets themselves, to manufacturer–retailer relations and to retailing-related legislation on competition policy and retail location planning, for example, in order to provide some evidence on the 'performance' of the retail sector. These are common themes in each of the individual-economy chapters, and although the text is not founded upon a statistically based 'structure, conduct and performance' model used by industrial organization economists (Bain, 1968), it is informed by such an underlying set of ideas, or more loosely upon a 'five forces framework' used in the analysis of corporate strategy (Porter, 1985). That is, the 'outcome' or performance of the retail sector is dependent upon pre-existing retailer structures and manufacturer–retailer relations together with retail location and other legislation, and 'performance' will include some idea of consumer satisfaction, profit performance, retailer product development etc. as well as changes in the structures of the retail sector and retailer–manufacturer relations.

Individual economies and governments

One particular theme across this study as a whole is the ability of governments to influence the performance of retail markets, and the contrasting national environments that they have created in this respect. Thus, a major distinction between two economies may well be their respective retail legislative environments. As Wrigley points out, disparities between, in the case of his research, the British and US grocery retailing sectors in the 1980s, in terms of market concentration, the use of market power, the geographical structure of retailing, and sales margins and returns on investment 'owe a considerable amount to the differential nature of the regulatory environments in which the industries operated' (Wrigley, 1992: 727). Quite specifically, a study undertaken for the UK Treasury by McKinsey, the leading management consultants, concluded that competition and productivity among UK grocery retailers was being hampered by planning consent regulations and that this was having an adverse impact upon consumers (*Sunday Times*, 10 January 1999). This text should create particular opportunities for examining Wrigley's hypothesis, given the contrasting policies among a number of countries covered. As Davies (1995: xvii) highlighted in respect of retail planning in the previous decade, while Belgium and West Germany 'strengthened their planning policies and returned to a restrictive stance', one of 'The most dramatic features of the 1980s … [was] the virtual abandonment of any retail planning in the UK'.

European retailing

A study of Europe, within the chosen concept of retail internationalization, makes sense in a number of ways. First of all, the various economies of the European Union are relatively homogeneous in terms of their state of economic development, while nonetheless providing opportunities for comparison between northern and Mediterranean histories and cultures, and among larger and smaller economies. Second, there is in certain areas a common background and influence regarding important environmental variables. Competition policy is one such area where there has been 'a remarkable convergence' of policy stemming from the importing of a basic philosophy from the United States into the German 1957 Act Against Restraints of Competition and the influence of this national legislation on the European Economic Community (EEC) treaty of the same year (see Neumann, 2001: 30). Such legislation has, of course, a contemporary significance as exemplified in the European Court of Justice November 2001 ruling in the matter of 'grey market' imports of Levi Strauss clothing by the UK Tesco and others. This ruling upheld the Trademark Directive and thus prevented Tesco and other such retailers from obtaining supplies of superior branded clothing from outwith the European Union and selling these garments at discounts of up to 40 per cent below the recommended price (see *Financial Times*, 21 November 2001). Third, although it is not a central theme of this study, senior management of larger retail groups in particular clearly see themselves as operating on a European stage, capitalizing perhaps on the relatively homogeneous competitive and regulatory environment. One recent example of this is the home-improvements market, with current (2001) annual sales of €107.8 billion and an annual growth rate of some 8 per cent, where the recently concluded Anglo-German alliance of B & Q (Kingfisher) and Hornbach creates 'a home-improvement network that stretches from B & Q in the United Kingdom, throughInsee [Kingfisher subsidiary] Castorama in France to Hornbach's interests and a sprinkling of eastern European assets owned by both groups' (*Financial Times*, 30 November 2001).

Structure of the book

The structure of this study, following this Introduction, is to provide material and analysis relating to retailing structures, competition and performance within each of seven EU economies: Denmark, France, Germany, Greece, Italy, Spain and the United Kingdom. The choice of these individual economies ensures not only a significant coverage of the whole of the European Union but also representation both of northerly and Mediterranean countries and both larger and smaller economies. The material in Chapters 1–7 focuses upon circumstances unique to the individual countries, but within a structure that facilitates the drawing out of comparisons and common themes. Thus, each of the individual-country chapters commences with a historical background to the present-day retailing economy, and this is followed by a more detailed examination of contemporary structures etc. In each chapter this is in turn followed by an analysis of particular retailing issues in the individual economy, and, in a separate section, by a consideration of the particular legislation in that economy relating to retailing. Finally, each individual-country chapter offers conclusions on the current state of retailing development and competition, and the imapct of government legislation in areas such as competition policy and land-use planning.

Finally, with regard to the study as a whole, in Chapter 8 an attempt is made to take a synoptic view of the individual-country studies, to identify common themes and contrasts, and to draw EU-wide lessons for those concerned with retail analysis, comparative international market performance, government policy and consumer welfare.

References

Alexander, N. (1997) *International Retailing*, Blackwell, Oxford.
Bain, J. S. (1968) *Industrial Organization*, Wiley, New York.
Burt, S. (1993) 'Temporal trends in the internationalization of British retailing', *International Review of Retail, Distribution and Consumer Research*, 3(4): 391–410.

Commission of the European Communities (1993) *Retailing in the European Single Market 1993*, Eurostat, Brussels.

Corstjens, J. *et al.* (1995) 'Retail competition in the fast-moving consumer goods industry: The case of France and the UK', *European Management Journal*, 13(4): 363–73.

Davies, R. L. (ed.) (1995) *Retail Planning Policies in Western Europe*, Routledge, London.

Dobson, P. *et al.* (1998) 'The welfare consequences of the exercise of buyer power', *Office of Fair Trading*, Research Paper 16.

Dobson, P. and Waterson, M. (1999) 'Retailer power: recent developments and policy implications', *Economic Policy: A European Forum*, 28: 135–64.

Howe, W. S. (1992) *Retailing Management*, Macmillan, London.

Howe, W. S. (1998) 'Conceptual, interpretative and practical issues in the use of retailer sales margin profitability data', in Neely, A. D. and Waggoner, D. B. (eds) *Performance Measurement – Theory and Practice*, The Judge Institute of Management Studies, Cambridge, pp. 483–90.

Kaynak, E. (ed.) (1988) *Transnational Retailing*, de Gruyter, New York.

McGoldrick, P. J. and Davies, G. (eds) (1995) *International Retailing: Trends and Strategies*, Pitman, London.

Neumann, M. (2001) *Competition Policy: History, Theory and Practice*, Edward Elgar, Cheltenham, UK.

Porter, M. E. (1985) *Competitive Advantage*, Free Press, New York.

Sternquist, B. and Kacker, M. (1994) *European Retailing's Vanishing Borders*, Quorum Books, Westport CT, USA.

Wrigley, N. (1992) 'Antitrust regulation and the restructuring of grocery retailing in Britain and the USA', *Environment and Planning A*, 24: 727–49.

1 Denmark

Hanne Gardner

There is something of Legoland about the Danish retail scene – small-scale but fits together and works well.

European Retailing 2000, Denmark, 2000

Introduction and background

Denmark is a small country with a population of 5.3 million covering 44,000 sq. km. The average population density is therefore 124 (Danmarks Statistik [hereinafter DS], 1999: 134). Over 20 per cent of the population lives in Copenhagen, and when taking the surrounding area into consideration, this increases to one-third of the population. This high concentration of population has had a significant effect on retailing in Denmark. The country consists of a peninsular and two major islands as well as a large number of smaller islands. Denmark is surrounded by seas apart from one land-fast border with Germany, which has changed location several times following wars. The shape and configuration of the islands have had a major influence on the way in which retailing has developed over time because of the impact on the transport and distribution of goods.

It was only during the last couple of years that the two main islands (Sjaeland and Fyn) have been connected by a combination of a bridge and dyke. Before then, the 1 h needed for ferry crossing made many from Fyn think twice about visiting Copenhagen by car, because of the time involved and the inevitable constraints and possible delays which a ferry places on travellers. Now it is much quicker and more convenient for car passengers, albeit more expensive. The second, recent major engineering achievement was the connecting of Denmark to southern Sweden by a tunnel-bridge between Copenhagen and Malmo. These two major bridge developments will have a significant impact on the whole way of life in Denmark, not only in terms of transport and shopping for the Danish population, but also in terms of the way tourists will travel and shop in Denmark. For example, the Swedes are much more likely to shop in Denmark for food and alcohol, in particular, as there are not the same restrictions on the sale of alcohol in Denmark as there are in Sweden, and prices in Denmark are generally much lower.

According to the OECD, Denmark has one of the highest standards of living in Europe. Among the population, the over sixties account for 20 per cent, and the under twenties account for almost a quarter of the population. The majority of these two age bands do not have paid employment, but because of the extensive and generous welfare system in place, they will increase the burden on the working population and this will no doubt have an impact on the structure and shape of retailing in Denmark. Life expectancy is 74 years for a man and 79 for a woman (DS, 1999: 37). The retirement age in Denmark is 67 years. However, a significant proportion of the over sixty-year-olds have been able to take early retirement under the relevant legislation (*efterlon og fortidspension*), and, if qualifying, will be provided with a proportion of their salary by the government until they reach normal retirement age. Those who retire will have more time to shop, and many will see shopping as a leisure activity. As a result, these consumers will not only become more experimental but also more demanding. The number of people living alone is well over one-third of the population, and a further one-third is accounted for by households of two people, many of whom are one parent and one child. Such household sizes and composition will have a significant impact upon, for example, not only the pattern of grocery sales but also features such as the sizes of packs of grocery products.

Car ownership in Denmark in the early 1990s was 305 per 1,000 inhabitants compared with 435 in the United Kingdom. In 2000, 43.1 per cent of households had one car and of these 9.7 per cent had two cars or more (DS, 2000: 376). Conversely, 47.2 per cent of Danish households did not have access to a car. This fact clearly has far reaching implications for retailing. Public transport is well organized and used by a high proportion of the population particularly in and around Copenhagen. This, combined with the excellent provision of bicycle paths, allows a relatively high proportion of the population to shop without the use of a car, but restricts the volume of shopping bought during any shopping trip.

Danish personal taxation is one of the highest in Europe. However, it is often misleading to look just at the percentage of direct tax as the items such as house mortgage payments qualifying for tax relief vary from country to country. Nonetheless, almost every Danish taxpayer pays tax at over 50 per cent. However, health care, education and public transport, as well as welfare benefits, all reflect high levels of public spending derived from this high level of taxation. MOMS, the Danish value added tax (VAT), is currently charged at 25 per cent on almost all goods and services, including food. This not only adds significantly to the consumer's shopping bill but also helps to provide much needed revenue to help fund the extensive welfare provisions in Denmark.

The Danes had a referendum on joining the Euro in 2000. This was rejected, albeit by a small majority.

Culture

National shopping patterns and trends, including the development of retail store formats, are determined not only by more obvious economic constraints upon shoppers but also by differences in national culture – factors often overlooked by retailers seeking to expand internationally.

The availability of ready-prepared meals in the United Kingdom, for example, has accelerated the growth of the multiple retailers' food sales. By contrast, in many other European countries, there is a long tradition of cooking and eating together at home, although it presupposes that time is available for such activities. This is, however, no longer always the case, particularly with the increasing number of women in full-time employment. Nonetheless, culture, eating habits and patterns determine to a quite significant extent the way in which customers shop, with France being a particular example.

The proportion of women in full-time employment in Denmark is one of the highest in the European Union. Childcare is plentiful and the cost is assessed based on income: an important feature, particularly if childcare is required for more than one child. Schools start at 8 o'clock in the morning and generally finish before or at 2 o'clock with only a very short break (20 minutes) for lunch (usually a packed one provided from home). After-school care is thus vital for all working parents and this is readily available, although often at a considerable price. This is another example of variables that will determine patterns of shopping, including location, and income available for higher value added merchandise.

Danish retailing in the first half of the twentieth century

At the turn of the last century, Denmark was very much an agricultural country, with a high proportion of the population engaged in working directly in farming in the area of dairy products or meat. In 1906, for example, 42.2 per cent of the population was employed in agriculture (Bryle *et al.*, 1991: 157). The strength of the Danish Co-operative Movement (*Faellesforeningen for Danmarks Brugsforeninger* or FDB) dates back to the nineteenth century. FDB was founded in 1896 through an amalgamation between two *Faellesforeninger* – one covering *Sjaelland* and the other covering *Jylland*. The purpose of FDB was to procure goods on behalf of the Co-operative Retail Societies at the most competitive prices. FDB started off by purchasing goods from wholesalers and manufacturers, but it became clear very quickly that in order to get the best products at the most advantageous prices the way forward for FDB was to acquire or set up factories which could supply the individual cooperative shops owned by the Co-operative Retail Societies. The first such venture was a coffee roasting plant, established in 1897.

The first half of the twentieth century was dominated by the two World Wars. Denmark was neutral in the First World War, but the event nonetheless had a marked influence on the country. In 1920, a plebiscite was held to determine how much of northern Germany should be returned to Denmark. Before the 1864 Prussian war, the Danish border with Germany had been south of Kiel. However, as a result of this war, Denmark lost Slesvig, Holsten and Lauenburg, and as part of the settlement, post-1864 the Danish border moved to just south of

Ribe. Following the First World War, and based on the 1920 plebiscite, the new Danish/German border was drawn just north of Flensburg (Ilsoe, 1960).

Retailing in the inter-war years was dominated by the small, independent retailers and cooperatives, and the only large retail outlets were the department stores. The 1930s were characterized in Denmark by falling prices for agricultural products, and as a result workers in those occupations lost their jobs. This in turn affected consumption and led to mass unemployment. In 1933, social reform became the foundation of the Danish welfare state as we know it today.

At the outbreak of the Second World War, Denmark again declared itself neutral, but on 9 April 1940 the country was invaded by German forces. This occupation lasted until 5 May 1945 when Denmark was liberated by allied forces. During the war years the Danish population was subject to rationing. Although food was plentiful, the occupying German forces commandeered what was available, causing great resentment among the Danish population. After the war, rationing continued for some time, and the retail trade also had price competition restrictions imposed upon it until the mid-1950s (Lov 102, 31 March 1955; *Tilsyn med monopoler og konkurrence begraensning*, p. 107, in Betaenkning, No. 1353, 1998). After this period, price competition started to become the dominant feature of Danish retailing. This is particularly relevant, because it also links into the establishing of multiple-shop organizations. The basis on which these operate in terms of central control and buying is to secure better prices for larger quantities of goods ordered. Retailer buying strength until this time had been a feature only of FDB in its exclusive role of procurer and manufacturer to the Co-operative Movement. This, combined with the dividend paid to members, was the reason for the very high market share of the cooperative shops. In effect, the dividend served as a way of reducing manufacturers' set prices – something about which manufacturers could do nothing.

In 1947 there were 53,042 shops in Denmark, having a total turnover of DKr 6,362,472 and employing 142,613 people. By 1957, the number of shops had increased by slightly more than 14 per cent to 60,653, turnover had risen to DKr 13,725,134 and employment had increased by one-third to 190,866 people. By far the most important proportion of retailing was made up of grocery shops, accounting for almost 59 per cent in 1947 and 54 per cent in 1957 (Fog and Rasmussen, 1965: 44).

Department stores, which can be compared more easily with other countries, give a further impression of the change in retail provision in Denmark. In 1947 there were only six, accounting for a turnover of DKr 206,785 and employing 3,418 people. By 1957, the number had risen to 11, with a turnover of DKr 421,436 and employing more than twice the number of people at 6,864.

With regard to the grocery trade, in 1947 there were 14,761 shops, and by 1957 this number had increased to 15,710 (Fog and Rasmussen, 1965: 63). Over this decade there was relatively little change in market concentration. For example, while in 1947 the smallest 25 per cent of grocery stores accounted for 7 per cent of turnover, by 1957 this had only reduced to 6 per cent of turnover. However, the top 10 per cent of shops in 1947 accounted for 30 per cent of turnover, and by 1957 this had increased to 38 per cent of turnover. Perhaps more significantly, the top 25 per cent of shops, which in 1947 accounted for 48 per cent of turnover, had seen this increase by 1957 to 60 per cent (Fog and Rasmussen, 1965: 64).

The development of Danish retailing in the second half of the twentieth century has been summed up as 'increased consumption, greater distances to be travelled to shop, and decreasing customer loyalty'. It has been estimated that consumption of groceries increased by 35–40 per cent since 1960 (Betaenkning, No. 1353, 1998: 107).

The impact of legislation on Danish retailing

In Denmark, as elsewhere in the European Union, national legislation has had a profound effect on market structure and competition in the retail sector, and this section considers the range of this legislation as it affects retail organization size, shop opening hours, the impact of land-use planning legislation, and restrictions on retailer promotional activity.

Retail organization size – *Naeringsloven*

Unusually, in Denmark this legislation has had a direct effect on the outlet-number size of retail organizations. The most significant legislation was *Naeringsloven*, which is the law that governs how and where retail businesses are allowed to operate. In effect this law creates the requirement for a licence to trade, and from 1931 *Naeringsloven* (para. 26, stk. 2) stated that a retail organization could have only one shop in each Kommune or municipality, when at that time there were 1,200 such municipalities. However, the law did not apply to Co-operatives as long as they traded only with their members. A second exception to the law was that, provided a factory's products were sold in shops owned by the same company, then not only could the outlets of such multiple-shop organizations sell those products but also similar goods. 'Irma', now owned by FDB, bought a dairy to enable the company to develop a number of shops, thus overcoming the restriction imposed upon most other organisations by *Naeringsloven* regarding multiple-shop ownership.

The new *Naringslov* came into force in 1966. This new law had a significant impact on retail structures in Denmark because it allowed multiple-shop retailers to operate without the earlier constraints. For example, Dansk Supermarked had been created earlier in anticipation of this change, and the particular impact of this legislation upon Dansk Supermarked is dealt with below under that organization. Thus, Denmark experienced from an early date legislation that prevented the development of multiple-shop retailers, unless that retailer also had a manufacturing unit or sold exclusively to members only. This operated to the unique advantage of retailers such as vertically integrated Co-operative Societies. Irma, a dairy/grocer very similar to the early years of J. Sainsbury in the United Kingdom, and now owned by FDB, is an example of a successful multiple. The *Naeringsloven* law allowed Irma to develop multiple-shops because of its dairy activities. This law had successfully prevented the rapid development of multiple retailers in Denmark and also explains why the Co-operative became, and still remains, Denmark's most dominant retailer. As indicated above, it was only when this law was changed in 1966 that the way was paved for other multiple-shop retailing organizations to develop in Denmark.

Lukkeloven – the law governing shop opening hours

The law governing opening hours in Denmark has been very conservative, with strong similarities to the German law in this area (Gov No. 1260, 20 December 2000). The old *Lukkelov* (No. 289, 1 July 1922) was modified in 1932, 1946, 1950 and 1987, reflecting changes in society over that period. Some of the most significant recent changes occurred in 1994, when it became possible for shops to remain open until 20:00 h during the week and until 14:00 h on Saturday, with the provision that on two Saturdays a month, shops could remain open until 17:00 h. Prior to this change, shops had to stop trading after 18:00 h. Monday–Thursday and 20:00 h on Fridays, and no trading was permitted after lunchtime on Saturday until Monday morning. The exception was bakers' shops, which were permitted to trade on Sundays, and special regulations also apply to small shops, convenience stores, petrol stations and kiosks, allowing such outlets to remain open for longer hours (Betaenkning, 1987: 17). One interesting feature of this law is that it is the police that are responsible for its enforcement, and any-one can telephone the police and report a shop breaking the law (Betaenkning, No. 1353, 1998: 130).

To a large extent the situation in Denmark with regard to shop opening hours was a legacy of the important influence of the trade unions and the church on the way in which retailers could operate. As Danish society changed and as more women began to work in paid, full-time employment, these shopping arrange-ments became impractical. Moreover, the development of hypermarkets and superstores forced a review of this legislation. Gradually large stores were open-ing longer hours, and breaking the law. As the law was amended, trading also first became permitted during every first Saturday afternoon in every month (*lang Lorday*). Most of the hypermarkets now trade late every weekday and until 17:00 h on a Saturday but not on a Sunday.

New legislation, revolutionary for Denmark, has amended the law from 1 July 2001 to allow retailers to be open four Sundays per year, although the Sundays cannot be on religious days such as Easter Sunday, Christmas Eve or Constitution day (5 June). From 2003, the number of Sundays will double to eight, although four must be in either July or August. Restrictions will, however, continue to exist which will limit the types of stores that are eligible to trade.

Land-use planning legislation

The local councils (*kommuner*) have to a large extent been able to control retail expansion over the years. From 1 January 1992 new laws governing planning were introduced (Lov No. 388, 6 June 1991, published by Miljoministeriet, j. nr.

D 3100-0009). These laws seek not only to safeguard the environment, but also to preserve historic and valuable buildings, thus being intended to create suitable environments in the towns and cities and countryside. Moreover, they seek to involve the public in the planning work as far as possible. The planning provisions apply on a regional as well as a local council level, allowing an overview to guard against developments not considered to be in the public interest. The new large stores and shopping centres have sought locations at major roads to maximize access for customers. This trend has been significant since the late 1980s (Betaenkning, No. 1353, 1998: 9). The Planning Law (Lov No. 388, 6 June 1991) was changed in 1997 in an attempt to permit developments which retailers might otherwise seek to pursue. However, the law seeks 'to strengthen town centres as vibrant and varied trade centres' (Betaenkning, No. 1353, 1998: 128)

It has been suggested that the ideal target customer base for potential development of large-scale retailing has been 25 towns, with a population of 30,000 inhabitants each (Betaenkning, No. 1353, 1998: 10). However, planning legislation has sought to contain such developments because of the impact this could have not only in town and city centres but also on neighbourhood shops. The legislation thus seeks to safeguard the '*svage forbruger*' (the weak consumer), defined as those who do not have a car and are more than 2–3 km from the nearest neighbourhood shops. For example, it is estimated that 2–3 per cent of the Danish population is without access to a car and lives at least 2 km from the nearest shopping area or *butikskoncentration* (Betaenkning, No. 1353, 1998: 10).

Promotional activities and Markedsforingloven

The Danish laws governing retail promotions – *Markedsforingsloven* – make price the natural focus of retail competition, and over time customers have become 'deal prone'. Price rather than store image becomes one of the overriding factors that determine consumer choice of shopping venues in Denmark. The perception of store image and what is seen as a well-presented store varies greatly from country to country. In the United Kingdom, hanging banners in yellow and black or red has often been said to cheapen the image of a store, whereas in Denmark hanging banners, including Danish flags, appears to be the norm and part of the most popular stores' visual promotional material. Shopping around for special offers has always been significant in Denmark, and evidence for this is provided by the sheer volume of free promotional material distributed by retailers to all Danish households each week giving details of retailer price cuts. The reason for this is that most of the 'below-the-line' activities such as money-off coupons and free samples, so widely used in the United Kingdom, are not permitted or are so closely controlled by law in Denmark as to render them ineffective. For example, *Markedsforingsloven* bans competitions with prizes, although competitions which require no purchase are permitted. Distribution of 'money-off' coupons (*rebatmaerker*) prior to a purchase is banned, but such reductions are allowed after a sale is completed provided that the amount is stated. Furthermore, a retailer cannot refuse to sell as many items of a product as a customer wants, so that in the context of special offers etc. a restriction of 'only two items per customer' is not permitted (see Betaenkning, No. 1353, 1998: 133).

Retailing structure and forms

Aggregated market structures

Table 1.1 gives a contemporary overview of the general size structure of Danish grocery retailing and changes in this during the last quarter of the twentieth century, and the data in Table 1.2 provide a picture of the situation over the last decade of that century.

The data in Table 1.1 show that, despite early restrictions on the development of multiple-shop operations outwith the cooperative retailers, the share of the latter remained constant over this time while that of the multiples expanded by almost one half. There was some noticeable movement in market shares between

Table 1.1 Number of shops and turnover by grocery retailers

	1975		1984	
	No. of shops	Turnover (%)	No. of shops	Turnover (%)
Co-operatives	1,796	31	1,409	31
Multiples	281	20	482	27
Wholesale chains	2,842	26	1,817	18
Buying associations	1,899	15	1,833	21
Independent grocers	1,347	3	365	1
Other	1,009	5	749	2
Total	9,156	100	6,655	100

Source: B. Fog and J. Vesterholt (1986) quoted in 'Handel med dagligvarer – og communal planaegning' (1986: 163) in Betaenkning, No. 1125 *Aabningstier, butikker, servicesektoren og den offentlige administration*, December 1987, Copenhagen.

Table 1.2 Grocery shops and turnover in 1988 and 1998

	1988	1998
Number of shops	5,702	3,593
Turnover (in DKr millions)		
Under 5	3,472	1,064
5–9	1,145	1,031
10–49	920	1,226
50–100	127	178
over 100	38	94

Source: Ehlers, S. (1999) *Dansk Dagligvarehandel 10 aarsstatistik 1988–1999*, Stockmann-Gruppen A/S, Lyngby, p. 10.

wholesale chains and buying associations. Taken together, the market share of these fell only slightly, from 41 per cent in 1975 to 39 per cent in 1984, but the former lost almost one-third of its market share, while the latter gained 40 per cent. The combined market share of the remaining categories of non-affiliated Independent Grocers and Others declined from 8 to 3 per cent.

It has been estimated that multiples accounted for three-quarters of the total Danish retail trade, which in 1996 was estimated to be worth DKr 204 billion, excluding MOMS (Betaenkning, No. 1353, 1998: 10). There has been a significant reduction in shop numbers in the grocery sector while other retail outlets have seen a less steep decline (Betaenkning, No. 1353, 1998: 8). Large stores and strong multiples have been progressing at the cost of the small independent stores including the small independent Co-operative shops (those not owned by FDB).

Examining the data in Table 1.2, it is clear, even allowing for the effect of inflation on the size category of shops, that there has been a considerable reduction in the smallest of these. The number of these smallest shops fell from almost 3,500 in 1988 to 1,064 in 1998, while the numbers in the largest size category rose by almost two and a half times over the period. The reduction in numbers of the smallest shops has implications for the granting of planning permission in the future and could have serious implications for small rural communities in particular, which may be left without any retail provision.

The picture is even clearer if one examines the number of shops by operator, and data on these are set out in Table 1.3 comparing the years 1988 and 1998.

The data in Table 1.3 show even more clearly the extent of increased grocery retail market concentration. This is particularly so in the case of Dansk Supermarked (DSM) where shop numbers rose two and a half fold over the period 1988–1998 and market share increased from 12.8 to 22.3 per cent. By contrast, the Co-operative Movement stood still in terms of market share over this period. However, although its market share remained almost constant at 38 per cent, its shop numbers fell by more than one-quarter, implying a significant increase in operational efficiency. The German Aldi, which entered Denmark in 1977, expanded very considerably over the decade – almost doubling its shop numbers, and seeing its market share increase from 3.1 to 4 per cent. On the other hand,

Table 1.3 Number of grocery shops and turnover by key retailers

	1988		1998	
	No. of shops	*Turnover (DKr billion)*	*No. of shops*	*Turnover (DKr billion)*
Co-operatives	1,557	22.037	1,156	27.380
DSM	130	7.515	324	15.958
Aldi	95	1.845	186	2.993
Grocers	3,920	27.325	1,927	25.180
Total	5,702	58.723	3,593	71.509

Source: Ehlers, S. (1999) *Dansk Daglivarehandel 10 aarsstatistik 1988–1999*, Stockmann-Gruppen A/S, p. 66.

the independent grocers saw shop numbers decline considerably and also experienced an absolute fall in total turnover, taking their market share from 46.5 per cent in 1988 to 35.2 per cent a decade later. When examining the figures for FDB and DSM, it is useful to look at the different retail formats operated by the two major retailers. As far as hypermarkets are concerned, each of the two has a total of 12, and further detail on both of these organizations is given later in this chapter.

Independent retailers

The number of independent grocers in Denmark has declined sharply over the last half century not only because of changes to the retail size and formats but also because of the importance of the discount sector. Many of the independent grocers were affiliated to wholesalers or buying groups. These groups attempt to obtain keener prices by purchasing collectively in order to combat the buying power of the two Danish giants FDB and DSM. Voluntary chains (*Frivillige kaeder*), wholesaler owned groups of shops, such as Dagrofa, and wholesaler associations, whose members often own one single shop, usually run by the owner, all seek to benefit from improved buying terms. These groups have been able to survive, often because their retail outlet may be the only one to have remained in a particular area.

Department stores

Department stores were originally very popular in Denmark, but changing lifestyles, the increasing number of women in full-time employment and with less time for shopping, and the development of hypermarkets have all had an adverse impact. In 1976 there were 13 department stores in Denmark, although it should be noted that a number of these were operated by the same group – most notably Magasin. However, it should also be noted that due to a peculiarity in the statistics, Salling's department stores have been counted as grocery outlets because Salling, which has department stores in Aarhus and Alborg, is owned by Herman Salling, part-owner of DSM. For the same reason FDB's Anva department store was excluded from the total of this retail format, and all of these retailers' activities in this sector were registered as grocers (Betaenkning, No. 1125, 1987: 143).

Department store trading in Denmark, which in 1994 employed 25,700 people (Betaenkning, No. 1353, 1998: 78), is becoming a much less popular retailing format. This is due largely to the lack of time on the part of traditional department-store shoppers to engage in city-centre shopping, with the result that, according to research at the Centre for Retail Trade at the Copenhagen Business School, 'It [the department store] is a type of retail format which is longer perceived as exciting' (quoted in *Politiken Weekly*, 24 January 2001). Thus, while until quite recently Copenhagen had a very good choice of department stores such as Crome & Goldschmidt, Messen, Haveman, Anva, Fonnesbeck and Daells Varehus, with one exception these have all now stopped trading and the future of the remaining store appears to be in doubt. The most up-market of the department stores, Illum founded in 1891, has announced that it will close in 2002 (*Politiken Weekly*, 24 January 2001). This department store is located in the heart of Copenhagen's most prestigious shopping street Ostergade, popularly known as 'Stroget'. 'Magasin du Nord', the other department store in the centre of Copenhagen, was put up for sale because of a significant trading deficit of DKr 108 millions (*Politiken Weekly*, 16 May 2001).

New developments

The most significant retail developments over the last 50 years in Denmark have been the emergence of hypermarkets/superstores and discount formats. In terms of size these are at the opposite ends of the spectrum.

The development of *hypermarkets and superstores* has been a gradual process. The two key players have been the Co-operative Movement FDB and DSM. Both have had to overcome significant difficulties, which the planning authorities have imposed on all retailers. However, most proposals have eventually been allowed. As a rule of thumb it has been suggested that every time a hypermarket opens – either FDB's Obs! or DSM's Bilka – that store takes one percentage of the Danish grocery market. Today these two retailers have 12 hypermarkets each. Hypemarkets have had a significant impact not only on more traditional grocers, but also on shops selling goods which traditionally could not be sold in grocery outlets such as electrical goods and clothes. The extended trading hours of hyper-markets have made them exceedingly popular shopping venues, not least for the working population, who, until the change in the law, were severely restricted by the almost simultaneous closing of shops and offices/factories. The one limiting factor in their development has been the requirement of a car, because most of the hypermarkets and superstores are situated out of town. The sheer volumes of goods purchased require a car for transportation home.

The European *discount stores* concept was pioneered and developed by Aldi in Germany (see Bennison and Gardner, 1995). The key feature was that the store stocked no more than 600 lines. The reason for this, before in-store scanning became commonplace, was that 600 prices were found to be the optimum number of prices a checkout operator could remember at any one time. Netto, the Danish discount-store format, was developed by DSM in response to Aldi's entry into Denmark in 1977. DSM is not a company to let other operators enter its territory without a fight. Hence the company decided to invent a discount format by taking the best ideas from Aldi, but adapting the format to meet Danish requirements.

The first Netto opened in 1981 and has proved an enduring format to such extent that it has become a Danish export to the United Kingdom, Germany and Poland. However, the beginning of discounting was slow to gain acceptance among shoppers in Denmark, just as it had been in Germany. It was the recession in the Danish economy in the 1980s which forced consumers to re-evaluate their spending and to realize that significant amounts of money could be saved by shopping at the discount shops. To put this into context, it was rather like introducing VAT on food in the United Kingdom: in other words, add 25 per cent to your weekly shopping bill and most consumers would have to either cut down or find alternatives. This, combined with relatively high levels of unemployment (over 10 per cent in the early 1990s), made discount outlets all the more appealing, and Danish consumers increasingly started to shop in these outlets. When the recession eased and unemployment levels fell, consumers continued nonetheless to shop in the discount stores.

FDB decided that it also needed a presence in the discount sector, and a discount chain Fakta was acquired in 1987. The chain included 74 Fakta stores as well as 14 Bonus stores, which already had been acquired (Stockmann, 1992). By 1992, FDB owned 201 Fakta stores, and by 1994 Aldi owned 159 stores, and 183 Netto had stores. Other smaller discount stores also operate, but none is on a scale of the three above. It was estimated that all the discount stores accounted for 9.9 per cent of the grocery turnover in Denmark (Stockmann, 1992: 279).

Brief history and background of the two major Danish retailers

Faellesforeningen for Danmarks Brugsforeninger (FDB)

The Co-operative Movement, which currently embraces the shop formats Obs!, Superbrugsen, Dagli'Brugsen, Kwickly, Irma and Fakta, has a very long history in Denmark and has contributed significantly to retail development. Although the FDB was not originally permitted to operate retail stores, this restriction was removed in 1968, and today FDB is the most important part of the Co-operative Movement with the majority of shops. Together, FDB and the independent retail Co-operative Societies account for one-third of the grocery market alone.

Although, as noted above, it was only from 1968 that FDB was allowed to own shops, it was not until 1972 that FDB exercised this right when it merged with Hovedstadens Brugsforening (HB). This is similar to the CWS in the United Kingdom in that it was prevented from running shops and set up CRS to rescue societies to overcome this problem in the 1930s. It was not until the CWS took over the Scottish CWS (SCWS) in 1973 that it became a retailer by virtue of that merger, as the SCWS already had owned shops in the Highlands and Islands (see Kinloch and Butt, 1981). As in the United Kingdom, the number of independent Co-operative Retail Societies has diminished significantly over the years in Denmark, and FDB has become stronger in terms of both shop numbers as well as market share. Examining the proportions in terms of turnover, FDB has always been more significant because of the manufacturing and procurement. In 1990, the number of stores operated by the Co-operative Movement in Denmark was 1409 (FDB, 1992).

The number of stores operated by FDB was only 317 compared with the independent Co-ops 1092. However, these numbers disguise the fact that FDB operated the Obs! hypermarkets until 1999 and these hypermarkets accounted for a very significant market share included in the overall market share. Today, Obs!

is operated and controlled jointly by the Norwegian, Swedish and Danish Co-ops. This collaboration was agreed among the Nordic Co-ops in order to achieve more efficient buying.

Dansk Supermarked

This company was founded in 1964 on a fifty–fifty basis between F. Salling (owner of department stores) and A. P. Moller, the shipping, container and airline, as well as oil and gas exploration and extraction company – Denmark's largest and most important business (see Hahn-Pedersen, 1997; Cortzen, 1993 for details of the company). The company's principal retail formats are Bilka, A–Z, Fotex and Netto. The organization is privately owned and very secretive, and as a result, little information is available on the individual store formats' performances. The motivation for the foundation of this multiple-store retailer was undoubtedly the anticipated change in the *Naeringsloven* legislation in 1966 which would allow companies to operate multiple stores across the country without having manufacturing facilities. The two founding companies and their owners saw the opportunity to become engaged in extensive retailing using different formats to challenge the supreme rule of the Co-operative Movement. The impact on Danish retailing of this legislation was very similar to the change in legislation in the United Kingdom in 1964 when resale price maintenance was abolished leading to the decline of the British consumer Co-operative Movement. This occurred because, under a system where manufacturers determined retail prices, the Co-operative customer dividend represented in reality a significant price reduction. When manufacturers were no longer able to dictate a uniform retail price for their products, and price-cutting retailers began to offer significant price reductions, the particular advantage of the Co-operative stores and their customer dividends was lost. In the year 1989–1990, the turnover of DSM was estimated to be in the region of DKr 13.8 billion.

Internationalization

Today many Danish retailers fear that global grocery and household goods retailers such as Ahold and Wal-Mart might enter the Danish market. Other global retailers such as IKEA in furniture and Toys'R'Us have been operating in Denmark for a number of years. One of the most recent developments, which might help prevent such entry into the Danish market, has been the June 2001 agreement between the Danish, Norwegian and Swedish Co-ops to pool resources and to seek to improve buying terms. Some may say that it is surprising this has not happened before now. As we have seen above, the Scandinavian Co-ops had already agreed in 1999 to run the hypermarkets Obs! as one operation in order to become more competitive. The advantages of buying for homogeneously sized stores could give the Co-operative Organizations the competitive edge they need. It is too early to comment on this development, but it would seem likely to go some way towards safeguarding the Obs! hypermarkets from the global predators at least for the time being.

One of the significant difficulties which these Co-operative Organizations have had to face has been the democratic structure of their governing body (Congress) and the inability of the demands of such a structure to be combined with efficient business practices. The members of Congress, often representing single-shop Co-operative Societies, make demands to have the same prices as the volume-related trading terms which FDB can command. Such demands make it almost impossible to run different business formats side by side efficiently. The members of Congress have always criticized the way that some of the smaller stores have been unable to secure the same competitive prices as the hypermarkets (Obs!) or discount stores (Fakta). These and other aspects of the democratic structure of Congress makes it almost impossible for the Co-operative Movement to compete with DSM. DSM for its part has never had that problem in that the different store formats have their own buying teams who make sure that the group's different store formats compete with each other.

Clearly the size of the population in Denmark would put off global retailers such as Wal-Mart, unless acquisition of Bilka or Obs! was considered appropriate. Danish planning laws would almost certainly restrict expansion and new, major out-of-town developments would be prohibited, particularly for global players. Danes have a history of supporting Danish businesses when faced with a choice. Moreover, it has been suggested that the Danish market is too small to be considered viable, in that it would neither provide the global retailers with the required return on capital, nor would the meagre Danish grocery retail margins meet the expected criteria set by most global retailers. Furthermore, it may be that such incoming international retail operators would be cautious about entering the Danish economy in the light of the difficulties currently experienced by Wal-Mart in the German market.

The population distribution in Denmark also indicates that a significant proportion of the population lives in rural communities not populated densely enough to attract new operators to such geographical locations. A sizeable proportion of the rest of the population – in the major cities or towns – often lives in flats close to the city or town centre. These shoppers thus find neighbourhood shopping convenient, either en route to and from work on a daily basis or as a social activity to get out of the home. The mode of transport is often on foot, by bike or public transport, all of which prohibit the volume of shopping bought and carried home. These factors help not only the discounters (Netto, Aldi and Fakta) but also the small independent butchers and bakers and speciality shops which have been able to survive.

Research has shown that Danes shop in at least two or three outlets per week, and there is a strong loyalty on the part of consumers to small independent retailers supplying luxury items which are used to top up shopping from different outlets. This is in stark contract to the population in the United Kingdom, many of whom prefer one-stop shopping. However, the one-stop, out-of-town shop requires not only a car (access to which not every Danish shopper has), but also parking spaces, which most of the small stores do not have, particularly in town and city centres in Denmark. Thus the lower level of car ownership in

Denmark, when compared with the United Kingdom, also helps maintain small retail stores.

Conclusions

A number of features of Danish retailing have endured over a considerable period of time, during which there have been significant changes in retailing structures in many other EU countries. This is partly because of aspects of Danish culture, and partly because of the geographical spread of the population. However, as with many of these other economies, the decline, in the number of small stores seems unstoppable when viewed over recent decades. Two dominant retailers, nonetheless, look set to continue to play key roles in the future, with the Co-operative Movement FDB and DSM having a combined market share of over 60 per cent (see Table 1.3).

The Co-operative Movement as a whole has continued to play a major role in Denmark, and recent developments in terms of collaboration with other Nordic Co-ops seem to have secured their competitiveness, at least for the time being. DSM also looks set to continue to grow at a steady pace. Both these retailers have reduced their vulnerability to other competitors by the very fact that they operate different shop formats.

Thus, despite the incursions of international retailers, and the impact of some changes in legislation and cultural variables, Danish retailers and retailing may continue to prove to be as enduring as Lego bricks!

References

Anderson A. B. (1991) *Arbejdsgruppen om Detailhandel*, Industriministeriet, Copenhagen.

Bennison, D. and Gardner, H. (1995) 'Internationalisation of limited line discount grocery operations', in McGoldrick, P. and Davies, G. (eds), *International Retailing, Trends and Strategies*, Pitman, London.

Bryle, C.-J., Brorup, M. and Ratjien, J. (1991) *Fakta Danmark*, Systime, Herning.

Butiksstrukturkommissionen (1998) *Butiker og Forbrugere – nu og i Fremtiden*, Betaenkning, No. 1353, Erhvervsministeriet, Copenhagen.

Cortzen, J. (1993) *Myten Moeller Maersk Mc-Kinney Moeller – han gor Danmark rigere*, Borsen Boger, Greve.

Cortzen, J. (1998) *Herman Salling en Gudbenaadet Kobmand*, Borsen Boger, Copenhagen.

Danmarks Statistik (1999) *Statistisk tiaarsoversigt*, Aarhus Stiftsbogtrykkerie, Aarhus.

Danmarks Statistik (2000) *Statistisk Aarbog 2000*, Danmarks Statistik, Copenhagen.

Ehlers, S. (1999) *Dansk Dagligvarehandel 10 aarsstatistik 1988–1998*, Stockmann-Gruppen, Lyngby.

Fog, B. and Rasmussen, A. (1965) *Danmarks detailhandel i 1980*, Einar Harcks Forlag, Copenhagen.

Hahn-Pedersen, M. (1997) *A. P. Moller og den Danske Olie*, Schultz, Copenhagen.

Ilsoe, P. (1960) *Nordens Historie*, Gyldendal, Copenhagen.

Kinloch, J. and Butt, J. (1981) *History of the Scottish Co-operative Wholesale Society*, CWS Print Works, Glasgow.

Stockmann, E. (1992) *Storre, Faerre – og Billiger, Dansk Dagligvarehandels Historie i Vort Aarhunderede*, Schonberg, Viborg.

Additional reading

Bahr, H. (2001) *Supermarkeds-Haandbogen*, Stockmann-Gruppen, Frederiksberg.
Industrministeriet (1987) Betaenkning, No. 1125, *Aabningstider – Butikker, Servicesektoren og den Offentlige Administration*, Stougaard Jensen, Copenhagen.
Informa Retail (2000) *European Retailing 2000+: Denmark*, Informa Publishing, London.
Jorgensen, H. *et al.* (1989) *Detailhandelsvirksonheder og Personaleplanlaegning*, Rapport nr.18, ATA-forlaget, Aalborg.
Planstyrelsen Miljoministeriet (1989) *Detailhandel I Regionplanlaegningen et vejledende materiale*, Planstyrelsen, Copenhagen.

2   France

Enrico Colla

Introduction

This chapter again follows the structural pattern of the others in this study. It commences with a historical background to French retailing, identifying the principal periods in its development, and this is followed by an overview of the range of structures in French retailing. The chapter then provides a clear summary of the principal features of the current French retail environment, and follows this with a more detailed analysis of a limited number of particular issues, including specific retailer strategies and the impact of e-commerce upon French retailing. As with all of the individual-country chapters in this study, a particular analysis is provided of the impact upon retailing structures and performance of government legislation; the chapter concludes with perspectives and forecasts regarding French retailer strategies and the impact of government legislation in this sector.

French retailing until the 1960s

Three major waves have marked the history of mass retailing in France until the latter part of the twentieth century: the period 1820–1860, the years 1890–1910, and the decade of the 1960s. Interestingly, these three main waves correspond quite clearly to periods of strong economic growth, suggesting that a surge in consumer demand was accompanied by developments in mass retailing (Marseille, 1997).

1820–1860

The first wave of development of mass retailing in France, inaugurated in the 1820s by the rise of 'novelty shops', saw the emergence of department stores. In fact, it was in France – even before the United States or elsewhere in Europe – that the very first department stores originated. La Belle Jardinière opened in 1824, Aux Trois Quartiers was created in 1829, Au Bon Marché in 1852, Les Magasins du Louvre in 1855, the Bazar de l'Hotel de Ville in 1856 and Le Printemps in 1865.

However, these department stores did not arise out of a commercial vacuum. They were inspired by the boutique concept popularized by small manufacturers and craftsmen who sold their own products (Bouveret-Gauer, 1997). This small-shop concept was the birthplace of numerous innovations often incorrectly attributed to department stores: fixed and clearly displayed prices, a low sales-margin policy, promotional sales, free entry, merchandise exchange and catalogue selling. Department stores, however, were able to apply and enhance these innovations, as well as other technical innovations such as electric lighting, lifts and escalators.

1890–1910

The second wave of development of French retailing saw the extraordinary growth of the department store La Samaritaine, which opened in 1869 and increased its turnover considerably throughout the following thirty years. This period brought the creation of the Galeries Lafayette, and the development of the Nouvelles Galeries and Magasins Reunis, which opened department stores at the turn of the century in French provincial towns. In addition, this period was especially fertile for grocery chain stores such as the Docks Remois, the Ruche Picarde, Casino, Goulet-Turpin, the Docks de France and the Comptoirs Modernes. Throughout the twentieth century until the 1960s, the number and market share of department stores grew continuously, albeit with peaks and troughs following economic cycles and successive European wars.

In France, as in the rest of Europe during the first two or three decades of the twentieth century, the competitive marketplace was being progressively modified. Single-price stores – originating in Great Britain under the name 'variety store chains' – began their ascent at the end of the 1920s and continued to grow throughout all of the following decade because of the economic depression. Those companies, such as Le Printemps and Galeries Lafayette, often managed both a department store chain and a variety store chain. With direct competition in the same sector and the diversification into single-price stores, many chains acted, one after the other, to improve service, modernize stores, decorate interiors and create a more pleasant atmosphere. Inevitably, this led to an increase in prices and costs, without, however, impeding moderate growth of the entire sales network. After the Second World War, department stores were modernized or completely rebuilt during the 1950s and 1960s, even managing to regain market share lost to the variety stores before the conflict.

The 1960s

Finally, the third wave of French retailing development brought self-service and the supermarket, with the Leclerc stores, Carrefour, Auchan, Euromarché, Promodès in the grocery sector and the rise of large specialized stores (LSS) such as Conforama, Castorama and Darty in other sectors.

The first French self-service store, created through the initiative of Goulet-Tourpin, opened in 1948 in Paris (Villermet, 1991). Several years later – in 1954 – the first supermarket opened, and by 1960 there were only 90 stores of this type

(Dayan, 1992). In the same year 1,690 French retail outlets, that is, 0.2 per cent of the total and with 2.5 per cent retail market share (4.5 per cent of the retail food market), operated totally or partially on a self-service basis. At the end of the 1950s there were approximately 1,050,000 retail establishments in France, with 353,000 in the grocery sector. These food retail outlets may be thought of as belonging to one of four categories. The vast majority – some 285,000 outlets, accounting for 83.1 per cent of the total – consisted of traditional or independent shops. The others – approximately 68,000 – belonged to a central buying group or voluntary chain and were part of a multiple store group or were members of cooperative chains that were especially prevalent in grocery retailing.

The second category of food retailers, comprising central buying groups, brought together independent retailers, who combined part of their merchandise purchase requirements. The largest of these groups in the food sector were Codec, founded in 1924, and Union of Food Traders (UNA). The latter had a purchasing unit in Paris, and the merchandise bought was shipped to 47 warehouses, and then delivered to between 20 and 120 members, depending upon the district served. In 1960, there were 2,650 members, and in that same year, the combined turnover of Codec and UNA was equal to that of all the other groups put together (Villermet, 1991). Within the voluntary chains were wholesalers who had initiated organizing the purchases of associated retailers. Together, they numbered 30,000, and their turnover represented about 2.1 per cent of all food purchases in 1960. The main voluntary chains in France as of 1 January 1958, were Spar France, affiliated with Spar Internationale (47 wholesalers and 5,200 retailers), Végé-France (23 wholesalers and 2,500 retailers), Luga (89 wholesalers and 8,000 retailers) Avam (40 wholesalers and 500 retailers) and Copral (9 wholesalers and 1,000 retailers).

The third category, retail chains with multiple stores, included in 1960, 24,000 establishments, more than 5,600 warehouses and 72 companies. The largest of these were Etablissements Economiques of Casino, Docks Lyonnais and Docks de France. In order to strengthen their market presence, several of these multiple-stores companies were grouped around a powerful central buying unit that consolidated orders. The best known of these in 1960 were Paridoc, Loceda and Ceda. Founded in 1927, Paridoc, the largest among these groups, comprised 28 companies and 8,650 points of sale in France.

Consumer cooperatives made up the fourth category in food trading in 1960. Their organization was characterized by the stake of their members, who were shareowners of the outlet or the company managing several stores. They also had the unusual feature of buying directly from producers. In 1958, these cooperatives comprised a total of about 8,500 retail outlets.

Overview of French retailing structural trends to date

Supermarkets

In France, supermarkets are defined – by Insee – as self-service stores with a broad range of predominantly food products, and a floor space of 400–2,500 sq. m.

The modernization of the retail trade and the development of supermarkets occurred around the 1960s in France. In 1970, the supermarket format rose to 13.6 per cent of the national food retail market. Growth slowed during the 1970s due, among other factors, to the impact of the Royer Law of 1973, discussed below (Dupuis, 1988); but by 1980, France had a total of more than 4,000 supermarkets, accounting for 21.8 per cent of the food retail market.

Between 1980 and 1990, the supermarkets developed parallel to larger hypermarkets. During this time, the life cycle of each coincided more in France than in Great Britain or Germany (Zaninotto, 1992). Even if their number continued to increase moderately, supermarkets began to lose ground beginning in 1990; and they were overtaken by hypermarkets, which commanded 36.4 per cent of the total food market in 1999, compared to 30.1 per cent for supermarkets (INSEE data). This trend can be explained not only in part by the conversion of numerous existing supermarkets into hypermarkets (a strategy frequently employed by independents) but also especially by a rapid market penetration by hard discounters, who were undisputedly the champions of supermarket store openings in the 1990s.

Table 2.1 below sets out the principal French supermarket groups in 2000 together with their store numbers and average store size.

Hypermarkets

Hypermarkets are defined by Insee as self-service stores with a broad range of food and non-food products, car parking facilities and a sales floor space of more than 2,500 sq. m. The creation of these outlets in France goes back to 1963 when Carrefour introduced the concept which had been a feature of US retailing since

Table 2.1 Supermarkets in France (2000)

Trade name (Group)	Number of stores	Average selling space (sq. m.)
Intermarché	1,541	1,410
Champion (Carrefour)	965	1,370
Super U (Système U)	523	1,488
Shopi (Carrefour)	402	564
Casino	399	1,105
Atac (Auchan)	321	1,254
Ecomarché (Intermarché)	265	587
Franprix (Casino)	255	647
Marché U (Système U)	169	747
Supermarché Match (Cora)	141	1,360
Centres Leclerc	99	1,695
Maxicoop	38	650
Coop	33	514
Others	478	–
Total/average	5,629	1,155

Source: LSA – Libre Service Actualités.

the 1950s (see Burt, 1994: 154). Until 1968, the number of openings of this retail format in France remained modest; but starting in 1969, the figure actually tripled, reaching 45 openings per year. This expansion proceeded at a very strong rate during the next five years, and then slowed under the effects of the Royer Law (explained below), notably in 1974 and 1975. However, the development continued throughout the late 1970s, often involving consolidation through the purchase by larger retail groups of individual hypermarkets, and even recovered new vigour at the beginning of the following decade.

The terms of the Royer Law limited growth in hypermarket outlets in France, but at the same time led to internationalization. By contrast, in France, small- and medium-sized regional retailers encountered fewer difficulties than their large competitors in obtaining the necessary authorizations to open new outlets. Consequently, large retailers created more joint ventures, making acquisitions in France and opening new stores mainly in Spain, Argentina and Brazil (Colla, 2001). During the first half of the 1980s, the rate of new hypermarket openings in France progressively declined, but recovered more intensely between 1985 and 1990.

During the last decade of the twentieth century, the growth of hypermarkets again fell off, and this occurred more substantially following new legislative restrictions – particularly the Raffarin Law of 1996. The 1,000-store point was passed in 1994 (with 41 new hypermarkets that year), and in 2000 the total reached 1,175 units with 11 hypermarket openings and 6 enhancements from supermarket to hypermarket.

Thus, during the whole of the last decade of the twentieth century, and despite legislation that discouraged their development, the market share of the hypermarkets again rose at the national level, although new establishments were opened mostly in foreign markets. French retailers increased their international growth and some of them became the leaders in many foreign countries. By 1991, 55 of Carrefour's 129 hypermarket outlets were overseas, with a particular emphasis upon Spain and South America (see Burt, 1994: 157); and by 2000, Carrefour was the second-ranked world retailer after Wal-Mart, the leading hypermarket operator in the world, and the foremost supermarket operator in Europe. The group achieved 52 per cent of its total sales outside France that year. It was the leading retailer in Spain, Belgium, Argentina and Brazil, and the leading foreign retailer in China and in the whole Asia (Colla, 2001). Auchan too achieved a strong position in Italy and in Spain, where it became the second largest retailer after Coop and Carrefour, respectively (Colla, 1999). Casino is now (2001) among the leading retailers in Brazil, after having acquired the local group Pao de Açucar, and it has made many more acquisitions in other South American (Argentina and Colombia) and Asian (Taiwan and Thailand) countries. Intermarché acquired the German Group Spar Haendel in 1997 and is now struggling to make it profitable.

Table 2.2 below summarizes data on the role of international activities by the major French retailers.

During the 1990s in France, the average size of the new hypermarket outlets continued to increase, but openings were more and more often mere

Table 2.2 Leading French retailers abroad (2000)

Group	Number of foreign countries	Total stores abroad	Hypermarkets	Supermarkets	Hard discount
Carrefour	26	5,670	518	1,306	3,152
ITM Enterprises	7	1,583	–	954	630
Auchan	13	416	120	296	–
Casino	13	909	189	590	130
Cora	8	18	17	1	–
Leclerc	6	14	9	5	–

Source: *Food Business News*, October 2001.

expansions or conversions of supermarkets, or even cash-and-carry and department stores.

This limitation to the internal development of hypermarkets encouraged the phenomenon of retailer concentration. This began most notably in March 1991 with the acquisition by Carrefour of Montlaur and more dramatically with its acquisition a few months later of the Euromarché group which at that time consisted of 76 hypermarkets, 47 DIY stores and 57 cafeterias (Burt, 1994: 157). At the end of that decade, and following the merger of the Carrefour and Promodès networks in 1999 (Cliquet, 2001), five major retail organizations (Carrefour, Leclerc, Auchan, Géant Casino and Cora) accounted for 87 per cent of French hypermarket floor space in 2000. Details of these are set out in Table 2.3.

Table 2.3 Hypermarkets in France (2000)

Trade name (Group)	Number of stores	Average selling space (sq. m.)
Centres Leclerc	408	4,408
Carrefour	218	8,406
Auchan	120	8,805
Géant	108	6,671
Intermarché	101	3,268
Cora	57	8,747
Hyper U (Système U)	34	3,624
Champion (Carrefour)	32	2,834
Super U (Système U)	31	2,699
Hyper Champion (Carrefour)	29	2,964
Others	36	–
Total/average	1,174	5,766

Source: LSA, 2001.

'Hard discount' (or limited assortment discount) chains

It was not until the end of the 1980s and the beginning of the following decade that limited assortment discount ('hard discount') retailing really caught on in France (Colla, 1994, 1997). At that time, small urban discount outlets remained relatively rare, and indeed it was only during the 1980s that discount supermarkets expanded (Colla, 1994). However, these discount supermarket outlets then underwent an upmarket changeover through increases in store space and number of stock units, and during this decade, the only real name in discount was Ed, of Erteco (Carrefour group), but its growth was sluggish and its financial performance disappointing.

A new impulse was to come from Germany, particularly from Aldi and Lidl, which began operating in France in 1988 and 1989. The sector quickly showed an extraordinary dynamism, with an annual growth rate in the number of outlets of more than 100 per cent, and the opening of numerous national retailer brands. This expansion was favoured by the tendency of French supermarkets and hypermarkets to trade up, and by legislation restricting large retail outlet construction and store opening hours. Economic downturns and changes in consumer behaviour also accelerated the market penetration of discount retailers (Colla, 1994). The conquest of market share by the discount retailers was limited at first, but progressed steadily until 1996, when the Raffarin Law of that year had the effect of reducing their growth. According to Nielsen data, the total grocery market share of the discount chains grew from less than 1 per cent in 1990 to almost 5 per cent by 1995, and reached 7.4 per cent in 1999 (Reidiboym, 1999). As an indication of the impact of legislation in this area, however, the number of new discount retailer store openings fell from an average of 285 during 1994 and 1995 to an average of 135 over the following two years; and the annual average number of such store openings over the years 1998–2000 was 64 (Insee, 2001).

While it was the first to penetrate the French market in 1988, Aldi slowed its new openings over successive years, contrary to the strategy of Lidl and Ed (Carrefour). The gain in market share by the German leaders Aldi and Lidl was relatively slow at first, but progressive, and there has been no slowing down in recent years. By contrast national leaders' store chains, after a strong growth from 1991 to 1994, began to reduce the number of store openings and to lose market share (Insee, 2001). As of 1 September 2000, the number of stores was respectively 811 (Lidl), 423 (Ed), 405 (Aldi), 316 (Leader Price), 196 (Le Mutant) and 171 (CDM). In the year 2000, Lidl controlled 32 per cent of the total discount market, with more than two billion Euros of sales; Aldi's market share was 15.8 per cent, with more than one billion Euros of sales; and the market shares of Ed and Leader Price were 15 and 12.7 per cent, respectively (Nielsen). Table 2.4 provides data on the number of stores and sales areas of the leading hard discount stores in France.

Convenience stores

The number of smaller, independent retailers fell considerably in France with the rise of large retailers. The total number of food stores fell continuously from

Table 2.4 Hard discount stores in France (2000)

Trade name	Number of stores	Average selling space (sq. m.)
Lidl	811	686
Aldi	405	666
Leader Price (Casino)	316	627
Ed le marché discount (Carrefour)	308	689
Le Mutant (Coop de Normandie)	196	597
CDM (Intermarché)	171	627
Ed l'Epicier (Carrefour)	115	324
Norma	96	661
Penny Prix Bas (Rewe)	67	662
Treff Marché	31	535
Others	4	–
Totals/average	2,520	672

Source: LSA.

1,050,000 in 1960 to 135,386 in 1998. More recently, the number of non-specialist food stores with less than 400 sq. m. of selling space fell from 27,643 in 1995 to 23,695 in 1998; and the market share of all small food stores fell from 10 per cent in 1995 to 8.7 per cent in 2000 (Insee, 2001). Only some of these small food retailers benefited from the possibility of conversion into modern convenience stores, depending upon whether their size and location were favourable. Several types of businesses adopted this structure, particularly:

1   the largest national grocery chains, often through franchise agreements (Carrefour/Promodès, Casino);
2   consumer cooperatives, within the framework of their network restructuring – activities that were often very strong in local markets (e.g. Co-op of Normandy);
3   independents and small, food and non-food chains (groceries and newstands) which diversified into convenience stores by introducing other products; and
4   petrol retailers which opened convenience stores near their service stations.

Details of these organizations are set out in Table 2.5.

Department stores

Beginning in the 1970s, both department stores and variety stores in France were confronted by a whole series of strategic threats, particularly the severe competition from hypermarkets. The country experienced significant geographical decentralization in the retail sector, as shopping malls – which the department stores never managed to penetrate – developed in the outskirts of towns around hypermarkets.

Table 2.5 Convenience stores in France (2000)

Trade name	Group	Number of stores	Average selling space (sq. m.)
8 à Huit	Carrefour/Promodès	620	227
Casino/Petit Casino	Casino	592	157
Coccinelle	Francap	425	210
Spar	Casino	313	192
Proxi	Carrefour/Promodès	291	188
Shopi	Carrefour/Promodès	194	220
Coop	Coop de Normandie	191	200
Relais des Mousquetaires	ITM (Intermarché)	144	175
Comod	Carrefour/Comptoirs Modernes	104	293
Eco service	Auchan Proximité[a]	94	191
Total/average		2,968	205

Source: LSA.

Note
a Sold to Casino in April 2000.

Demographic growth and prosperity explained the growing number of automobiles in city centres, with consequent access and parking problems. The large outlets in Paris were able to defend their positions; but the same was not true in the provinces, or in suburban shopping centres, where a number of department stores were forced to close.

From the 1970s onwards, department store floorspace continued to shrink, and the situation did not improve until the 1990s. However, from the mid-1990s onwards, a trend towards urban centre renewal took hold, and the department store environment progressively improved. Notable consequent characteristics included a decline in outlying neighbourhood and suburban shopping centres, economic growth and a drop in urban crime, an improvement in the social environment, a tendency to uphold past traditions, an environmental movement combating air pollution, and the sociological rediscovery of the city (Colla, 2001).

Following these socio-demographic changes, a new balance between suburban and city retailing began to take form. Saturation, and the difficulty of opening large outlets in the suburbs, were such that retailers rediscovered opportunities for growth in the city centres. Beginning in 1998, the leading retail names in Paris – Galeries Lafayette, Printemps and Bon Marché – were able to improve their positions due not only to the economic recovery and an upturn in consumer spending but also through their new marketing policies relating to product assortment, promotional strategies and their sales environment. Merchandise assortment became more specialized, with more perfumes, *prêt-à-porter*, accessories, and more luxury and 'prestige' brands. The sales environment has been restructured and segmented by gender and lifestyles. However, the retail market share of department

Table 2.6 Main department stores in France (2000)

Group	Trade name	Number of stores
Galeries Lafayette	Galeries Lafayette	37
Galeries Lafayette	Nouvelles Galeries	40
PPR	Printemps	24
Galeries Lafayette	BHV	7
LVMH	La Samaritaine	1
LVMH	Le Bon Marché	1

Source: LSA.

stores remains very limited: 1.4 per cent in 2000, with 0.4 per cent in food and 2 per cent in non-food (Insee, 2001) (Table 2.6).

Variety stores

The total retail market share of this type of retailer peaked in 1960 at 7 per cent, then declined to 1.4 per cent in 1991 and to 0.6 per cent in 2000, when it had a market share of 1.1 per cent in food products and 0.4 per cent in non-food products (Insee, 2001). This downward trend can be explained mainly by the difficulty that these companies faced in meeting the intensified competition triggered by the entry to the market of new retail formats such as hypermarkets, discount supermarkets (Leclerc, Intermarché), and more recently, large specialized retailers, or category killers. Originally, the variety store chains differentiated themselves from the department stores, targeting a clientele with more modest means. This change favoured concentration in the sector: two chains, Monoprix, a unit of the Galeries Lafayette group, and Prisunic, of the Printemps group, dominated the sector until 1997, the year of their merger. Monoprix then became the only remaining significant competitor, and in 2001 its stores numbered about 270 (Charrière and Gallo, 2001). Marks & Spencer was the only other retailer of this type in France, with 18 stores, but the group decided to abandon completely international activity in Europe by closing all its stores at the end of 2001, at which stage it was reported that the firm was to sell its 18 prime stores to the department-store group Galeries Lafayette (*Financial Times*, 24 December 2001). Table 2.7 sets out the principal variety store chains in France prior to the withdrawal of Marks & Spencer in 2001.

Table 2.7 Main variety stores in France (2000)

Group	Trade name	Number of stores
Monoprix/Prisunic/Inno	Galeries Lafayette	270
Marks & Spencer	Marks & Spencer	18

Source: LSA.

Large specialized stores

The LSS emerged in the 1960s in France, where, despite the rise of department stores, variety stores and mail order catalogues, traditional retailing in the form of specialized and small independent stores offering a full retail selling service was the overwhelming form. It was at this point that the rapid development of hypermarkets and large supermarkets completely shook up and transformed retailing of all self-service non-food goods. The hypermarkets seized substantial market shares in groceries, household goods, small appliances, hardware supplies, cosmetics and beauty, underwear etc. Nevertheless, they did not manage to achieve the very high level of market share in non-food as they had done in food, which explains the still significant strength of specialists.

At their outset, the LSS competed head-on with specialized outlets, and in markets where these had been especially dominant (brown and white appliances, furniture, home improvement), traditional retailers virtually disappeared. After the small shops, the LSS began to threaten hypermarkets as well, and little by little, the competition between these two categories became more direct and bitter. The LSS have constantly increased their market share throughout the past few years. The situation varies, naturally, from one sector to another, and it is in home improvement, sports and home furnishings that large specialized retailers achieve their best results, with a market share of around 60 per cent. On the other hand, in toys and small appliances, the large grocery stores – hypermarkets and supermarkets – have seized more than 50 per cent of the market.

Table 2.8 sets out the market shares of the various forms of retailing in a range of product categories, highlighting the role of the large specialist stores;

Table 2.8 Market shares of store types by product category in France (1999) (%)

Product category	LSS	GS[a]	Traditional stores	Others
Home improvement	61.3	10.5	5.2	23.0
Sports	58.6	9.1	28.5	3.8
Furnishings	57.0	2.0	28.0	13.0
White household appliances	41.9	18.9	34.0	5.2
Shoes	39.4	10.6	38.7	11.3
Gardening	38.0	19.0	33.7	9.3
Brown household appliances	37.0	26.0	33.0	4.0
Microcomputers	33.0	33.0	30.3	3.7
Telephone equipment	31.7	30.3	34.7	3.3
Apparel	30.6	16.3	30.2	22.9
Small household appliances	24.3	53.8	10.4	11.5
Toys	23.5	50.7	10.0	15.8
Cultural products[b]	21.0	40.0	23.0	16.0
Pets	12.6	67.4	13.0	7.0
Automobile repair	11.3	10.4	66.4	11.9

Source: Rhode (2000).

Notes
a Grocery stores (hypermarkets and supermarkets).
b Mainly books and recorded music etc.

and Table 2.9 identifies the major large specialist retailers in France by merchandise category, with data on average store size, number of stores and market share.

Table 2.9 Large specialized stores in France (1999)

Trade name	Average selling space (sq. m.)	Number of stores	Market share (%)
DIY			
Castorama	7,823	141	18.2
Leroy Merlin	8,329	73	14.5
M. Bricolage	1,781	320	5.7
Bricomarchè	1,512	430	8.3
Household			
Ikea	20,000	10	n.a.
Conforama	3,248	164	n.a.
Mobilier de France	1,667	99	n.a.
But	2,532	227	n.a.
Fly	1,200	143	n.a.
M. Meuble	1,500	160	n.a.
Habitat	1,708	32	n.a.
Electricals			
Hypermédia	2,705	12	n.a.
Darty	1,117	173	n.a.
Textiles and accessories			
C & A	2,000	51	1.1[a]
Kiabi	1,800	86	2.3[a]
Halle aux Vêtements	1,000	215	1.6[a]
Gemo	1,240	214	1.4[a]
Vétimarché	1,000	118	0.6[a]
Sport			
Décathlon	2,411	183	n.a.
Go Sport	1,441	95	n.a.
Centre Intersport	516	365	n.a.
Toys			
Toys'R'Us	3,254	31	n.a.
Jouéclub	278	230	n.a.
Cultural products			
FNAC	2,650	49	n.a.
Virgin Megastore	1,520	11	n.a.

Source: Rhode (2000).

Notes
a = 1998.
n.a. = not available.

Mail order

In France, mail-order sales remain relatively healthy, with a total retail market share in 1999 of 2.4 per cent. This form of retailing has, however, become particularly concentrated in certain product categories such as clothing, books, recorded music etc., and housewares. Another characteristic which is unique to the French market is the substantial use of the Minitel for ordering. In 1994, there were actually more than 6 million owners of this simple electronic terminal (see the next section under E-commerce). This result was made possible by tremendous financial support from the state, which launched the device by distributing it free of charge to households.

French retail environment

Concentration and manufacturer/supplier relationships

Relationships between manufacturers and large French consumer goods retailers have always been difficult, and conflict has always been the norm. The main reason for this has been the very high level of price competition in the retail market, which forces retailers to reduce their buying costs. The decentralized structures of the associated independents have also contributed to the lengthening and difficulty of negotiations. The negotiating power of the retailers continues to grow: a consequence, above all, of the increase in retailers' size and their market concentration. French chains have constantly expanded their networks of outlets, as the acquisition of increased market share implies growth in purchasing volume, which leads in turn to more favourable terms being granted by manufacturers.

Table 2.10 Market share in the French grocery market by retail trade name (%)

	1999[a]	2000[b]
Carrefour (HM)	18.1	17.4
Leclerc (HM + SM)	16.1	16.5
ITM (HM + SM)	12.7	12.5
Auchan (HM)	12.0	12.2
HD[c]	8.2	8.8
Champion (SM of Carrefour Group)	7.0	7.1
Système U (SM)	5.8	6.1
Géant (HM of Casino Group)	4.3	4.2
Cora (HM)	3.6	3.6
Atac (SM of Auchan Group)	2.0	2.1
Monoprix (VS)	1.9	1.9
Casino (SM of Casino Group)	1.2	1.1

Source: LSA, based upon Secodip data.

Notes
a October 1998/September 1999.
b October 1999/September 2000.
c All stores of all firms.
HM = hypermarkets; SM = supermarkets; HD = hard discount; VS = variety stores.

Furthermore, smaller retailers, even with fewer expansion opportunities, have also tried to reduce their purchasing costs by associating with other retail companies, forming buying groups, voluntary chains and cooperatives. Such operators and small retailers are thus able to enjoy the same advantages as the larger retailers without having to give up their entrepreneurial independence. These developments have progressively led to a trend towards a high level of market and buying-power concentration both in terms of retail trade names (enseigne), as set out in Table 2.10, and in terms of firms and buying groups.

This market concentration has grown significantly over the last decade, and has led to a situation where France now has the highest retail market concentration of the five largest economies in Europe. This outcome was achieved through a series of acquisitions on the part of the leading retailers: Carrefour took over Comptoirs Modernes and Promodès, Auchan acquired Docks de France, and Casino bought Franprix and Leader Price. These acquisitions were very much encouraged by the Raffarin Law of 1996, which required retailers to obtain authorization in order to open new stores.

Following the acquisition of Promodès by Carrefour in 1999, the market share of the five largest retailers in France was 83 per cent: a figure which had risen from 60 per cent in 1994 and 73 per cent in 1998. The current situation is set out in the data in Table 2.11.

Table 2.11 Market shares of five largest French grocery retailers, 2000 (%)

Carrefour (Carrefour, Champion, Ed)	30
Intermarché	15
Leclerc	15
Auchan (Auchan, Atac)	13
Casino (Géant, Casino, Franprix, Leader Price)	10
Total	83

Source: Nielsen.

Finally, if we take into consideration the concentration of buying groups in France, the five largest of these hold 90.2 per cent of the grocery market in the year 2000. Details of these are set out in Table 2.12.

Table 2.12 French grocery central buying group market shares, 2000 (%)

Carrefour (Stoc, Continent, Champion, Ed)	25.4
LUCIE (Leclerc, Système U)	25.4
ITM Enterprises (Intermarché)	13.8
Groupe Auchan (Atac)	13.1
OPERA (Géant, Casino, Franprix, Leader Price, Cora, Match, Monoprix)	12.5
Total	90.2

Source: Secodip.

The size of French retailers also increased following their expansion in foreign markets. Not only Carrefour, Auchan and Casino, but also Intermarché, and to a lesser degree, Leclerc, have substantial operations outside of France (Colla, 2001). In 2000, Carrefour was the second largest retailer in the world, after Wal-Mart, with 47.5 per cent of its activity located in foreign countries: 26.3 per cent in Europe, 14.8 per cent in South America, and 6.4 per cent in Asia. Finally, it is worth emphasizing that in France a very significant concentration of retail sales are in large stores. According to Nielsen data, hypermarkets in France hold 52 per cent share of the food market, which is the highest proportion in Europe (Bell, 2001a).

Retail concentration and its market relationship implications have led manufacturers to compete among themselves to obtain trade services from retailers: listings, favourable in-store display of their products, promotions etc. (Dupuis and Tissier-Desbordes, 1996). Manufacturers then tend to differentiate their trade terms as a reflection of the level of service they obtain from their retailer customers, and the greater the power the retailer has in this relationship, the more generous the manufacturers are forced to be in respect of trade terms. Moreover, the differences in such terms which depend on the contractual power of retailers are not systematic: the privileged clients are not always the same ones, and the nature of these differences can vary over time. In addition to manufacturer promotion budgets devoted to stock unit listings, the types of trade discounts most commonly adopted by manufacturers are those related to the total sales or sales increases at the end of the year and trade cooperation agreements such as slotting allowances for shelf space and promotion display, and participation in advertising and promotion. Details of these are set out in Table 2.13.

Unfortunately for retailers, their competitive advantage is unstable: better trade buying terms and conditions lead to lower retail prices, which allow competitors to identify the manufacturers involved and to negotiate the same conditions for themselves. This leads to a levelling off of the terms retailers are able to demand, and then those with more trade buying power obtain a new advantage and the cycle

Table 2.13 Discounts and allowances from suppliers to retailers in France

Event	Practice
Initial order	Bonus for listing the product
New product	Shelf facing allowance
Promotion	Purchase of selling space
Retailer advertising	Participation in copy and catalogue costs
Store opening	Financial participation Free products
Merchandising	Product labelling and installation on shelf facings
Retailer investment	Participation in store renewal costs

Source: Adapted from Dupuis and Tissier-Desbordes (1996).

begins again. However, one avenue to achieving longer lasting competitive advantage for retailers is the progressive expansion of their own private label brands; retailer policy and trends in this area are discussed in the following section.

Trends in retailer own brands

In France, retailer own brands were little known before the launch of Carrefour's 'Produits Libres' (Brand Free) in 1976. Casino and other chains had introduced private labels, but the competition, especially from associations of independent retailers such as Leclerc, who were opposed to retailer brands, was essentially on price and less in offering differentiation.

The Produits Libres from Carrefour were imitated by other unbranded products ('white products' from Continent, 'family products' from Mammouth, 'orange products' from Euromarche, 'simple products' from Cora). They were economical products, but which nevertheless offered acceptable quality, and they were all called 'produits drapeaux'. Their packaging was simple, one-colour – often white, as in the case of Carrefour – the manufacturer's name was visible and the retailer's brand was discreetly mentioned. The launch of these products was often supported by huge advertising investments, which favoured their success.

However, following their initial success, there was a strong negative reaction by most producers and by some other retailers, and the number of own brands and their market share did not grow very much. In the case of Carrefour, from a total of 50 in 1976 the number of these products reached only 105 by 1982. For Euromarché the figure that year was 163, and the contribution of own brands to the total sales of these two retailers in 1982 was 5 and 8 per cent, respectively. For Mammouth, Cora and Continent, the proportions of sales were much lower (Thil and Baroux, 1983).

During the 1980s, these private brands were progressively replaced by 'classical' (branded) private brands, referred to as 'counter-brands' by certain authors (Kapferer, 1995); and the market share of all of these private brands rose from 8.4 per cent in 1975 to 11.2 per cent in 1980.

The next stage of retailer own brands in France was generic products, sold with no brand and positioned as the lowest price product. They were significantly cheaper than leading brands, but their quality was also appreciably lower. These products were later given brand names: usually manufacturer brands, but also sometimes retailer brands, although this was not necessarily obvious. From the beginning of the 1990s, these products were often called 'lowest price products' and were used by hard-discount competitors. Some retailers such as Intermarché preferred to have different brand names for different product lines. Others, by contrast, used only one brand name for all their products in the lowest price range (Leader Price of Franprix). In the former case, the retailer brand is less apparent, and the link with the retailer name is less obvious than in the latter case.

A third phase in the growth of retailer own brands is that of products carrying the same name as the banner of the store adopting them. These are good quality items, packaged similarly to leading brands, but generally slightly below them in price; although at times their prices are very close to the prices of the large brands, and even, in some cases, higher. The same name being adopted for both the product and the retail store clearly states that the retailer endorses the product. Retailers using this strategy are more and more committed to offering high-quality products or else innovative items. The retailer own brands of this generation are thus setting out to impose their brand name in and of itself, in head-to-head competition with national brands (Bell, 2001b). All the major retail chains (especially Carrefour and Casino) have expanded these brands, while in the merchandise assortments of associated groups such as Leclerc and Intermarché, the lowest price and economical brands still dominate.

In 1980, according to Secodip, the percentage of all types of retailer own brands in grocery was approximately 11.2 per cent at the national level; and ten years later, also according to Secodip data, it had passed the 15 per cent mark. However, it was in the 1990s, with the growth of the third phase of retailer own

Table 2.14 Grocery retailer own brands in France (%)

1975	8.4
1980	11.2
1990	15.2
1995	17.4
1996	17.2
1997	18.0
1998	19.4
1999	20.0
2000	23.9

Source: LSA (Secodip).

Table 2.15 French retailer own brands in 2000 (%)

Stores	*Market share of grocery products*
Intermarché	31.2
Casino	24.3
Carrefour	24.2
Total (HM + SM)	23.9
Champion	22.7
Système U	22.0
Stoc	21.6
Leclerc	20.8
Continent	20.8
Géant	19.4
Auchan	18.2
Cora	18.1

Source: LSA (Secodip).

Notes
HM = Hypermarkets.
SM = Supermarkets.

Table 2.16 Proportion of own label in European multiple grocers (1999)

Country	Volume share	Value share	Price index
United Kingdom	45.4	43.5	96
Belgium	34.7	26.0	75
Germany	33.2	27.4	83
France	22.1	19.1	86
Netherlands	20.6	18.4	89
Spain	20.5	14.8	72
Italy	17.1	15.5	91

Source: A. C. Nielsen.

brands, that their market share significantly increased, due not only to the growth of these products at Casino, Carrefour and Intermarché, but also because of their general adoption by all the other retailers, albeit at a lower rate. Details in the rise in this proportion over time are given in Table 2.14.

In 2000, the proportion of grocery own brands reached 23.9 per cent, and as shown in Table 2.15, Intermarché Group was the leader.

It should be noted that these proportions are substantially below those of leading European countries, set out in Table 2.16.

However, it must be noted that at the beginning of the 1990s France underwent an economic recession that fostered the growth of hard discount retailing, and consequently a resurgence of price competition. This only began to subside towards the end of that decade; and with more qualitative competition now under way for the coming years, the prospects for own brands remain very favourable.

Particular issues

Overview of the hypermarket structure and corporate strategies

The hypermarket in France has the most complete life cycle of any retail format in Europe, and it is thus interesting to analyse how its features – size, location, trade name offerings and policies – have changed at each of the different stages of its cycle (Colla, 1992, 2001).

At the very beginning, during the introduction stage in the 1960s, companies were experimenting with a selling structure whose potential was not clearly understood, and thus at this stage stores were not very large. Then, during the growth stage in the 1970s and 1980s, the firms which had the most experience with the format, such as Carrefour and Auchan, discovered they could improve productivity by expanding the size of their stores. The average selling space increased from 3,400 sq. m. in 1966 to 6,274 sq. m. in 1973. However, from this year it began to slow down slightly until 1980 when it reached 5,625 sq. m., and, with the exception of 1981, continued to decrease until 1990 when it was

5,386 sq. m. By this stage less skilful followers were entering this market, and independent associates such as Leclerc were increasing the number of their smaller sized stores. During the maturity stage of hypermarket development in the 1990s, store openings fell off due to the increased degree of competition and the competitive reaction of retail organizations. Nonetheless, the average store in terms of selling space resumed its growth, and from 1992 to 2000 this increased steadily from 5,428 sq. m. to 5,734 sq. m. (Insee, 1999, 2000).

During the launch and growth stages, the first hypermarket to open in an urban area gained appreciable market share quite easily, regardless of its location. The competitive environment was still relatively favourable because the main competitors in the grocery sector were small- and medium-sized stores, as well as single-price (variety) stores. Against this type of rival, it is obvious that hypermarkets enjoyed considerable competitive advantage, enabling them to leverage even further their economies of scale. However, everything completely changed with the advent of the maturity stage towards the mid-1990s. Established French hypermarkets now had to cope with several new competitive variables:

- other hypermarkets whose commercial offer was differentiated;
- hard-discounters and discount neighbourhood and suburban supermarkets;
- LSS with aggressive commercial policies; and
- the decrease in the availability of large commercial locations, due mainly to the saturation of the market and the impact of the Raffarin Law.

Commercial offerings also varied according to the life cycle stage of the structure. At the time of launch, the assortment was wide and shallow, with consequently, a rather limited number of stock units. During the growth stage, retailers introduced new products and expanded their selling areas. In food, fresh refrigerated products, bakery and pastry, frozen foods and counter sales took up more and more space. In non-food, apparel was more and more common, and particularly, cumbersome product categories such as gardening, do-it-yourself, automotive accessories, household appliances and furniture were also more and more visible.

On reaching maturity, the hypermarkets turned towards retail offerings previously exclusive to specialists, such as non-prescription pharmaceuticals, jewellery and optical products. Also, the number of stock units listed in certain categories increased. For example, expensive and slow-moving goods such as wines, liqueurs, foie gras and smoked salmon were added. Furthermore, hypermarkets also offered a whole range of financial services, credit and insurance, travel and leisure. It was also during this stage that these companies introduced exclusive manufacturer's brands or even actual retailer's own brands.

These innovations stemmed from the overall change in the competitive environment. With the increase in competition from other categories (particularly hard discount and LSS) and from other hypermarket retailers, differentiation of the offer began to appear, in addition to price competition. This differentition was implemented through location, size of outlets, type of assortment and the marketing of the offering itself.

As far as size is concerned, some chains (Carrefour, Auchan) managed to build a network entirely of large stores, while others (Cora, Geant, Casino, Leclerc) had mixed networks composed of stores with a smaller average size. The main obstacles hindering the creation of larger new stores included, in addition to restrictive legislation, insufficient financial resources, less experience in non-grocery, and a corporate culture which was sometimes incompatible with the demands of organizational independence and decentralized management.

With regard to location, we can distinguish isolated hypermarkets from those located in shopping malls. The former were generally surrounded by a shopping arcade offering minimal other services. It must be pointed out that these hypermarkets are less and less numerous because their draw and profitability are insufficient. Their main advantage is rapid construction. By contrast, hypermarkets located in shopping malls have an advantage, because they benefit from the strong pull of the mall, which ensures greater profitability. But they are also more complex to build because of the substantial financing they require, as well as the management coordination efforts between the hypermarket itself and the other tenants in the mall.

Differentiation of the offering can occur in several ways, with the hypermarket company choosing some parts of its assortment that it can enhance according to its specific expertise, the local market and competitor behaviour. The main objective of the services provided is to save the customer time and to create customer loyalty. Factors both outside and inside the individual store outlet come into play, and among the primary factors is the signage on the road leading to the point of sale, and the availability of adequate parking. Secondary factors include in-store signage and department indicators, together with a range of facilities which speed up payment and store exit: scanners, automatic credit and debit card terminals, express check-out registers for customers buying few items. Various financial services such as savings accounts, insurance policies, member cards and loans have multiplied, with the aim of creating repeat customer business. Leaders of the format are also pursuing store remodelling by creating 'shopping universes' based upon consumption patterns rather than traditional retail product categories, with the objectives of improving their discount image and enriching the shopping experience through the creation of a specific store atmosphere (Filser, 2001).

The importance of associated independents

In France, groups of associated independent retailers, notably Leclerc and Intermarché, dominate the supermarket sector, and also hold extremely strong positions in the hypermarket sector. These retailer groups are not only able to withstand competition from large multiples (corporate chains), but also boast higher growth rates than them. In non-grocery, the chains are the leaders in LSS, while independents and franchises lead in small specialized stores. Associations of independents in France are different from German or Italian purchasing cooperatives, and also the voluntary groups in the United Kingdom, in that no member can own more than two (or three) outlets. This enforced dispersion of ownership thus hampers a trend towards holding companies. Each store is, in effect, a small business which forms a cooperative with others in order to manage wholesaling and transportation on a local basis. All these local store owners belong to a national buying organization (Galec for the Leclerc group) that is in charge of buying activity for all the stores (with the exception of a limited amount of local buying) and also coordinates national promotions. Overall strategies and policies of these associated groups of entrepreneurs are mainly developed by the store owners themselves through some specialized working committees, each dealing with one general issue (private brands, advertising, new stores openings, international developments etc). This common management is strengthened by the rule of 'one third time' which imposes on each store owner the duty to devote two days a week to managing group activities through these committees.

Despite some of their ownership, management and operational characteristics which might otherwise have restricted their growth and dynamism, these groups have been able to reinforce their strategic and operational cohesion as a result of growth (the conversion of supermarkets into hypermarkets, for example, at Leclerc) and because of increasingly centralized decision making (Colla, 1991). Their particular pattern of ownership and management is not without importance in maintaining a certain degree of motivation on the part of members. They are able to expand their stores, and thus enhance their profits, but they are unable to open new stores. The associations have also benefited from the progressive centralization of transport functions, and from the growing importance of retailer own brands. This trend is particularly apparent at Intermarché where these policies exist side by side with initiatives, among others, toward upstream integration.

Vertical integration strategies in manufacturing and transport

Manufacturing integration

Not satisfied with controlling distribution channels through creation of their own brands, certain French companies (especially Intermarché and to a lesser extent, Casino, Leclerc and Promodès) have adopted policies of complete backward vertical integration in respect of a number of manufacturing operations. This strategy is not very common and is rarely applied systematically, but in some circumstances a few companies have pursued it.

The main objectives of backward or upstream integration for these companies are as follows:

* First and foremost, to reduce purchase costs, and consequently, selling prices, while at the same time maintaining the same margins by recovering part of production margins. If the existing distribution channel is not efficient, production margins can be excessively high and give rise to high profits which are eliminated with vertical integration.
* To be able to rely on the availability of suppliers who are capable of ensuring uniform quality and meeting demand. This is a more probable attraction

when the retailer has a large assortment of own-label products, and wants to reach and maintain an upmarket positioning.

- To take advantage of low-priced corporate acquisition opportunities, obtain highly useful information and strengthen the retailer's position relative to suppliers in a given sector.

The subsidiaries which are most often involved in retailer upstream integration frequently are found in traditional sectors (wine growing, table wine making and bottling, coffee bean roasting, basic canning, chocolates and confectionery, jams and sauces), to which fresh products have been progressively added: meats, cold cuts, bakery-pastry, gourmet items, cheeses. In particular, it is noteworthy that for meat products, many companies (including Promodès, Casino, Intermarché and Leclerc) have integrated the most critical stage of the chain – slaughtering, while for wines, they often handle the bottling. In such cases, the retailer is thus able to control the sanitary quality of the meats, and obtain several economic advantages (Dupuis, 1988): weight verification at the slaughterhouse, elimination of various costs (slaughtering and processing under the same roof avoids costly transport of carcasses and fats in controlled temperature atmospheres) and higher productivity of the butchers working in centralized plants in the vicinity.

Among retailers who have adopted this backward or upstream integration, we can distinguish those who have merely taken several uncoordinated initiatives of this type, and those who have made such moves a cornerstone of their entire strategy. Some groups, like Leclerc, have chosen to operate only in certain sectors which are strategic (among others, slaughtering) or especially important for their corporate policy (e.g. goldsmithing). Intermarché and Casino, on the other hand, belong to the second category. The former has integrated animal slaughter, frozen meats, non-alcoholic beverages, wine, fish, bakery and pastry (Paché, 1999). This strong vertical integration has enabled the group to become the leader in France in retailer private brands, with a market share of over 30 per cent. Casino has been involved in food processing since the beginning of the century, and its market share in meat products is particularly high.

Integration of physical distribution

In France, the system of physical distribution to retailers remained almost completely in the hands of the manufacturers until the 1980s (Filser *et al.*, 2001). They delivered directly from their central warehouses, regional distribution centres or through wholesalers. Then, the situation changed slightly, as large retailers began to set up their own warehouses and – less frequently – their own fleets of transportation vehicles. Centralization of logistics later began to accelerate, and in 1994, French firms had caught up with those of the United Kingdom, which had been the first to integrate logistics.

The retailers decided to integrate transportation logistics and create the necessary infrastructure above all for economic reasons (especially through reducing inventories), but also in order to provide better service to their customers. Deliveries became more flexible, and so the risk of running out of stock in the stores diminished. As a further development, some retail groups delegated central warehouse management and merchandise transportation to logistics service contractors in order to conserve their human and financial resources for purely commercial operations. British retailers are the leaders in this strategy, but in France too there are very significant operators, such as Carrefour, who have made the same choice.

E-commerce

While Europe is behind compared to the United States in e-commerce, France finds itself in a totally unique position in Europe. Internet penetration reached 15 per cent of the population in 2000, whereas it was 13 per cent in 1999. This is significantly lower than in Scandinavian countries (54 per cent) and in Germany (24 per cent). But this proportion rises to 34 per cent if we add the Minitel. Sales on the Internet topped 324 million euros in 1999, or 0.14 per cent of retail trade, but if we add sales over the Minitel, they amount to 1.6 million euros, or 0.7 per cent of total retail sales, against 1.2 per cent in the United States and 0.2 per cent on average in Europe (BCG, 2000a). If we consider all sales on the Minitel and the Internet, France is thus the leading country in Europe in terms of market share.

On the other hand, France is behind relative to all other European nations – except Italy, Spain and Portugal – when we only take into account Internet sales. The breakdown of electronic commerce sales by sector is also strongly influenced by the presence of Minitel. Contrary to the rest of Europe where the three main sectors are travel, computers and books, in France we find, in order, textile/apparel, travel and furniture/appliances.

E-commerce and Minitel

In fact, the buyers and the leading operators are different in the two channels. Mail-order retailers represent 75 per cent of all sales on the Minitel, and already account for 21 per cent of total sales on Internet, as well as being the fastest growing business on the Web. The largest operators are exclusively virtual sellers ('pure players'), which hold 40 per cent market share, while the multi-channels (excluding mail-order) reach 39 per cent.

The 'pure players' operators in France have a greater market share than the European average (34 per cent), and less than the share in only one country – Italy (BCG, 2000a). In the travel and leisure sector, Degriftour is an example. First appearing on the Minitel, it is now on the Internet. On the other hand, the creation of new virtual retailers who began initially on the Internet is more limited in France than in other European countries, and even more so than in the United States. The level of concentration is rather high, since for all types of activity, the five largest retailers represent 34 per cent of the market, and the ten largest

49 per cent. The concentration within sectors of activity is even higher. The three leading retailers in any sector typically account for 65 per cent of its sales. Competition here is very tough and the leaders already have established strongholds (BCG, 2000b).

Trends in Minitel and web sales

The growth in Internet sales is thus in part linked to the decline of the Minitel. In fact, Minitel sales in 1999 underwent a 6 per cent drop and returned to 1.3 million euros. This erosion in sales varies depending on the sector. It is higher in food and lower in textile/apparel, brokerage and travel. All sectors, however, have experienced significant Internet growth in France.

However, the decline in Minitel sales is proceeding slowly, and the transfer is not necessarily smooth. Nevertheless, companies selling on the Minitel have begun their transition towards the Internet, creating, in a number of cases, electronic commerce sites. But it must be emphasized that customers who have Minitel access do not have the same profile as those who buy on the Internet, and they will continue to use the Minitel. It is simple to use, and connections are fast and do not require initial waiting as on the Internet. And finally, the revenues from France Telecom cover or exceed the operating costs of the Minitel, and thus maintain the profitability of this channel, which is host to some 400 operators. Clearly, the Minitel is facing a decline in its activity. Threatened with competition from the Internet, it will need to focus on core competencies where it remains particularly effective, for example, orders for catalogue retailers, providing basic information. But if the dominant position of the Minitel seems to have hampered the rise of the Internet at its start, today it can also be noted that Minitel has accustomed many customers and operators to online commerce.

Government regulation in the French retail sector

Public intervention in the retail sector has been quite significant in France, particularly concerning the freedom to open stores, and rules regulating manufacturer/retailer relationships, especially resale prices.

Store openings – the Royer and Raffarin Laws

The first law passed on the freedom to open stores was the Royer Law of 1973. The Royer Law imposed an authorization requirement to open stores with selling space of more than 1,000 (or 1,500, depending on the size of the urban area) sq. m. The authorization was granted by a local commission where retail trade groups were heavily represented. The overall objective of the law was to limit the expansion of large retail stores, especially hypermarkets, in order to slow down the decline in the number of small, traditional retail shops. The steep drop in the number of these smaller retail outlets during the preceding years had created strong trade union protests which had concerned politicians. This law succeeded in limiting the expansion of large retail stores. It did not, however, have the effect of blocking them, and, as we have previously seen, hypermarkets continued to gain market share.

After a governmental freeze on authorizations to open large stores in 1993, the Raffarin Law of April 1996 required an authorization for any construction or expansion of a store with more than 300 sq. m. This law was supposed to limit large store openings, and contribute to the realignment of urban centre and neighbouring area shops. In fact, its main objective was to limit the growth of hard discounters – particularly, the German retailers who were very effective in France – whose average selling space was under 1,000 sq. m. Requests for store openings have to be submitted to department Commercial Construction Commissions (CDEC in French) which were made up of seven (under the Royer Law) and then six members with three elected official representatives, and three representatives from professional organizations (retail trade) and consumer groups (Chinardet, 1999).

Resale price regulation and the Galland Law

The Galland Law of 1 January 1997 modified the ordinance of 1986 relating to freedom in pricing and competition, which itself had superseded the 1945 ordinance on price regulations. Its main objectives were to prohibit retailer selling at a loss, to introduce more trade pricing transparency, and to permit manufacturer refusal to supply.

Thus, under the terms of this law, retailer sale at a loss is forbidden, except in the case where a store – under 300 sq. m. for a grocery and under 1,000 sq. m. for non-grocery – does so in order to meet a competitor's price in its geographic area. In calculating the threshold for resale at a loss, all trade price reductions 'acquired at the date of sale and directly linked to this operation' must be taken into account and must appear on the manufacturer's invoice. With regard to transparency of trade pricing, other trade discounts which are supposed to compensate for commercial and marketing services performed by the retailers (merchandising, promotions, market surveys etc.) – generally called 'commercial co-operation' – must under the Galland Law be separately invoiced, contrary to the ordinance of 1986. The Galland Law also forbids retailer listing fees for new product introductions, unless they are accompanied by purchase orders of the normal qualifying size. The refusal of a supplier to sell to a retailer, which was forbidden in the Fontanet Regulation of 1960, and which was confirmed under the 1986 ordinance, was finally permitted under the Galland Law.

The New Economic Regulations Law (NRE)

In May 2001, within the framework of a general law on NRE, a series of measures was introduced concerning relationships between manufacturers and retailers. These measures emphasize certain components of the Galland Law.

- Large retailers' promotions on fruit and vegetables are subject to an agreement between farmers' and retailers' trade associations, and the law specifies the mandatory completion of the contract terms (decided by the minister) in times of crisis. This measure was a response to the preoccupations of small farmers, who maintained that large retailers launched product promotions at the beginning of the season at prices which were below farmer production costs, aware that farmers would have to meet these retailer prices in their trade prices. The Galland Law regarding retailer selling at a loss would thus be complied with, but farmers would nonetheless experience losses.

- Stricter regulations were adopted concerning manufacturer payments for stock unit listings, and the amount of notice to be given preceding a break in commercial relations. The law recognizes, in this regard, the validity of agreements between farmers and retailers, but imposed a doubling of delisting notice time for manufacturers of retailer own brands.
- A study commission was appointed to publish recommendations and opinions on commercial practices between manufacturers and retailers. In the case of anti-competitive practices, the law introduced harsher sanctions of up to 10 per cent of the consolidated turnover of any group found guilty.

Consequences of the commercial legislation in France

The consequences to date of the Raffarin Law on store openings have been: a slowdown in the creation of hard discount stores, a certain amount of protection for the pre-existing market shares of established, smaller retailers, a push towards retailer concentration, and an encouragement of retailer international growth.

The Galland Law regarding retail pricing and retailer–supplier relations has had material consequences both on the competitive environment and on developments in trade relationships.

- The law has been totally effective at eliminating retailer sales at a loss. The selling prices invoiced to retailers have become almost completely uniform – corresponding to the minimum purchase price.
- Retail prices to consumers have also been aligned, upwards. The prices of the 2,000 most popular branded products went up by 3.6 per cent in the year following the Galland Law (Panel International, quoted by Chinardet, 1999). Consequently, as a result of the law, the largest retailers no longer really compete with each other on price for national brands. This has also helped the retailer own brands, as retailers have been able to increase their trade margins and prices for these products, or else increase the competitive price differential of own-label products relative to brand names. By reducing their competition on price, the stores have thus moved towards a competition increasingly based on the other variables of the retailing mix (corporate communication, promotion, own-brand expansion) and also upon productivity gains. In retailer own brands, for example, the retailers who are the most behind are now seeking to catch up lost ground. Among them, Leclerc is stepping up efforts in this direction, and Auchan has launched a vast programme of Auchan branded products (Bell, 2001b), where before it had preferred to expand its private labels under separate brands. Retailer own

Table 2.17 Change in 'commercial co-operation' (trade discount) on national brand products (% of the retailer buying cost)

1995	12
1996	16
1997	17
1998	23
1999	30

Source: LSA.

brands have in fact, recovered their growth in France starting in 1997, according to Secodip (see Table 2.14).

- Negotiating terms of sale between manufacturers and retailers is now moving from price charged towards trade discounts ('commercial co-operation', see page 46) which has become a significant differentiation factor for the manufacturers negotiating with retailers. The level of these contributions has increased significantly over recent years and, as shown in Table 2.17, has now reached a very high threshold. In many cases, the products – particularly very well-known national brands – are priced by retailers at the manufacturer invoiced purchase cost (before the Galland Law, they were sold even at below cost), the retailer making his entire gross margin from the 'commercial co-operation' payments.

Negotiations between the two parties, previously more based on adversarial arguments (price, price alignment rights) are now slowly giving way to negotiations premised on the mutual interests of manufacturers and retailers. Faced with changes in the competitive environment (concentration in the sector, growth of hard discount retailing in the 1980s, expansion of retailer own brands, technological changes and the impact of government legislation) manufacturers and retailers had already begun to improve their relationships with one another, moving from conflict towards cooperation (Manzano, 1997). At the end of the 1980s, this cooperation became particularly apparent with 'trade marketing' initiatives of an *ad hoc* style (Auchan) or implemented on a more repeated basis (Carrefour, Casino and Cora). These initiatives were essentially for advertising/promotional events customized at the point of sale (Chindardet, 1999).

With the advent of efficient consumer response (ECR) in the United States and Europe, manufacturers and retailers created ECR France, which has attained a particular position in retail logistics, due also to the efficient development of the electronic data interchange (EDI) network in France. The generalized use of scanning in France is among the highest in Europe with 93 per cent of the grocery volume, and with all major retailers scanning all of their sales. However, France does not appear as a leader in Europe concerning the most advanced category management practices. Very few retailers (among them Casino) have fully adopted these techniques. On the other hand, the marketing and merchandising departments of a number of leading French retailers are functionally linked to purchasing groups (Auchan), or work on product 'universes', but always separate their buying divisions from their commercial development divisions (Carrefour) (Chinardet, 1999).

Conclusions

Perspectives for the main grocery formats

At the end of the last decade of the twentieth century, the hypermarket was the dominant retail format in France. But stores of this type – particularly small- and medium-sized ones – began to have trouble fending off the competition as they continued to expand. As the consummate non-specialized store, the hypermarket occupies a market position that is difficult to defend against attacks from specialists. The exception is very large hypermarkets that enjoy both a favourable image and strong consumer credibility in non-grocery merchandise. However, stores combining these two conditions are rare, and only the two leaders in the French and European markets (Carrefour and Auchan) have reached this level. It is anticipated that the smaller hypermarkets will decide to focus on grocery and will limit themselves to only a few non-grocery departments with very professional management. A wider offering of non-grocery products would then be the exclusive domain of the largest hypermarket outlets.

In France, discount retailing has wrested a much smaller share of the market than in Germany, certain bordering states and Northern European countries. As noted earlier, the initial progress of this format was favoured by the tendency of supermarkets and hypermarkets to trade up, and by commercial legislation restricting large store openings and opening hours for stores. Economic downturns and changes in consumer behaviour have also accelerated discount retailing's market penetration (Colla, 1994). The factors that could lead one to predict the further advance of this format France are: very price-sensitive consumer attitudes, the size of the German leaders Lidl and Aldi, and the large number of French companies still operating in the sector. However, the Raffarin Law will continue to slow down the opening of new stores.

The convenience store format still has good prospects for growth in France. Although the number of small shops continues to decline considerably, convenience stores may find that such outlets offer good opportunities for conversion, provided their location is favourable.

Perspectives for the main non-grocery formats

Department stores are now mature in France and have to defend their market shares against attacks from LSS, and especially from the new specialized chains, recently merged groups and franchise networks.

Threatened by large supermarkets and LSS, variety stores are also experiencing a downturn, and are managing only with difficulty to conserve their market share by implementing new policies aimed primarily at differentiating their offerings.

On the other hand, the LSS are taking off in France and they are already the market leaders in some sectors, competing against food hypermarkets, department stores and variety stores. They are concentrated in number, and the leading names are very well known and enjoy a positive consumer image.

Mail order, after a period of stagnation lasting for quite some time, has been revitalized with the advent of the Internet. The competencies of mail-order organizations in delivery and direct marketing make them indispensable operators in the new forms of home shopping conducted online, and the Internet opens up new growth opportunities in different consumer categories for them. But this sector has become a competitive arena open to new entrants: web specialists on the one hand, and large retail groups on the other, who are attempting to integrate their bricks-and-mortar sales with online clicks-and-mortar. The latter have made serious incursions into the grocery business, while mail-order companies dominate in non-grocery sales.

Competing retail formats respond not only to overall consumption trends but also to particular patterns of buying behaviour. Consumers are ever more willing to shop in specialized stores which are able to satisfy their demands in terms of merchandise choice, buying comfort, overall shopping experience, after-sales service, and particular features such as size, breadth and depth of assortment, layout of the sales floor and services. French retailing is now characterized by a multitude of specialized retailers adopting a true differentiation strategy with several bases of segmentation. Possibilities for segmenting customers are quite varied, and consumption differentiation offers numerous opportunities to the more attentive retailers.

Trends in the competitive environment and retailer strategies

Over the past few years, as several retail formulae in France have entered the maturity phase of their life cycle, direct competition among retail groups has become considerably more aggressive.

With changes in consumer behaviour and the new competitive environment, retailers have reacted, first and foremost, by applying cost-reduction strategies. This has meant having to achieve economies of scale and reduce purchasing, transportation and administrative costs. In their search for cost savings, retailers have set out to develop their markets through internal expansion, acquisitions, collaborative buying arrangements and other alliances.

The expansion of retail groups has also occurred more and more frequently through diversifying operations, and retailer financial resources have been directed towards formulae with a high potential for growth. Retailers have generally preferred diversification through internal growth. However, France has also witnessed numerous strategic agreements and acquisitions, particularly abroad. A high level of concentration in retailing, including associated independent retailers, has thus ensued. These groups – Leclerc, Intermarché and Systeme U – have also undertaken a process of organizational and decision-making integration, in order to achieve economies of scale, to increase own-brand market shares and improve merchandising techniques as a means of confronting more effectively the competition from multiple branch store retailers.

The globalization of French retailers has surged over the past ten years. European retailers have intensified their efforts in Europe through measures to consolidate the market. However, new regions have opened up to investment, particularly Central and Eastern European countries, Latin America, and several Asian markets. These countries provide French retailers with opportunities for growth as development in their home markets is limited by restrictive legislation and a certain degree of saturation (Colla, 2001).

But along with growth, retailers have also adopted the strategy of differentiating their offerings. This has consisted of broadening their assortments and promoting their corporate image, while also pursuing less easily imitated options such as launching retailer own brands, which have met with considerable success in recent years. The rise of these private labels has been a feature of the entire retail sector in France. The store brands of super- and hypermarkets initially positioned themselves midway between the lowest price products and the major manufacturers' brands. But thereafter, their quality level became considerably closer to that of the leading national brands, which enabled them to create a favourable image with consumers.

Legislation, trends in manufacturer/supplier relationships, welfare effects

The Galland Law and the successive law on NREs advantaged manufacturers of major brands: loss leader sales have practically disappeared and consumer prices have increased. The new invoicing system introduced under the law enables manufacturers to monitor retail prices, and has had positive effects for national brands in terms of profitability and image. Only a few large multinational manufacturers – for example, Procter & Gamble – dislike the French system, claiming that the prices charged to retailers are too high and are too much the same for all retail formats compared to other European countries, notably Anglo-Saxon nations.

The small- and medium-sized companies that produce the retailers' own brands are quite satisfied, because sales of these brands are increasing, and their positioning has improved because of price increases in branded products. Other small- and medium-sized manufacturers, however, are encountering more problems because the costs of trade allowances (merchandising support, trade deals and slotting allowances) have reached very high levels, and constitute real barriers to retail shelf access. Indeed, in practice, retailers impose on small supplying firms the same trade contributions they receive from the leading brand manufacturers.

Large integrated retail chains have no cause for complaint about the legislation's consequences. There has been a rise in the prices of leading brand products as well as in trade contributions. Margins have, therefore, also increased. So, consequently, have major retailer profits and share prices, which make it easier for these groups to pursue strategies of international differentiation, diversification and growth. Another consequence of the legislation is that retailers and brand manufacturers work together more and more frequently in France to reduce costs, improve all interface operations, and differentiate their respective offerings, which provides both parties with new competitive advantages.

The only opposition to this legislation has come from the chains of independent associates, in particular the Leclerc group, which have always pursued a strategy of dominance through reducing trade costs. The Galland Law and the ban on selling at a loss deprive these groups of a competitive weapon they used to turn to systematically. But after an initial year of difficulties, they introduced new promotional tools that enabled them to offer consumers deferred discounts – calculated on the basis of a shopping basket of purchases – without breaking the law.

Consumers, however, have suffered negative consequences in terms of retail prices, which have not only risen but which have become more uniform in all stores. Price-conscious consumers and buyers of discounted products are the most penalized compared to those who are more concerned with quality and service. But all have felt the negative impact of this governmental intervention. Defenders of the law affirm, on the other hand, that the rules protecting the small- and medium-sized manufacturers – the ban on payments for a stock unit listing not accompanied by a purchase order, time deadlines for delistings – are designed to offset the impact of excessive market concentration on the part of retailers and other large-scale manufacturers, and to promote greater variety for the benefit of consumers. But it is still too early to judge whether this objective has been achieved.

Final considerations

As the development and growth of the modern retail concept in France has now for the most part reached its limit, the coming years are likely to see a strong surge in the German hard-discount retailers together with increased penetration by LSS and e-commerce. Nevertheless, the global impact of e-commerce is not likely to be quantitatively very significant. Rather than increasing actual sales, the Internet will offer marketing synergies to the traditional retailers – especially with regard to communication and customer loyalty and service – as these all become 'brick and click' operators (BCG, 2001). Such trends in French retailing seem to confirm the fact that rarely do changes in distribution occur suddenly or rapidly. With quite long life cycles being the norm, retailing formats 'become sedimentary rather than disappear' (Badot, 2001). Their survival, however, implies constant transformation in order to adapt to evolving consumer expectations, as well as continual differentiation in order to be distinct from competitors.

Following the implementation of new strategies in differentiating retail offerings, together with innovations concerning assortments, store layout and atmosphere (Moati, 2000; Filser, 2001), considerable transformations will occur for all types of store, and new concepts will appear. Retailer own brands in France will increase appreciably, and their image and positioning will improve relative to manufacturers' brands. The internationalization of French retailers will continue to develop, and they will try to consolidate their current positions while also conquering new countries.

French government policy with regard to retailing will be directed mostly to resist the undesirable effects of highly aggressive price competition, and also to defend both consumers and small- and medium-sized producers against possible abuses of power by the large retail groups formed through consolidation. In this, the French government will be supported by the vigorous anti-monopoly policies of the European Commission.

Thus, in the coming years, French retailing will be characterized by fewer differences with the rest of Europe. However, segmentation of markets, and the variety and differentiation of concepts and trade names will become more significant.

References

Badot, O. (2001) 'La prospective en distribution: pour un élargissement d'un cadre d'analyse hérité de la micro-économie dans une perspective dépassant la seule problématique du commerce avec ou sans magasins', *Conférence d'introduction à l'atelier de prospective de la distribution GVPI*, IAE de Caen Basse Normandie.

Bell, R. (2001a) 'Grocery retailing in France', *The European Retail Digest*, 30: 27–31.

Bell, R. (2001b) 'Uniquely Auchan', *The European Retail Digest*, 30: 23–6.

Boston Consulting Group (2000a) *The Race for Online Riches*, BCG, London.

Boston Consulting Group (2000b) *Le Commerce électronique en France*, BCG, Paris.

Boston Consulting Group (2001) *The Multi-channel Consumer*, BCG, Boston.

Bouveret-Gauer, M. (1997) 'De la boutique au grand magasin', in *La révolution commerciale en France*, Le Monde, Paris.

Burt, S. (1994) 'Carrefour – Internationalising Innovation', in McGoldrick, P. (ed.), *Cases in Retail Management*, Pitman, London, Case 13.

Charrière, V. and Gallo, G. (2001) 'La mutation des magasins populaires: le cas Monoprix', in Bloch, A. and Macquin, A. (eds), *Encyclopédie Vente et Distribution*, Economica, Paris.

Chinardet, C. (1999) '*Négocier avec la grande distribution*', Les Editions D'Organisations, Paris.

Cliquet, G. (2001) 'The megamerger: Carrefour-Promodès', *The European Retail Digest*, 30: 32–5.

Colla, E. (1991) 'I centri Leclerc: un gruppo di indipendenti al bivio dell'internazionalizzazione', *Commercio*, No. 40.

Colla, E. (1992) '*Gli Ipermercati. Sviluppo e maturità della grandi superfici di vendita in Italia e in Europa*', Etas Libri, Milan.

Colla, E. (1994) 'Discount development in France: the introduction of the format and the competitive response', *Journal of Marketing Management*, 10: 645–54.

Colla, E. (1997) 'Le développement du hard discount en Europe: une analyse compétitive', *Révue Française du Marketing*, No. 161.

Colla, E. (1999) 'Les tendances de la grande distribution en Italie et les facteurs critiques de succès pour les enseignes françaises', *Market Management*, No. 3.

Colla, E. (2001) *La Grande Distribution Européenne*, Vuibert, Paris.

Dayan, A. (1992) *Manuel de la Distribution*, PUF, Paris.

Dupuis, M. (1988) *Distribution: la nouvelle donne*, Les Editions d'Organisation, Paris.

Dupuis, M. and Tissier-Desbordes, E. (1996) 'Trade marketing and retailing: a European approach', *Journal of Retailing and Consumer Services*, 3(1): 43–51.

Filser, M. (2001) 'Reenchanting the shopping experience: case studies from France', *European Retail Digest*, 30: 23–6.

Filser, M., des Garets, V. and Paché, G. (2001) *La Distribution: Organisation et Strategies*, Editions ems.

Insee (1999, 2000, 2001) Comptes du Commerce.

Kapferer, J.-N. (1995) 'Stealing brand equity: measuring the perceptual confusion between national brands and copy-cat own label products', *Marketing and Research Today*, 23(2): 96–103.

Manzano, M. (1997) 'The relationship between manufacturers and retailers in French marketing channels*', Proceeding of the EAERCD 9th International Conference on Research in Distributive Trades*, Leuwen, Belgium.

Marseille, J. (1997) *La révolution commerciale en France*, Le Monde, Paris.

Moati, L. (2001) *L'avenir de la grande distribution*, Editions Odile Jacobs, Paris.

Paché, G. (1999) 'When logistics threatens to become a source of competitive disadvantage: The Intermarché co-operative case', in Dupuis, M. and Dawson, J. (eds), *European Cases in Retailing*, Blackwell, Oxford.

Reidiboym, M. (1999) 'Le hard discount à la française sort du lot', *LSA* 1627: 4–51.

Rhode (2000) *Un panorama des Grandes Surfaces Spécialisées en France*, DECAS, Paris.

Thil, E. and Baroux, C. (1983) '*Un Pavé dans la Marque*', Flammarion.

Villermet (1991) *Naissance de l'hypermarché*, Armand Colin, Paris.

Zaninotto, E. (1992) 'Il pluralismo delle forme organizzative proprietarie' in Caccia Dominioni, L., Zanderighi, L. and Zaninotto, E. (eds), *Le Forme di Impresa nel Commercio Europeo*, EGEA, Milan.

3 Germany

Klaus Barth and Michaela Hartmann

Introduction

This chapter follows broadly the structure of others within this study. It commences with a historical overview of the development of retailing in the German economy, and a consideration of the particular characteristics of German consumers and the present technological environment of German retailing. This is followed by a contemporary account of current developments in retailing in Germany and the range of store formats. Particular consideration is then given to the internationalization of retailing in the German economy, the importance of e-commerce, and manufacturer–retailer relations. More detailed consideration is given, because of its particular significance, to the legal environment of German retailing, and conclusions are then drawn on the interaction of all of these influences.

The development of retailing in Germany

'Middle class' growth

Throughout the last century until the 1950s, the German retail economy was dominated in particular by medium-sized retailers – part of that group in the German economy and society referred to as the *Mittlestandbewegung* (see Gellately, 1974). At the start of the 1950s, this sector still accounted for 80 per cent of all retail turnover (Lingenfelder and Lauer, 1999: 25). Small sales-area size of retail business combined with an emphasis upon outlet operating efficiency, together with an atomistic market structure (i.e. one comprising a large number of small-scale competitors), characterized the retail business sector at that time. Demand significantly exceeded supply, and the greatest priority for the retailers was the procurement of sufficient quantities of goods. The acquisition of new customers played only a minor role, if any.

Increase in affiliated retailers and retailer cooperatives

The burst of growth in the postwar period soon resulted in an excess of retail outlets, and at the end of the 1950s, a selection process began, leading to a reduction in the number of non-affiliated retailers. During this time, retailer cooperatives – that is, independent retailers such as Edeka or Rewe adopting the same trading name – grew in importance. At the same time affiliations of retailers – where the manager of the multiple-shop branch is an employee of the organization – also spread. Most of the estimated 120–150 affiliated retailers which existed in the 1950s came from the food and luxury-products areas (Berekoven, 1987: 86). Expansion was the main goal of these large multiples. Since, the construction of new stores required both organization and capital, the increase in individual store sales areas over the period 1950–1960 was rather limited. The *Arbeitsgemeinschaft des Lebensmittel-Filialbetriebe*, one of the principal trade organization committees, calculated that the number of stores rose from 4,353 in 1950 to 6,200 in 1960. The first moves towards consolidation began to emerge at the end of the 1950s. These led to the closure of smaller and unprofitable stores, while the remaining stores were developed and extended in terms of the product range they carried. As a result of this, the market share of the large multiples increased from 5.3 to 12 per cent of the entire food retail trade in the decade from 1950 to 1960.

The four department store companies Karstadt, Kaufhof, Hertie and Horten were particularly successful. In 1956 they reached a combined market share of 7 per cent of all retail turnover. The product ranges of the department stores were substantially developed during this time. In particular, the food departments of these stores were so significantly extended that it was not unusual for them to account for 20 per cent of the department store turnover. By 1965 department stores themselves accounted for some 10 per cent of all retail turnover (Schmalen, 1999: 471).

Retail self-service developments

An important feature of the development of German retailing in the 1960s was the development of the self-service principle. Schulz-Klingauf described the outstanding feature of self-service as 'Shop as you please, pay as you leave' (Schulz-Klingauf, 1960: 15). In 1951 there were only 39 self-service shops in Germany; and even in 1957 there were still serious discussions as to whether the self-service principle was at all tolerable for the German consumer (Tietz, 1993: 87). However, the triumphant advance of the self-service was not to be stopped, and by 1961 there were 22,619 self-service shops. This equated to a market share of 14 per cent of all grocery shops (Lingenfelder and Lauer, 1999: 27). The introduction of the self-service concept in turn led to the rise of the grocery supermarket retailers; and this sector of the market was particularly exploited by the large, multiple-shop organizations. One aspect of this introduction of the self-service principle was that the choice of goods and a number of shopping activities, which up to that point were carried out by retail personnel, were delegated to the consumers and manufacturers. One result of this was that manufacturers were then obliged to increase their advertising activities directly to consumers in order to ensure sales of their products. Furthermore, for retailers the continued introduction of self-service had the major effect of replacing the importance of personnel with sales area. This substitution was linked with substantial increases in fixed-cost investments, which were not possible for many small retailers. Thus, the spread of self-service retailing accelerated the already existing market concentration tendencies in the retail sector. Between 1960 and 1970, the total sales area in the food retail trade rose by around 120 per cent, while the number of grocery shops in the same period declined by 20 per cent.

Increasing importance of greenfield locations

The trend towards increased sales areas, the application of the discount principle to broad product assortments as well as the increasing mobility of shoppers led to the emergence of new large-scale retailer store formats on greenfield sites. As a consequence, German city centres became less and less attractive as retail locations. The outcome of this was that independent retailers lost their customers and closed down, their facilities and equipment were left unused, and the supply of retail services in city centres worsened. This trend led to developments in consumer markets and superstores, discussed below. These threatened not only specialized retailers, but above all, the department stores as well.

Additionally, the mid-1960s heralded the arrival of out-of-town shopping centres. The bundled settlement of different shopping stores on greenfield sites was inspired by and modelled on the development of American shopping malls. In Germany, the subsequent development, where shopping centres were built not only on greenfield sites, but also in edge-of-town locations, in the suburbs as well as in city centres, proceeded so rapidly that already by the end of the 1960s more than 200 shopping centres had been constructed. Of those, however, 90 per cent had sales areas of less than 30,000 sq. m.

Mail-order retailing

Mail-order retail occupies a special position in German retailing. In the years after 1945 it was possible to identify a slow upward trend for mail-order retail (Kirchner, 1974: 224). Following the currency reform of 1948 a large expansion of this form of retailing began, and by 1950 the number of mail-order transactions was estimated at 4,000. However, the majority of the organizations consisted of one-man operations and small businesses. In the 1950s, the mail-order business experienced a significant boom. Official statistics from 1960 show that in 1958 approximately 3,600 mail-order companies achieved turnover of some 2.8 billion DM. This represented a market share of 3.6 per cent of all retail turnover at that time. However, the six largest mail-order companies represented over half of this share (Berekoven, 1987: 86, 99).

In the 1960s, a merger and consolidation process began in this sector, the net effect of which was the closure of many small specialized mail-order businesses. Overall, the mail-order sector performed very well in the 1960s. Its share of the entire retail turnover did not rise as significantly as in the 1950s, but still increased from 3.8 to 4.5 per cent. During this period, efforts on the part of the mail-order business towards sales offices and internationalization began; and the entry of both Quelle and Neckermann into the travel industry in 1962 was extremely successful.

Spread of the discount principle

In addition to the increase in average business size and the spread of the grocery supermarket multiple retailers, price competition in German retailing increased significantly at the beginning of the 1960s. Such downward movement in prices was not solely delivered via special offers, but rather the discount principle of permanently low prices across a wide merchandise range became increasingly widespread. In the 1960s, the discount principle became a matter of considerable public discussion in Germany. One of the reasons for this was the success of the American 'discount houses', and following this, Karl and Theo Albrecht introduced the discount concept in Germany through their Aldi store chain. The essential feature of the discount principle, which is clearly bound up with the self-service principle, is based on an aggressive pricing strategy, consistent trading down and a product assortment structure that is based on rapid turnover alone. The main discount store formats are the grocery supermarket retailer, the consumer market (see below) and the superstore. Aldi, the corporate chain store, deserves particular mention here. In the 1950s, the two Albrecht brothers had already developed the family grocery shop into a large retail enterprise, with a market presence of 300 stores in 1960 (Lingenfelder and Lauer, 1999: 43). With the opening of the first Aldi store in 1962 in Dortmund they moved to the price-aggressive discount principle. The stores, equipped with the most modest store fixtures etc. and an 'everyday low prices' (EDLP) programme, offered some one hundred articles. This new and successful store concept was spread rapidly by the opening of new stores, so that by 1975 Aldi already had 1,000 stores in Germany (Brandes, 1998: 28).

The environment of German retailing

The consumer

Over the past few decades, German consumer profiles have changed in many ways. The demographic structure has shifted; and nowadays consumers demand much greater choice and their behaviour is much less predictable, making a clear definition of target groups much more difficult. The following are some of the trends currently confronting retailers in Germany.

The rising average age of the consumers

The average age of consumers in Germany is constantly rising. The population aged from 50 years and upwards is increasing, while the proportion of young people is declining. According to calculations of the German Federal Statistics Office for the year 2000, the age of the German population is split as follows: 15 per cent under 15 years, 17 per cent aged between 15 and 30 years, 32 per cent 30–50 years, 19 per cent aged 50–65 years, and 17 per cent aged 65 years upwards. Not only does this development have repercussions for retailers' product policy, but it also demands an appropriate adjustment of their marketing approaches.

Rise of single and two-person households

A continuous rise in the number of households with a simultaneous decrease of the average household size to single and two-person households has also to be borne in mind. This change in household structures is accompanied by alterations in consumer demand. The increasing desire for convenience deserves particular attention, because single people tend to want to complete their purchases in a time-saving and stress-free manner.

Convenience shopping

The desire of consumers for convenience also extends to their shopping habits – reflected, for example, in the preference for home-based shopping. In addition, it also relates to products. They should be designed in such a way that the consumer experiences the greatest possible benefit, combined with the least possible time expenditure. This can be best illustrated by the example of modern prepared dishes, the preparation of which takes little time but which nevertheless represent an adequate meal. Also, dining out has become more important. While in 1997, dining out constituted approximately 30 per cent of the German food market (by comparison, in the USA it was already 45 per cent in 1995), a rise of up to 40 per cent is expected by 2010 (o. V., 1999: 71). Similarly to developments in the United States, Eatzi's, Germany is also witnessing the importance of so-called meal-solutions-models. Supermarkets are expanding their offer of cold or hot pre-pared dishes, which place the emphasis on freshness. As a consequence, the share of turnover for prepared meals is rising.

Increasing environmental and health consciousness

Consumers have been strongly concerned with subjects such as the environment and health, leading to an increase in ecological products, bio-food and lifestyle food. Examples of the impact of increased health consciousness are the fall in per-capita consumption of strong alcohol from 7.5 litres per year in the 1990s to a current level of 5.9 litres, and the increase in per-capita consumption of yoghurt by 3.5 kg to almost 16 kg over the same period (o. V., 2001b: 17).

'Smart' and 'hybrid' shoppers

For some time now the German retail trade has been confronted with the customer types referred to as smart and hybrid shopper. Smart shoppers, who represent approximately 30 per cent of all consumers, are characterized by unpredictable consumption patterns. Forecasting their purchasing behaviour turns out to be particularly difficult. On the one hand, they often engage in shopping for fun; on the other hand, they conform to the rational model of information search. They are permanently searching for attractive offers, but if necessary they may pay DM 3 for a can of Cola. The term 'hybrid' is used to show that the customer is split. On the one hand s/he is brand loyal and corresponds to the customer segment described by Veblen: for the customers a relatively high price denotes a high benefit – the principle of conspicuous consumption (Veblen, 1899: 172). On the other hand, hybrid consumers search for good deals and bargains. A possible cause of this focus on price is that shopping budgets in Germany have become impinged upon by mobile phone bills and pay-TV subscriptions. The impact on marketing is that the definition of segments with clear features becomes increasingly difficult, and in particular that the strict segmentation of the consumers into non-prosperous discount customers and prosperous speciality shop customers is no longer possible.

Technological environment

The rapid changes taking place in the technological environment, in particular within the area of information and communication technologies, are central driving forces of the developments in the retail sector. The first German scanner store was opened on 15 October 1977, and by 1996 the number of scanner workstations had already reached approximately 85,000 (Lingenfelder and Lauer, 1999: 31). At present, scanning as a subject has fallen into the background. Current attention is centred on new technologies for gathering and analysing data, for example. Key terms such as datawarehouse or datamining and their potentials are widely adopted, and above all the Net and its pervasive impact offers a challenging field of inquiry and provides enormous potential for the retailing sector.

As examples, it is possible to list the following effects, opportunities and risks of new technologies. Modern retail information systems contribute to the optimization of information retrieval and information analysis and can improve the decision quality substantially. Via integrated databases, ordering and sales processes can be entered and large quantities of customer data can be won. In this way, one receives information about customer needs and purchase histories, which can be made usable with the application of marketing tools. This information availability approaches an 'anywhere, anyhow and anytime' scenario. Datawarehouses include data which can be passed on to manufacturers, logistics service providers etc. via extranet or Internet. Consequently, the value chain partners will be linked more closely together. The Net can serve as a medium for promotions and advertising. Further, the Net offers new possibilities for market research. Companies can use the Net to investigate the word-of-mouth and referral behaviour in various consumer newsgroups. The Internet as a new global sales channel enables not only retail business enterprises but also manufacturers or completely new alliances to sell goods and services. The point is, that retailing without retailers is possible, and the Net leads to increasing vertical competition.

The store format structure of German retailing

The individual store formats adopted by retail business organizations vary according to the sector of the trade, the chosen operating form, the scale of retail outlet, the product range, the location, the price level and the particular way in which stores or store groups are to be managed. These store formats in the retail trade are subject to a constant modification process, referred to as *the dynamics of store formats*. From time to time new store formats develop, existing store formats change, lose their impact or withdraw from the competition. The dynamics of store formats reflect consumers' needs, since only those store formats which adapt best to the individual and overall needs of consumers will succeed. As a result of the complexity and dynamism of store formats, classification of these is difficult. Consequently, the distinction of store formats is based on a combination of structural and other variables. Since the retail trade in Germany has many variations (see Barth, 1999: 86), the following explanation is limited to the most important and, for the purposes of this work, relevant store formats.

Speciality stores

These offer a closely related and usually sector-oriented merchandise assortment, such as men's clothing. This may consist of products of different qualities and price positions, and which are sold with a high level of customer service. If these outlets specialize in a particular merchandise sub-range they are called single-line stores. Beyond the fact that the product assortment is wider than that of a standard specialized dealer, the product assortment is appropriate for the particular quality requirements of customers. Generally, customers are also offered a high level of service.

Department stores

These are large retail outlets with a sales area of 3,000 sq. m. and upwards. Goods from a range of branches, including groceries and semi-luxuries, are offered. Apart from the food department, in which the principle of self-service prevails, most goods are sold with a full level of customer service. The rise of the consumer markets and superstores in the 1960s led to a so-called 'store erosion' of the department stores in the 1970s. In turn they reacted to this trend with trading-up approaches, and these achieved varying degrees of success. During the period 1950–1980 the number of department stores rose from 140 to 406. However, by 1995 it had fallen again back to 345. The department stores achieved a peak market share of 10 per cent of the entire retail turnover in 1972 (Berekoven, 1987: 133). However, the competition from the consumer markets and superstores was so strong, that turnover of the department stores decreased in the second half of the 1970s, and simultaneously their proportion of shop numbers and sales area decreased. Consequently the department stores were forced to rationalize their entire organization. In addition, a trading up strategy was implemented by the department stores in order to position themselves in relation to greenfield site competition. The emphasis of the product assortment policy was based on wide assortments, sales areas were transformed and the management of unprofitable departments was delegated to outside firms. In 1993 the number of department store companies was reduced from four to two, when Karstadt acquired Hertie, and Horten was taken over by Kaufhof.

Convenience stores

This retail format is characterized by a broad, flat and fast-selling product range. The convenience store is the epitome of ease of consumer buying. Stores are located in the neighbourhood or directly beside main streets. The product assortment consists mainly of goods for daily use and is offered to the customer on a comparatively small sales area. In Germany typical examples are the petrol station/garage forecourt shops and the kiosk or neighbourhood store. For the customers of convenience shops, price frequently moves down the order of priority, in favour of convenience. Although the number of articles per purchase visit as well as the average value per sales receipt is small, customer frequency and high trade margins in this sector make it a very attractive one for retail organizations; and in 2000 convenience stores in Germany achieved a retail market share of 6 per cent.

Non-store retailers

These retailers do not offer and sell goods from a shop outlet, but mainly by catalogues or brochures as well as field service personnel. Customers order via mail, by telephone or electronically and receive their purchases to their homes through the postal service or other transport organizations. If the product assortment of the mail-order business dealer is restricted to a few areas of goods, this would be described as a 'specialized mail-order business'. In addition to this, there is still also the 'product assortment mail-order business', which usually carries a product assortment similar to that of a department store without food. 'Universal mail-order businesses' operate product assortment mail-order business and specialized mail-order business. With a total turnover of 37.5 million DM in 1998 the mail-order business gain a market share of 3.9 per cent of all retail turnover (EHI, 2000: 81). Based on the net turnover not including foreign-based subsidiaries, Quelle is the largest German mail-order business, followed by Otto Versand and Neckermann.

Affiliated retailers

These are not specific store formats, but instead they represent the attempt of individual retail business enterprises to increase sales by operating in a number of locations, with individual local stores organized under a single, uniform brand. A 'large multiple' would be defined loosely as one where more than ten stores belong to the one retail business enterprise. The success of affiliated retailers is based on the fact that the operational and strategic marketing decisions are centralized (Lingenfelder and Lauer, 1999: 34). Within this, a risk and a yield balance among the individual stores can be achieved, which allows the occupation of risky locations. The development of this format in the 1990s has led to a situation, at least in the food retail trade, where the sector is currently dominated by large multiples, and where there are almost no non-organized retailers. In 1950, affiliated retailers in the food retail trade accounted for a market share value of 5.3 per cent, but by 1994 this had risen to 80 per cent. An exact classification of retail businesses is becoming more and more difficult, since the growth of co-operating chain stores and affiliated retailers has led them to continue to seek links and group purchase arrangements in order to acquire bulk purchasing advantages.

Discount retail business enterprises

The discount principle is similarly not a retail organization structure format, but is a particular trading formula which may be applied to a range of retail store formats. Since it is mainly large retail business enterprises that are able to achieve the article-specific purchase volumes necessary for the aggressive price strategy of the discount principle, this trading formula is almost exclusively operated by large retail enterprises trading through large numbers of branches. The grocery discount stores, first and foremost Aldi (further examples would be Le-Di, Lidl & Schwarz, Norma), have experienced continuous growth since the 1960s. According to a market analysis carried out by the *Europäisches Handelsinstitut* (EHI) (European Trade Institute) discount stores in Germany already had a lead over the grocery supermarket retailers in 1999. On 1 January 2000, 17.5 per cent of all store-based grocery shops were discount stores and their proportion of the entire sales area was 23 per cent (EHI, 2000: 81; Groner, 2000: 10).

The discount principle has also met with success in other German retail sectors. In particular, the specialized discount stores in the textile, clothing, leather goods and footwear sectors were able to adapt to the fashion requirements of the consumers and doubled their turnover from 1970 to 1980 (Berekoven, 1987: 126).

Grocery supermarket retailers

The product assortment of these retailers covers food, non-food products for daily and short-term requirements and semi-luxury merchandise. Self-service is the main style of selling, and floor coverage generally ranges between 400 and 1,000 sq. m. Grocery supermarkets are mainly located in good city locations and residential areas on main and side streets. Since the appearance of the first German grocery supermarket retailer in 1957, the number of these has increased constantly (Lingenfelder and Lauer, 1999: 42). Only in 1997 did the number fall:

from 9,610 to 9,596. At this time, turnover was 62.3 billion DM and the market share of all retail turnover was 6.5 per cent. In 1998 the grocery supermarket retailers' turnover fell back to 58.7 billion DM and their market share declined to 6.1 per cent of all retail turnover. This trend continued to the year 2000 by which time the number of grocery supermarket retailers continued to fall to 9,230. Since then, however, while the number of stores in the grocery retail business has generally declined, the actual proportion of the grocery supermarket retailers to the number of all grocery shops rose from 12.9 per cent in 1998 to 13.1 per cent in 2000. The sales area of the grocery supermarket retailers amounted to 6.83 million sq. m. in the year 1998, and therefore accounted for some 28.1 per cent of the sales area of all grocery shops. In the year 2000 the sales area of the grocery supermarket retailers rose slowly to 6.89 million sq. m. However, their share of the total sales area of the food retail trade fell to 27.8 per cent. According to research by the Institut der deutschen Wirtschaft, on 1 January 2000, 13.6 per cent of all grocery shops belonged to the grocery supermarket retailers. Consumer markets, superstores as well as the discount stores are a particular threat to the existence of the grocery supermarket retailer.

Consumer markets

According to official statistics, these markets have a sales area of at least 1,500 sq. m., and the principal idea of this concept is to attract consumers by means of a low-priced broad merchandise assortment. This product assortment covers mainly food, but also includes semi-luxuries as well as excise goods and consumer goods, which are sold in self-service either on the basis of continuously low prices or a special offer policy. A further typical characteristic of consumer markets is their low-cost locations. Furthermore, they are mostly automobile-customer-oriented, so that they usually adopt a traffic-favourable location. Depending upon location they are situated either alone or within shopping centres.

Superstores

These are usually retail business enterprises with a sales area of at least 5,000 sq. m. The emphasis of their product assortment is focused on food, which is predominantly sold, as in the consumer market, using self-service and with continuously low prices or a special offer policy. Superstores also seek out low-cost locations. They too are automobile-customer-oriented, and stand either by themselves or are located in shopping centres. The 1970s was the decade of the consumer markets and superstores. These two store formats experienced an unequalled boom during this time. Consumers were willing to undertake long journeys for the low-priced and broad assortment, particularly since sufficient parking spaces were available. At the end of the 1970s there were already 1,300 consumer markets and superstores, which accounted for a market share of 10 per cent of all retail turnover.

In 2000, superstores achieved a turnover of 31 billion DM and represented 16.3 per cent of total retail turnover (Nielsen, 2001: 15).

Speciality discount markets

These markets offer goods in their chosen specialist merchandise field at low to medium price levels in a generally large sales area. The broad and deep product assortment is based upon goods areas, requirement areas or target group areas. Although self-service is a feature, customers may have access to technical and assortment-specified service if desired. Owing to their focus on car-owning customers, specialized markets are mostly located in peripheral locations or outside city centres. Leaders in the specialized discount market concept were the drugstore markets and the building and do-it-yourself (DIY) markets. Also, as a result of strong increases in rates charged by tradesmen, building markets profited from the DIY trend; and consequently the number of specialist discount building markets rose to 400 in 1978 and almost doubled by 1980.

Factory outlet centres (FOCs)

These developed from the conventional factory store. The factory store as a direct sale system of the manufacturer is a simply equipped, medium to large-scale business. In particular, it offers b-grade goods and excess stock remainders at sustainable lower prices than in the normal retail trade. The concept of the FOC, which originated in the United States, combines the settlement of factory stores with off-price stores under one roof, with the offer of additional leisure and catering services, which should create a kind of 'event-discount shopping' (Zentes and Swoboda, 1999: 113). The clear target group of these store formats is the so-called smart shopper or bargain hunter who wants to purchase high-quality and well-known labels instead of cheap unknown brands. The current 1,500 German factory stores listed in special 'good deal' guides provide ample proof of an existing demand for appropriate purchase opportunities (Schmalen, 1999: 481). FOC itself represents a philosophy – to sell branded articles below the regular retail price level – which is a threat to the old and established retail business. The Federation of the German Retail Trade has described its position on this topic in a current notice as follows: 'Responsible persons should be fully aware of the following: in Germany, FOCs are not required … unless the following applies: FOCs may not be permitted to exist in an unrestricted manner in peripheral sites. Such FOCs are nothing other than large-scale retailers on greenfield sites, where they compete with the core product ranges available in city centre retailers. The net effect of this is a detrimental impact on city centre retail, and thus a threat even for mature city centre locations because FOCs are able to shift retail trade from the city centre to peripheries' (Wenzel, 2000: 4). Despite, at times, substantial resistance from the retail trade, 33 FOCs are currently in the planning stages in Germany.

Urban-entertainment centres (*UECs*)

These are a special form of shopping centre and represent a synergistic combination of entertainment, event shopping and communication. Thus, in addition to the possibility of completing daily or weekly purchases at a central place under one roof, UECs offer entertainment, leisure activities etc. City centres with a good tourism base and a large number of local visitors, or high purchasing power potential are considered as suitable locations (Falk, 1999: 1,088). These city-centre locations generally avoid the necessity for self-transport to the UEC. While in the period 1964–1995 one-quarter of all shopping centres was opened in green-field sites, the current trend is different. Since 1998, a unique trend towards the city can be identified. Of the 30 shopping centres opened in the last two years just 3 were located in greenfield sites, 16 in the city centre and 11 in suburban areas. Of the 279 shopping centres existing in Germany at present, 217 are situated within cities. The question of how many of these 217 shopping centres can be called UEC, depends on how well the respective entertainment and event shopping offers are developed locally.

Special issues in German retailing

With regard to current trends and challenges in the German retail industry, one can identify three features in particular – internationalization, e-commerce and retailer–manufacturer relations – which deserve special attention; and this section offers an overview of the key issues in each of these.

Internationalization

The increased concentration and the significant price and locational competition in the German retail trade have led to a situation where the number of retail organizations trying to cover their domestic turnover losses with international expansion is constantly rising. Two initial large internationalization waves were observed: first the EC-domestic market initiative in the 1980s, and the second, instigated by the economic and political opening of the Eastern European States at the beginning of the 1990s. At present the non-food retail sector in particular is demonstrating a high degree of internationalization, even if the number of foreign companies operating successfully in the German market clearly exceeds the number of German companies operating abroad. Examples of international retail organizations having an influence on the German commercial landscape include the Swedish Ikea and Hennes+Mauritz, Woolworth and Body Shop from the United Kingdom, and Toys 'R' Us from the United States. On the other hand, with regard to the food sector, Aldi, Tengelmann and Schlecker are examples of German companies operating abroad. In 1996, Aldi gained about 29 per cent (12.5 billion DM) of its total sales abroad. For Tengelmann this proportion was as high as 49 per cent for the same year (Lingenfelder and Lauer, 1999: S.51).

One of the most significant events in the internationalization of German retailing has been the arrival of Wal-Mart into the German market. Wal-Mart's approach to entering the German market was to acquire an existing dominant player. It was thus in December 1997 that it acquired the Wertkauf hypermarket chain of 21 stores – one of the most profitable hypermarket chains in the country – from the Mann family of Germany. Having determined that building new hypermarkets in Germany would be ill advised due to the mature European market and the strict German retail zoning laws that preclude greenfield operations, Wal-Mart spent more than two years exploring potential acquisitions, including Britain's Tesco, Metro also from Germany, and Makro of the Netherlands. Wertkauf's stores, similar in format to Wal-Mart's, featured high-quality personnel and locations, and were larger than the average German hypermarket. In 1998, Metro was the second largest retailer in the world, behind Wal-Mart. In 1997, some 7 per cent of its total sales were generated outside Germany, compared with 4 per cent in 1995 and 5 per cent in 1996. In 1998, Metro took the major step of acquiring S. H. V. Makro of the Netherlands. Metro's consolidated sales revenues for 1998 are estimated at 108 billion DM, out of which foreign sales would represent 37 per cent.

In the list of the 200 Top Global Retailers, which was published in the fourth annual report *Global Powers of Retailing* by Deloitte & Touche in 2000, Germany was represented by 13 companies. The most important ones are: Metro AG (rank 4), Tengelmann (rank 13), Rewe (rank 16), Edeka (rank 17); further ones are Otto Versand, Aldi, Karstadt Quelle, Lidl & Schwarz, Bertelsmann, Anton Schlecker, Tchibo, Globus Handelshof and C & A (Diehl-Wobbe, 2001: S.248).

Virtual retailing concepts add a new dimension to the current trend towards internationalization, in which retailers can offer products and product assortments anywhere in the world. The importance of a physical presence becomes irrelevant, thus substantially lowering the barriers to market entry; and only the logistical challenges of non-digital goods limit the possibilities of complete locational independence.

E-commerce

While the success of the Internet was initially born in the United States, the virtual business has been having an increased impact in Germany as well. However, according to a 1999 study carried out by the EU Commission, Germany's rating in terms of the penetration of Internet and e-commerce facilities was still only average when compared with the other countries of the Union. Meanwhile one in every four German citizens between the ages of 14 and 64 surfs the Internet. According to current estimates from the *Gesellschaft für Konsumgüterforschung* (Society for Consumer Goods Research) in Germany, there are approximately 13 million Internet users at the moment (Heinzmann, 2000: 64). Between 1997 and 2000 the number of Internet users more than doubled. In addition, the number of Internet addresses increased enormously, and the 2 million level has already been exceeded. In the light of these numbers, all market research institutes forecast immense growth rates for the Net. Most retail businesses recognize the importance of e-commerce, plan an Internet appearance or have already installed a representation of their product assortment. Often there is a link to an electronic mall or a local community, within which many different retailers appear combined under one network address. The largest German-language virtual shopping centre so far was launched in 1997. It is called Mall Shopping 24 (http:\\www.shopping24.de). Further examples of virtual shopping centres are Netzmarkt, launched in 1995 (http:\\www.netzmarkt.de) and the pilot project my-shop.

Looked at from the viewpoint of retail managers in terms of the benefits and risks, the major benefits of e-commerce are increased purchase efficiency, maintaining closer contact with customers, increasing sales internationally within the existing customer segment and the development of new target groups. On the other hand, risks perceived include increased price competition through more efficient comparisons in this dimension of competition, decreasing customer loyalty as online customers are less loyal, expanded geographical competition as businesses from around the globe compete among each other and the high level of new investment required – for example, the financing requirement to set up an e-commerce capable Website amounts to approximately \$43 million.

The Net creates a completely new communication situation. Information sovereignty will transfer to the consumer, because s/he determines, due to the interactive nature of the medium, the time of communication. Beyond that the Net gives rise to a new transparency of merchandise and prices, and consumers will have a shopping power they have not previously enjoyed. As a result, the relationship between consumer and retailer will change fundamentally. Retailers will need to adjust to a new world order; and it is thus important for them to control e-commerce properly.

However, the online presence of German retail business is very limited to date. Many retailers maintain only a passive website, which serves for representation, but does not enable transactions. In 1999, e-commerce turnover only accounted for 0.3 per cent of total turnover. In the Christmas 2000 period, despite a record turnover, the Internet trade only reached 0.6 per cent, although this already represented an increase of 100 per cent on the previous year's results. According to research, less than 40 per cent of e-commerce businesses will achieve positive results in the year 2002. In the absence of the expected sales volumes in e-commerce, hopes are now turning to *m-commerce* (mobile commerce), in which consumers are offered services via mobile telephone – and also pay via this mobile device.

Manufacturer–retailer relations – efficient brand marketing

Manufacturer branded articles as a proportion of the total product assortment of German retail business enterprises in 1999 amounted to 90 per cent in the field of pharmaceutical/chemist consumer goods and 70.3 per cent in the area of the food products (Markenverband e. V., 1999 Annual Report). Thus, faulty brand marketing can be hazardous for a manufacturer. Price plays a significant role in consumer purchase decisions, particularly in the area of substitutable brands, and this consumer price sensitivity is further promoted by a marketing strategy of the retail business enterprises that is predominantly focused on price. Consequently, the manufacturers' price positioning of brands is undermined (Skimutis, in preparation).

In the context of brand marketing, the external (manufacturer and retail industry) and internal (marketing and sales) interface management represents one of the greatest challenges for the brand-article-manufacturer. However, due to the strong buyer power in trade relationships, the manufacturer sales department often regards brand marketing and brand penetration as secondary fulfilment criteria. In addition, the negotiations between the manufacturer's sales personnel and the retailer's supply personnel are predominantly based on trade terms and conditions. An almost exclusive focus on quantitative targets promotes a one-sided concentration on these terms, and leads to the situation where qualitative criteria are left aside in the negotiations. As a result, the customer is only considered to a limited extent. Therefore the retail industry, whose target is obviously to promote the profile of the business outlets and not that of any one product in particular, has limited interest in brand maintenance, as emphasized by the manufacturer. The completeness of the brand appearance at the point of sale, which, from the manufacturer's viewpoint, is reflected in favourable placement and proper presentation in keeping with the market appearance, leads in the eyes of the retailers to additional costs which do not bring about appropriate increases in returns. Therefore, the generation of demand suction by the final consumer is necessary for the manufacturer. This market stimulation is generated by the use of pull measures such as advertising. This means that the final consumer is made aware of the brand names and is stimulated to buy them by the manufacturers' marketing activities. Consequently, retailers are not only buying the brand programme of the manufacturer but also a strong demand. As a result, those brand articles which fulfil this prerequisite best, become possible product assortment foci of the retail business enterprises. On the one hand, attractive display stands and associated material promote the sales of the retail business enterprise. On the other hand, they lead to retail-specific savings of handling costs, sales areas and sales units. Retail-partner-oriented trade marketing concepts of the manufacturers (in particular, key account and category management), improve the coordination between manufacturers and retailers in the long run and can work against the aggressive sales promotion of both the large-scale retailers and the cooperatives.

The legal environment of German retailing

Although it constitutes but one part of the retail environment, because the law impinges so much upon German retailing policy and operations, this matter is dealt with below in some detail.

Although competition-policy legislation in Germany can be dated back to the *Verordnung gegen den Mißbrauch Wirtschaftlicher Machtstellungen* (Law Against the Abuse of Economic Power) of 1923, the foundation of modern German competition policy is the 1957 *Gesetz gegen Wettbewerbsbeschränkungen – Kartellgesetz* (Law Against Restraints of Competition). In Germany the purpose of economic policy is to arrange and regulate the economic activities between business partners. The Federal Secretary for Economics describes the function of the domestic trade policy as follows: The German domestic trade policy is aligned to protect a free space for trading ventures, which they need to grow and to develop and exhaust new opportunities for rationalization (Ahlert and Schröder, 1999: 245). Domestic trade policy is not an independent area of policy, but a conceptual summary of all domestic trade measures, and the regulations relating to the sector's structure, competition and economic policy. The most important instruments for the implementation of these objectives are laws and regulations governing the sector's trade, competition, structure, building and planning law. Basic legal requirements represent restrictions (e.g. with the formulation of slogans or the regulation of prices) as well as protection against competitors. The legal basis in Germany is very wide, and the following sub-sections describe the essence of the principal regulations.

Gesetz gegen Wettbewerbsbeschränkung – GWB (Law against Restraint of Trade)

Currently, Section 20 paragraph 4 GWB is the most discussed legal regulation of the GWB. The Restrictive Trade Practice Act of 1996 regulated the conditions under which a sale below cost price is forbidden. Since this new regulation came into force, its practical application has been tested again and again. Principles of interpretation are currently being discussed, the objective of which is to create more clarity and an effective application. This paragraph 20 should prevent below-cost selling from taking place for a longer period and the use thereof from serving to damage or destroy competitors. The idea is to lay down the boundaries of admissible price competition and to prevent in advance a deliberate or power-based displacement of medium-size competitors, in the interest of the long-term competitiveness of the sector. The German Cartel Office sets the cost price based on the list price of the suppliers. Additionally, price-related conditions such as trade discounts, discount payments, turnover-related rebates etc. are taken off. If the cost price is proven to be undercut, the Office accepts only, for example, the introduction of new products or a temporarily limited reaction to the price reduction of a competitor as a justified reason for below-cost prices. It was also determined that prices falling by 3 per cent below the cost price would be considered as slight. Warnings have already been issued to Wal-Mart, Aldi North and Lidl.

A paradox exists in this respect within a united Europe. While the Office of Fair Trading in Great Britain has acted to protect consumers from excessive prices further to alleged price-fixing arrangements in the food trade, the German Cartel Office must prevent the retailers from delivering their products more cheaply than is permitted. It is clear that German consumers benefit by billions of DM in savings from the price war in the food trade. According to statistics from the *Hauptverband des deutschen Einzelhandels* (HDE) (Main Association of German Retailers) this saving stood at some 4–5 billion DM in 1999 (o. V., 2000a: 1). For discounters in particular, this regulation is a clear restriction, because Section 20 prevents them from undercutting the prices of competitors if the cost price has to be undercut. As a result they are not able to maintain their position as price leaders.

Fernabgabegesetz (Remote Delivery Law)

In connection with the increasing importance of e-commerce, the so-called 'remote delivery law' was passed, and came into force on 30 June 2000. Under its provisions, Internet companies in Germany must grant consumers the right to return goods within two weeks, and the charges associated with returning these goods fall on the Internet company starting from goods valued at DM 80.00. However, the right of return for online orders does not apply to electronically supplied goods. For example, if software, music or other data is supplied to the computer of the consumer, then it will be considered as bought. Additionally, the law regulates the handling of confidential data, such as in particular credit card numbers. In cases of misuse, the bank of the consumer is generally held liable.

Gesetz gegen unlauteren Wettbewerb – UWG (Law against Unfair Competition)

The general clause of the Section 1 UWG outlaws unfair behaviour. Examples of this type of behaviour would include (1) customer attraction by deception, compulsion, utilization of emotions, inexperience and others, (2) obstruction by discrimination, boycott etc. (3) piracy of intellectual properties. Section 2 UWG is particularly worth mentioning. While comparative advertising was illegal in Germany for a long time, it has been permitted since 2000. The objective of the legislators in this area is to provide more transparency concerning different offers and better information from the consumers' point of view. However, to date it has scarcely been used by retailers, but is more commonly used by service providers, such as telecommunications companies and banks.

A current (early 2002) example of the application of this law has, however, reached the English-language business press. In January 2002, the Belgian clothing retailer C & A offered its German customers a 20 per cent discount to all shoppers paying with a credit card. This offer was made during the period of the initial introduction of the Euro currency, and was designed to smooth the introduction of the new currency, but the discount was, a few days later, extended to all customers irrespective of the payment method. The injunction against C & A by the Düsseldorf court of the first instance – which now relates to such discount sales being offered outwith clearly specified times of the year – was brought under Section 7 of the UWG at the instance of the German Association for the Fight Against Unfair Competition, an organization of 1,600 companies and trade associations, in a move which is clearly interpreted as being motivated by a desire to take advantage of current German law to continue to protect small, family-owned German stores (see *Financial Times*, 8 and 9 January 2002). The current (March 2002) situation is that the court has fined C & A €1m. for this offence, but that the company intends to appeal against this (*Financial Times*, 30 March 2002).

Baunutzungsverordnung – BauNV (regulations on the use of buildings)

The regulations on the use of buildings were first adopted in 1962. The most important legal regulation for the location decisions of retail business enterprises is Section 11 Abs. 3 BauNV. This deals with the establishment of large individual retail businesses (in particular, superstores and consumer markets) and shopping centres outside of the city centres. This regulation determines that the establishment of large retail businesses and shopping centres is only allowed in central areas or specially designated areas. The reasoning behind this is that it is through the strong expansion of price-aggressive large-scale retailers on greenfield sites that the medium-size retailers and also the classical large-scale retailers (in particular, department stores and limited-line stores) are threatened. Additionally, the local authorities saw their structural policies coming under threat, and they particularly feared a depopulation of the city centres.

The new edition in 1977 of Section 11 Abs.3 BauNV fixing a size-area definition of such stores or centres was the first success. The construction of retail businesses with a gross area of more than 1,500 sq. m. (that is, with a sales area of approx. 1,000 sq. m.) is only permitted in central areas, that is, in locations within the city, or in special areas as designated by the local authorities. From 1 January 1987, these limits were reduced to a business size area of only 1,200 sq. m., and in the retail trade decree of 7 May 1996, the approved sales area (not the business size area) was further lowered to 700 sq. m. Since no local authority can be compelled to designate special areas where such larger businesses may be permitted to develop, large-scale retailers can more or less be prevented from expanding. It is also worth pointing out that representatives of the German middle class associated with smaller scale retailing frequently have a strong influence in local authorities.

However, in most cases the desired effects of this legislation – especially the protection of the middle class – did not occur even though the intensified actions of the legislators led to a tremendous slowing down of superstores and consumer markets. These large-scale retailers reacted in an unexpected way: by developing new store formats and by diversification. As a result, low-cost locations were sought out by speciality discounters of furniture etc., and nowadays these speciality markets are competing as discounters with the traditional city-centre speciality stores. Thus, competition in the city centres has substantially increased and there has been an expansion of sales areas.

At present, municipalities are particularly using the BauNV as a tool against the establishment of large shopping malls and, in particular, factory outlet centres on greenfield sites. Between 1996 and 1997, only one in every seven planned greenfield shopping centres was actually established. This is the main reason for the factory outlet centres in Germany being in the very initial stages of their development.

Ladenschlussgesetz (Law regulating the closing time of shops)

The *Ladenschlussgesetz*, which was first passed on 28 November 1956, regulates retail business hours. It refers exclusively to store-based retail formats, while non-store-based retail formats are free to arrange their opening hours. Also excluded are pharmacies, kiosks, petrol stations, automatic vending machines and sales offices at railway stations and airports.

Originally the *Ladenschlussgesetz* served as an instrument to protect the employees. However, it was also intended to prevent what was considered as undesired competitive behaviour and to guarantee equality of opportunities in retail trade competition.

Section 3 is a central point to be considered here, governing as it does the times at which sales outlets for the business trade with customers generally *have to be closed*. These times cover:

- Sundays and national holidays
- Mondays to Fridays until 06:00 and starting from 20:00
- Saturdays until 06:00 and starting from 16:00
- the four consecutive Saturdays before the 24th of December until 06:00 and starting from 18:00
- 24 December, if this day is a working day, until 06:00 and starting from 14:00.

Thus, the *Ladenschlussgesetz* determines when retail outlets must be kept closed, but does not compel these outlets to be open during the legally possible shop-hours.

The issue of store opening hours has been under discussion in Germany for years. The discussion is basically dominated by the same questions over and over again: Who benefits from liberalized shop opening hours? Should one support the convenience of consumers? Are additional shop-hours tolerable for the employees in the retail industry? Will additional opening hours create additional sales, more prosperity, more employment in the retail sector? How might the life rhythm of people be influenced (more trouble on Sundays and in the evening)?

Matters currently stand as follows. According to an initiative of the *Bundesrat* (the Upper House of the German Parliament) store opening hours should be extended on weekdays from 06:00 to 22:00 and on Saturdays from 06:00 to 20:00. On Sundays all affected shops should remain closed. This liberalization would undoubtedly be in the interest of the city centres as well as out-of-town retail developments. However, the *Bundesregierung* (Federal Government) does not see any need for changes in the current legislative period. This means that further liberalization of the *Ladenschlussgesetz*, and therefore an alignment with the corresponding regulations of neighbouring countries, will not take place in the near future.

Rabattgesetz und Zugabeverordnung (rebate law and addition regulation)

Rabattgesetz und Zugabeverordnung govern the granting by retailers of price deductions to final consumers. Rebates are price abatements, which a supplier grants his customers by a reduction on the required or published price. Rebates are only permitted in a few cases. In particular, the rebate in the form of cash or a cash coupon may be granted only to a maximum value of 3 per cent.

Rabattgesetz und Zugabeverordnung substantially limit retailer pricing strategies in Germany. In particular, the ability to discriminate amongst customers is very limited.

Examples:

- According to *RabattG* Sections 1, 9, differentiated treatment based on different existing or future importance (e.g. a bonus grant towards children as 'buyers of tomorrow') is forbidden. Thus, mark-downs or sales promotion may not be targeted towards a particular group or directed towards single customer groups.
- Referring to *RabattG* Section 4 Abs., the turnover on which the grant of a rebate or a coupon is dependent may not amount to more than DM 50. So-called yearly rebates, which are differentiated by quantity or turnover, are legally forbidden.
- A quantity-dependent price distinction is only permitted if the combination is not arbitrary or unusual. For example, while the offer of a package of three pairs of socks at a more favourable total price – 'three for the price of two' – is permissible, an offer of a package of ten electronic pocket calculators is judged as uncommon and thus legally forbidden.
- The possibility of a daytime-dependent price distinction is also limited in the rebate law. However, the legislator's formulation is very vague. A lower price at mid-day is only forbidden if it is understood as a discount or rebate from the customer's viewpoint. However, if this price reduction is understood as a general price reduction, and thus not as a rebate, it is admissible.
- Additions are basically forbidden in Germany (ZugabeVO, Section 1). Special actions like 'buy one, get one free' are not possible. According to UWG Section 1, any such linking of a gratuity to the purchase of a commodity is an offence.

While in other industries within Germany there are different versions of the rebate legislation, and while such legislation in other countries can be defined as liberal, the German rebate law and addition regulation significantly limit the possibilities of price reductions as a reward for customer loyalty and thus heavily circumscribe this dimension of retailer competition.

Verpackungsverordnung (packaging regulation)

The *Verpackungsverordnung* of 1991 has a significant impact on the retail trade. It was introduced in order to deal with constantly increasing waste quantities and to be able to convey valuable raw materials back into production. The regulation contains the obligation to take packaging back, to begin using reusable packaging in some areas, to recycle certain packaging, as well as to encourage a commitment on different packaging. However, the legislature created the possibility of leaving the fulfilment of these obligations to a private collection system, which collects the used packaging and returns it for recycling. This function is carried out by the '*Duales System Deutschland Gesellschaft für Abfallvermeidung und Sekundärstoffgewinnung* (DSD) GmbH' (Dual System Germany, Society for Waste Avoidance and Secondary Material Production Ltd), established in 1990. A particular feature of the Dual System is the 'Green Dot' identification of packaging, for the use of which a royalty is raised, which serves to finance the system. The *Verpackungsverordnung* forced the retail businesses to restructure their retro-distributional systems, not only for sales packaging, but also for transport packaging and cover packaging. This had a substantial impact on costs. Currently, discussions are under way concerning the amendment of the packing regulations. The target is an obligatory pledge regulation. This would establish a general pledge obligation against all 'ecologically unsuitable' beverage packaging. The Secretary responsible is planning to bring this regulation into force – 'if at all' – by October 2001 at the earliest. Since an obligatory pledge must necessarily go hand in hand with a return obligation, it could create a substantial additional cost for the retail trade.

Conclusions

The EU domestic market initiative, the opening of the Eastern European markets and, last but not least, the changed potential within the area of e-commerce have had an enormous impact on the environment and available strategies for German domestic trade. Even though it is barely possible to detect and assess the full effects of all the changes, past economic and local-political decisions are increasingly being questioned. Demands for a new administrative policy, where politics and markets are to be more closely linked, are getting louder and louder, as is criticism of the present basic legal conditions.

The impact of the legislative environment on German retailing

With respect to the sales-area limitation of the *Baunutzungsverordnung*, a primary criticism is that the dynamics of the trade are ignored (Tietz, 1993: S.761). The arrival on the market of new store formats and new enterprises form a substantial basic condition for the operability of the German free-market economy. However, each form of sales-area limitation impairs the development of different varieties of retailing and shifts the sands of competition. Additionally, in practice legal restrictions and rights pertaining to sales area have led to a situation where managers spend a lot of time arguing with authorities and federations. It would be better, rather, if managers could concentrate in particular on consumers and goods.

With respect to the law regulating shop closing times, comparable limits do not exist in neighbouring countries. The main point to note here is that rigid store opening times are not customer friendly or requirement-oriented at all. The fact that a substantial demand for shopping opportunities outside the legally allowed times exists is demonstrated by visitor numbers and sales figures of the petrol station/ garage forecourt shops and railway station shops. Additionally this law leads to a warping of competition, because for all areas excluded from the provisions of this law (mail-order business, Internet trade, petrol stations, railway station shops etc.), there is a clear competitive advantage. They alone can use opening times as a marketing instrument, in order to increase their turnover and market shares. For all the other store formats, the restrictions lead to a limitation of the strategy parameters, delivery availability or demand-responsive sales times. And, as the convenience store example shows, consumers are quite ready to enjoy additional time comforts. Referring to the increasing convenience orientation of German consumers and the past success of the convenience store, the demand for convenient opening hours undoubtedly exists. For example, more than 43 per cent of the income of the petrol station tenants of Aral AG, one of the largest petrol retailers, came from the sale of magazines, cigarettes and food. Four out of ten customers of forecourt shops arrived without cars (o. V., 2000a: S.206). From this, Aral AG drew a logical conclusion and subsequently opened in Cologne the first petrol station shop – without a petrol pump!

With regard to *Rabattgesetz und Zugabeverordnung*, German legislation is considered by many to be outdated, and rightfully so given that the *Rabattgesetz* originates from the year 1933! In addition, the rebate law does not conform to EU directives. Such a limitation of discounts is not included in the EU directives on electronic business. Therefore, the repeal of both *Rabattgesetz und Zugabeverordnung* is currently under discussion. The Federal Government wants to delete both of them without any replacement. However, the HDE is against the abolition of these laws. The protection of the 'middle class' is put forward as one main reason. Should abolition take place, a replacement regulation in the UWG is being sought. To put it in a nutshell, in order to adjust to modern marketing opportunities and new technologies as well as the rules of the European Union, liberalization in the German retail sector is essential.

The impact of information technology

Another important challenge for the retail business enterprises is the professionalization of information processing. Gaining a competitive edge without being an information leader is hardly conceivable. Regarding the increasing flood of data and the complex decision factors, the decision-makers must give greater consideration to this subject. Any commercial enterprise must, if it is to stay competitive, secure its own market position. A good opportunity in this respect is to position itself as an information specialist. Businesses deal with integrated commercial information systems, which are not merely limited to stock control. Instead, such information systems can be used even for further marketing, personnel or financial decision making. For example, they can be used to gather information about price acceptance, about the sales performance of individual employees or about the existing liquidity requirement for incoming goods at a certain point in time. Beyond that, supplier and customer data can be analysed under profitability criteria. Therefore, integrated commercial information systems are an important instrument for improved positioning for commercial enterprises.

Managerial implications

Apart from the external environment which can partly be influenced and partly – like the legal conditions – not, the competitive scope of action or the performance of the business enterprise is limited by financial and human resources, that is, respectively the expertise, calibre and imagination of the executives and managers. The identification of competition-relevant resources or core competencies is thus a central function. Consequently, topics such as operational comparison, customer satisfaction research or the integrative consideration of financial and non-financial, quantitative and qualitative as well as operational and strategic factors in the context of a balanced scorecard are playing an increasingly important role in the German retail trade.

However, in order to fully exploit market opportunities, the identification and control of innovative fields is an urgent requirement, because old methodologies are rarely beneficial in reorganizing within a new competition structure. The necessity for innovation has been widely recognized in political-economical discussions a long time ago, as far back even as Schumpeter (1883–1950). Only those retail organizations that succeed in stimulating demand, building traffic and exhausting the purchase frequency and readiness of the customers again and again, will be able to maintain or to develop their market position. As has become clear, the purchase mentality of the German consumers has changed. Falling customer loyalty and decreasing customer satisfaction are evident in reductions in conventional retail shopping and a switch to other providers. Therefore, the creation of position features, which offer a greater benefit than those offered by competitors, is of central importance. The customer linkage rests on three particular bases (Barth and Stoffl, 1997: S.8). These are, first, reducing costs by process innovations, optimization through the whole distribution channel elimination of those functions which do not provide value; second, increasing flexibility, for example, based on process organization or a risk diversification by balanced programme, target group and market structure; and third, diversifying performance through performance innovation, development of the service proportion and intensification of customer loyalty tools. This last point may be demonstrated by referring to a specific development. At the moment a large number of retailers offer home delivery as an additional service. Of course home delivery services, as offered by beverage or electrical appliance dealers, are not new. What is new is that supermarkets now accept and also deliver goods orders for an appropriate fee. The order can be transmitted by fax, telephone or through the Internet. This concept is called remote ordering.

Last but not least, the fact remains that German retailers currently share a common interest in value-oriented management. In order to be more attractive to investors, shareholder value concepts or value management concepts are ranked as more important. Thus, on a long-term basis, an enterprise can only be successful if it pays attention not only to the interests of its customers but also to those of its shareholders. Shareholder importance is based on their position as financiers. The situation in the capital market is that there is strong competition for capital and the shareholder expects a risk-reflecting appropriate interest on the provided capital in the form of the yield on shares. The greater the yield on shares, the better the gain prospects of the financial sources and the better the ability of the business to raise capital. Thus, the yield on shares is an important measure for the determination of the performance. In this respect characteristic measures for value-oriented management – such as Economic Value Added – are still at the initial stages in the German retail industry. However they are becoming more significant (Ehrbar, 1999: S.22).

Final observation

Altogether the following should have become obvious. Change in the German retail sector is more dynamic and more unpredictable than ever. Market potentials can be neither clearly defined nor forecast. In terms of consumer behaviour, retailer–manufacturer relations, retailer competition and the impact of government legislation, retail management that is based on non-existent stable and controllable conditions and the reduction of complexity, cannot be successful in the long term. Consequently, the focus shifts from an optimization of trade marketing under the assumption of a certain status quo to a marketing concept in which environmental changes are not understood as disturbance but as substantial inputs. Success is based on both forecasting and controlling the discontinuities in the market and finding generators for success and growth.

References

Ahlert, D. and Schröder, H. (1999) 'Binnenhandelspolitische Meilensteine der Handelsgeschichte', in von M. Lingenfelder (hrsg.), *Meilensteine im deutschen Handel*, Frankfurt/Main, pp. 241–92.

Barth, K. (1999) *Betriebswirtschaftslehre des Handels*, 4. Aufl., Wiesbaden.

Barth, K. and Stoffl, M. (1997) 'Hat das Marketing im Handel versagt? Die Kundenorientierung als Ansatz einer Neubesinnung', in *Handelsforschung 1997/98, Jahrbuch der Forschungsstelle für den Handel*, Berlin e. V., Wiesbaden, pp. 3–19.

Berekoven, L. (1987) *Geschichte des deutschen Einzelhandels*, 2. Aufl., Frankfurt/Main.

Brandes, D. (1998) *Konsequent einfach: Die Aldi-Erfolgsstory*, 3. Aufl., Frankfurt/Main/ New York.

Diehl-Wobbe, E. (2001) 'US-Firmen dominieren die Weltspitze', in *Textilwirtschaft*, 23.01.2001, 56. Jahrgang, p. 248.

EHI (2000) *Handel Aktuell 2000*, Köln.

Ehrbar, A. (1999) *Economic Value Added*, Wiesbaden.

Falk, B. (1999) 'Perspektiven der Shopping Center', in von O. Beisheim (hrsg.), *Distribution im Aufbruch*, München, pp. 1083–100.

Gellately, R. (1974) *The Politics of Economic Despair: Shopkeepers and German Politics 1890–1914*, London.

Groner, B. (2000) 'Zwang zu steigender Betriebsgröße im LEH', in *Dynamik im Handel*, 01.01.2000, Heft 10, pp. 10–13.

Heinzmann, P. (2000) 'Internet – Die Kommunikationsplattform des 21. Jahrhunderts', in von R. Weiber (hrsg.), *Handbuch Electronic Business. Informationstechnologien – Electronic Commerce – Geschäftsprozesse*, Wiesbaden, pp. 59–90.

Kirchner, G. (1974) *Versand-Handel*, Stuttgart/Wiesbaden.

Lingenfelder, M. and Lauer, A. (1999) 'Die Unternehmenspolitik im deutschen Einzelhandel zwischen Währungsreform und Währungsunion', in von M. Lingenfelder (hrsg.), *Meilensteine im deutschen Handel*, Frankfurt/Main, pp. 11–56.

o. V. (1999) 'Meal Solutions-Modelle', in *Lebensmittelzeitung-Spezial*, 01/1999, pp. 71–3.

o. V. (2000a) 'Verkauf unter Einstand', in *Lebensmittel-Praxis*, 15/2000, pp. 1–2.

o. V. (2000b) 'Jean Pascale will durch übernahmen wachsen', in *Textilwirtschaft*, 06.04.2000, 55. Jahrgang, p. 8.

o. V. (2001a) 'Tankshop ohne Kraftstoff', in *Fokus*, Heft 4/22. Januar 2001, p. 206.

o. V. (2001b) 'Branchenspektrum', in *Handelsjournal*, Nr. 1, Januar 2001, pp. 14–22.

Schmalen, H. (1999) 'Handel zwischen Gestern und Morgen: Ein Spannungsfeld von Kunden, Konkurrenz und Gesetzgeber', in von O. Beisheim (hrsg.), *Distribution im Aufbruch: Bestandsaufnahme und Perspektiven*, München, pp. 469–92.

Schulz-Klingauf, H. V. (1960) *Selbstbedienung, Der neue Weg zum Kunden*, Düsseldorf.

Skimutis, A. *Die Kompatibilität von Marken und Vertriebsstrategie*, Dissertationsschrift (in preparation).

Tietz, B. (1993) *Binnenhandelspolitik*, 2. Aufl., München 1993.

Veblen, T. (1899) *The Theory of the Leisure Class*, London.

Wenzel, H. (2000) *HDI Aktuell*, Nr. 20/2000.

Zentes, J. and Swoboda, B. (1999) 'Standort und Ladengestaltung', in von M. Lingenfelder (hrsg.), *Meilensteine im deutschen Handel*, Frankfurt/Main, pp. 89–122.

4   Greece

David Bennison

Introduction

The last decade of the twentieth century saw changes in the structure and organization of retailing in Greece that were unprecedented at any other time in the history of the country. Within 10 years a system of traditional retailing based on small, independently owned and operated outlets, whose antecedents can be dated in millennia, had a modern system of multiple-shop retail enterprises operating a wide range of formats superimposed upon it. The impact of these changes, in which the operations of international retailers have been pivotal, has been profound on power relationships within the channels of distribution, management practices, shoppers' behaviour and the urban landscape. In this experience, Greece is hardly unique, but it forms an excellent example of a phenomenon that has been taking place across southern Europe, and extending beyond into Turkey and the Middle East.

An analysis of Greek retailing cannot be divorced from the geographical and historical features of the country, and it is first necessary to outline these to provide the appropriate context for the chapter. Modern Greece now has a population of approximately 10.5 million, over 40 per cent of whom live in the Athens region. Thessaloniki, in the north of the country, is the second city, with a population of about one million. Below these places there is a network of small- and medium-sized towns, while the rural population live mainly in nucleated villages. Most of the mainland is mountainous, broken up by a number of plains, and there are more than one hundred inhabited islands. The road and rail infrastructure was for many years poor, but great strides have been made in the last two decades. The new Athens Metro, the international airport at Spata, and a range of other developments associated with the hosting of the 2004 Olympics, are the most prominent symbols of the country's modernization.

Greece was the location of the first civilization on the European mainland, and its philosophical, scientific, literary and political heritage permeate the present. However, the modern Greek state that emerged gradually from the Ottoman Empire after 1830 was a poor country, overwhelmingly rural in character. Athens was established as the capital in 1832, but at that time was little more than a village clustered around the foot of the Acropolis. The disintegration of the Ottoman

Empire was a slow process, but over the following century, the Greek state extended its territorial boundaries in a series of wars. The last part of the mainland to be incorporated was the regions of Macedonia and Thrace, in 1913. Nevertheless at that time there still remained a substantial Greek population in Istanbul (Constantinople) and along the western coast of Asia Minor. The 'Great Ideal' for Greeks was to incorporate all of these people within the Greek state, and so war continued in 1921–1922 to achieve this aim – but it ended in defeat. This 'catastrophe' was to prove a defining moment for the modern Greek state: the Treaty of Lausanne in 1923 agreed an exchange of minority populations between the two countries. The consequence for Greece was the influx of over one million refugees. For a poor country with a population then of 5 million, this was to have two critical outcomes. First, in order to provide people with a basic living, land reform was initiated. The semi-feudal rural estates, inherited from the Ottomans, were abolished, and the land given in small parcels to the people, resulting in the creation of a landowning peasantry. Second, the majority of the refugees were town dwellers, many with occupations in commerce and the professions. The foundations of a fluid, meritocratic and more entrepreneurial society were laid, but one where ties of family and kinship were extremely strong.

The impact of these momentous changes was not to emerge fully, however, for another 30 years. The Axis Occupation of the country during the Second World War was destructive, but possibly even more so was the 3-year Civil War (1946–1949) that ensued. At the end of all this, Greece in 1950 was impoverished, with poor infrastructure, and politically unstable. However, the country's strategic location ensured foreign aid, especially from the United States, and the economy began to grow. With few natural resources, income from shipping, remittances from emigrants, and, increasingly, tourism became the major sources of foreign earnings.

One of the legacies of the Civil War was to ensure that government was right-wing and patrician in nature. When it seemed in the late 1960s that a left-wing party might be voted to power, the military intervened (in 1967) to 'save' the country. A repressive dictatorship held power for 7 years until collapsing in 1974 under the weight of popular disenchantment and a disastrous intervention in Cyprus. Since then democratic government has become firmly established. In the first post-junta election, the New Democracy (conservative) party gained power, and held it until 1981 when it was replaced by PASOK, the socialist party. In 1990 New Democracy were returned to government, and lasted until 1994, when PASOK regained power.

The entrenchment of democratic government that came to Greece after 1974 was both rewarded and reinforced by accession to the EEC in 1981. The formation of the Single European Market in 1992 necessitated a painful harmonization process during which longstanding structural problems were addressed – not least high rates of inflation, and a large black economy estimated at one time to be worth 30 per cent of GDP. This meant several years of constraints on consumer spending, but in 2001 Greece was allowed to join the Single European Currency.

With economic growth since 1950, a process of accelerating urbanization occurred, fuelled primarily by large-scale rural emigration. Farmers sold or rented their land to others, raising the capital or income to set up small enterprises and/or to invest in property. This activity focused on Athens, and the city grew very fast: in the period 1951–1961, for example, its population increased by over a third to about 1,900,000, accounting for 22 per cent of the total population. This polarization of economic and social activity became even more accentuated, and only Thessaloniki in the north of the country acted as a counter-balance to the metropolis.

Retailing 1950–1990

Against the background of the fundamental changes in Greek society and economy that have taken place since 1950, retailing in the country for long seemed extremely resilient to any type of change. Data on retail stores and employment in Greece are available in a series of censuses conducted by the National Statistical Service of Greece (NSSG) at irregular intervals between 1951 and 1988. Table 4.1 shows clearly how resistant to change the Greek retail system was until the 1980s, with its basic organizational structure in 1988 virtually identical to that of 1951.

Table 4.1 Retail outlets and employment (1951–1988)

Year	Number of retail outlets	Food/drink (%)	Average size of outlet (persons employed)
1951	81,965	69.8	1.6
1958	104,700	61.3	1.7
1969	134,898	53.2	1.8
1978	160,599	39.8	1.8
1984	184,892	34.4	1.6
1988	184,281	29.5	1.8

Source: National Statistical Service of Greece, summarized in Bennison and Boutsouki (1995).

Until the 1980s each census recorded an increase in the number of shops, with an average yearly growth of nearly 4 per cent. As disposable incomes grew, the demand for consumer goods was met through the provision of more and more small shops. In contrast, the numbers of food/drink shops remained almost the same, reflecting the relatively slow growth of the total population of the country. However, the average size of the retail outlets expressed in terms of persons employed remained virtually unchanged at the very modest level of 1.8 in 1988. The practice and philosophy of this kind of retailing in Greece prior to the 1990s was uncomplicated. Goods were bought in, and then sold to customers at a margin, and features of modern retailing – whether effective merchandising, systematic stock control, or use of own-label merchandise – were all but absent in the country.

Over this period the marketing of consumer goods in Greece involved the activities of domestic manufacturers, wholesalers, importers and other foreign trade intermediaries feeding into a fragmented structure of small-scale retailers (Figure 4.1). Wholesalers were a vital part of the distribution channel and it was their role to supply food products and other manufactured goods to small retailers across the country, although they too were predominantly small, family-owned and operated enterprises, except for the activities of large import-wholesalers located in Athens.

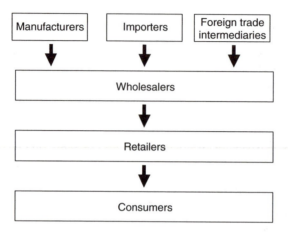

Figure 4.1 Channels of distribution in Greece until the 1960s.

Source: Boutsouki and Bennison (1997).

The resilience to change demonstrated by this multiplicity of small, essentially family-owned and operated shops can be attributed to a variety of reasons. First, relatively low incomes and a correspondingly low rate of capital accumulation combined with limited employment opportunities to make retailing an attractive way to earn a living for many people. Money earned either by temporarily working abroad or by the sale of land could be easily used to set up a small shop since the entry requirements were low, and there was virtually no legal impediment to prevent it (see below). Even now, it is still very common for the operation of a shop to be only one of a number of sources of family income, and this results in considerable inertia, especially in rural areas where outlets may be operated with minimum margins. In addition, credit had historically been relatively easy to obtain from suppliers, again reducing even further the barriers to entry to the sector.

Second, the geography of the country, outlined earlier, has an important effect on store numbers. The dispersal of about half of the population who still live outside the two major conurbations in a large number of smaller towns and villages, the mountainous character of much of the mainland, and the many populated islands all combine to sustain the large number of small shops serving very localized and limited catchment areas. Even small settlements with a population of less than a hundred are likely to support at least one general store/coffee shop *(kafeneion)*.

Third, the family and kinship traditions of Greeks, combined with strong sentiments of personal independence and self-esteem, underpin a society where individual entrepreneurship is highly valued. Owners of businesses invariably have a strong desire to retain control within their family, and pass it on in time to their children. Outside investors, who may seek control in exchange for funding, have not usually been encouraged. Overall, across all sectors, Greece has one of the highest rates of self-employment in Europe, for example, 32.7 per cent of the labour force in 1991 was classified as owners and a further 14.2 per cent as family members, leaving only 48.6 per cent as salaried employees (Michaelidis, 1992). The absence of a well-developed system of equity financing has been a related feature.

Fourth, and perhaps most critically, a number of legislative restrictions on retail operations severely constrained the level of competition in the market, making it very difficult to respond quickly or effectively to changing consumer demands. The most important of these were limits on opening hours to 50 a week, restrictions on the sale of fresh bread, meat and fish to specialist shops, strictly enforced price controls on food and other convenience goods, and an effective prohibition on the employment of part-time labour. These controls and regulations were originally intended to prevent the exploitation both of consumers and employees at a time of scarcity and limited job opportunities, and were enforced by a special Market Police. However, as the economy developed after 1960, they increasingly became an impediment to the development of more modern formats and the growth of multiple enterprises, since competition on price and service levels was difficult, and operational flexibility impossible. Such increases in channel productivity that were observed could be attributed almost entirely to increases in average transaction size rather than to any structural, organizational or technological changes (Preston, 1968; Bennison, 1979a). The most powerful elements of the channels of distribution remained the wholesalers and the manufacturers of consumer goods.

During the 1970s and 1980s, the first signs of structural and organizational changes in Greek retailing began to manifest themselves. Although at first they were relatively small scale, and mainly confined to the food sector, they were the harbingers of the fundamental changes that took place from 1990 onwards. Between 1984 and 1988, the Census of Commerce records the first signs of pressures building up in the retail system, when total shop numbers declined very slightly – by 0.3 per cent – for the first time (Table 4.1). In fact, this was entirely due to a sudden drop of 14.5 per cent in those classed as food/drink: the number of non-food outlets rose by a further 7 per cent. Although there had been no relaxation in the legal constraints on retailing at this time, the more enterprising food retailers had started to make productivity gains through changes in their layout and format by introducing self-service, and designating their shops 'Supermarkets', typically with a single checkout – while the more traditional general store (*pantopoleion*) began to disappear.

Even more important at this time, some significant organizational changes began to occur. Local chains of small supermarkets began to develop as the more entrepreneurial owners opened more outlets to secure economies of scale, and a fall of 11 per cent in the number of traditional grocery stores was recorded in the 5 years leading up to 1990 (Michaelidis, 1992). However, the major development in this period that set the scene for the dramatic changes of the 1990s, was the first foreign involvement in the sector, mainly in relation to the transfer of managerial expertise. Two of the country's largest supermarket retailers, Marinopoulos and Veropoulos, became associated with the French company Prisunic and the Spar organization, respectively. They expanded their product ranges and introduced more sophisticated merchandising and marketing activity. In turn, some of the country's other large supermarket chains such as Sklavenitis and Vassilopoulos began to follow their example. Economies of scale enabled these supermarket chains to gain a competitive advantage over smaller retailers, but the continuing existence of legally enforced upper and lower price limits restricted competition on price and minimized any possible competitive advantage deriving from it. As a result, the emerging large-scale retailers focused on the improvement of their service provision and/or acquired smaller operations in order to increase in size in an attempt to gain further competitive advantage. The structure of the channels of distribution became more complex (Figure 4.2) and market interactions between suppliers and retailers increased, at least in those cases where both parties had increased their bargaining power, while the role of the traditional wholesaler diminished. For the first time, long-term relationships between major retailers and their manufacturers began to be developed, whereas in the traditional part of the distribution channel, relationships between retailers, wholesalers and manufacturers/importers remained unchanged (Boutsouki and Bennison, 1997).

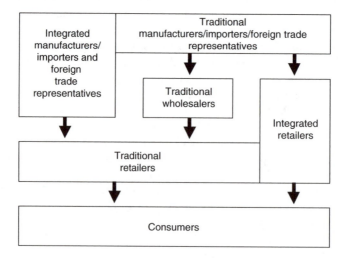

Figure 4.2 Channels of distribution in Greece in the mid-1980s.

Source: Boutsouki and Bennison (1997).

Despite these developments, much of the retail system in Greece at the end of the 1980s was not hugely different from that which existed 40 years earlier. Indeed, with its small family-owned and operated enterprises, often with an artisan element, it had many similarities to the one that would have been found in Classical times. There were few signs then of the fundamental changes that were about to occur, and which are described in the next section.

The retail revolution 1990 to the present

The changes that began at the start of the 1990s were not of a gradual, evolutionary nature, but, by the standards of retail change, were sudden and occurred with great speed. Although in the early days of this 'revolution' the number of outlets involved was relatively small, their impact on both retailers and consumers was to be profound. New management practices were introduced, and Greek consumers began to experience the choice, quality and service levels of modern retailing. The effects on the smaller indigenous retailers, and other traditional members of the channels of distribution have inevitably been far-reaching, while the physical outcomes in the form of new types of outlets and shopping centres are clearly apparent in the urban landscape. This is not to imply that by the year 2000 the change was complete, but rather it is to emphasize that the processes of change had become firmly rooted in the system, and that the inertia of previous decades – even centuries – had passed. The two main urban centres of Athens and Thessaloniki have been where most of the significant new developments have originated. But they have quickly percolated down the urban hierarchy to the major provincial centres such as Larissa, Heraklion and Patras, and below these to the smaller market towns of the various regions of the country.

There are several reasons for this transformation of the Greek retail system at the beginning of the 1990s. The pressure of changing consumer demands, much facilitated by a rapid growth in car ownership, could not be fully met while the legislative straightjacket on retail operations remained in place. In 1991, however, the New Democracy party returned to power, and it was more ideologically suited than PASOK to the task of deregulating retailing (and the rest of industry and commerce) as part of the harmonization programme for the introduction of the Single European Market in 1992. Almost overnight, the strict price controls were lifted, opening hours were extended to 68 hours a week (excluding Sundays); and the prohibition on the use of overtime and part-time labour was removed. The sale of fresh bread, meat and fish was also no longer made the preserve of specialist shops as they had been. At once retailers could at last compete effectively on price, and they were given the flexibility to provide the kind of goods and services that shoppers demanded.

The other major influence on retail change was a parallel upsurge of interest in Greece by foreign retailers operating in a number of sectors. At that time many companies – in western Europe particularly – were becoming involved in internationalization activities, at least in part because of high levels of competition in their domestic markets and concerns over saturation. The sudden liberalization of the Greek market opened up the opportunity for them to enter, and although the market was relatively small, it was concentrated in the two major conurbations, and considered worthy by many of exploitation since the indigenous competition was perceived as being so weak.

The developments since 1990 that have taken place are best dealt in two sections. First, the food/grocery sector needs special attention because it is here that the scale of change has been the most dramatic, and then, second, a summary of change in other sectors will be presented. (It should be noted at this point that there are no statistical data available from the National Statistical Service that enable direct comparisons with the situation pre-1990, and that information has been collated from a combination of industry and journalistic sources.)

The food/grocery sector since 1990

The early manifestations of change seen during the 1980s were but the precursor to the dramatic changes of the last ten years. The lifting of price controls in particular meant that price immediately became the main weapon of retailer competition. Its effect was all the more striking because Greek consumers at that time were feeling the impact on their incomes of a prolonged economic recession and rising unemployment. The 'price wars' that were unleashed in 1991–1992 made it imperative for grocery retailers to reduce their cost base and to tap economies of scale, and this led to a number of profound structural and organizational changes in the sector. The most significant of these has been the polarization of the sector, with the emergence of a handful of large companies at one end, and the continuing existence of a myriad of mainly single-outlet operations at the other: it has been estimated that 80 per cent of all food shops are still trading from units of less than 100 sq. m. (Nielsen, quoted in *Financial Times*, 2000).

This growth has been achieved both organically and by extensive merger and acquisition activity, with the large companies buying up smaller businesses – often owned by local entrepreneurs who have built one or two supermarkets as a speculative venture with the explicit intention of selling on. The involvement of major foreign retailers in the sector has provided a further powerful stimulus for change to the indigenous operators.

The major developments in this sector from the last decade of the twentieth century are discussed below.

The introduction of the hypermarket format

The appearance of these stores in 1991–1992 was the most conspicuous sign of radical change in the nature of Greek retailing, and the contrast with existing stores at that time could hardly have been greater. With over 7,000 sq. m. of floorspace and over 40 checkouts, extensive car parking, very wide merchandise ranges, and the inclusion of clothing, electrical goods etc., they brought a whole new shopping experience to Greek consumers, but one to which they readily adapted. The format was introduced by the French company Promodes in association with the largest Greek retail company, Marinopoulos, and traded under the Continent fascia. Stores were built in Athens, Thessaloniki, Herakleion and Larissa. At about the same time, two Mega hypermarkets were opened in Athens by the long established Greek firm of Vasilopoulos, which was subsequently acquired by the Belgian Delhaize group in 1992. A third company, Masoutis, also developed six stores in northern Greece in the 1990s. The sector was re-energized by the arrival of Carrefour in 1999 which opened its first store in Thessaloniki, and at that time had another three under development. Within a year it merged with the eight Promodes Continent stores and the Marinopoulos supermarkets to form the largest single food/grocery operation in Greece as measured by turnover, with sales of approximately 370 billion drachmas in 2000, and employing 9,000 people (Bistis, 2000). All the stores now trade under the Carrefour fascia; one Continent store in Thessaloniki was closed as it was too near to the new Carrefour. As of 2001, there are approximately 19 hypermarkets in Greece, and Carrefour has plans to build more in the larger provincial towns as well as continuing development in Athens.

The rapid growth of supermarkets of up to 2,000 sq. m. floorspace

Although these outlets are far less impressive to an outsider than the hypermarkets, their rapid development at all levels of the urban hierarchy throughout Greece is the most ubiquitously visible sign of the retail revolution in Greece. Competition at the local level is increasingly strong, and the growth in store numbers has been sustained: in 1995 there were 999 stores belonging to chains, and by 1999 there were 1,719 (Bistis, 2000).

There was much merger and acquisition activity over the decade of the 1990s as companies sought to tap economies of scale. Many essentially local companies were absorbed by the emergent major chains, although many still remain to be so. In 1998, for example, there were 74 companies operating between 3 and 20 stores, 59 of them with fewer than 10. In contrast, the number of companies operating over 20 stores rose from 7 in 1991 to 18 in 1998 (Michaelidis Publications, 1999). Consolidation amongst the larger players is also occurring, spurred on by the actions of Carrefour. In February 2001, for example, Veropoulos (ranked 4th in turnover) took over Panemporiki (ranked 10th).

A sign of the rapidly developing maturity of the grocery sector was the beginning of substantive market differentiation in 1995 when Promodes launched a limited line discount operation, Dia Hellas. This has grown rapidly, and there were 152 stores by 2000, an impressive 50 being opened during 1999 alone. In 1998, the German discounter Lidl entered Greece, and by 2001 there were 27 stores, mainly in the north of the country. However, the next phase of the company's development will see the growth of its presence in the Athens region, where Dia Hellas is strongly represented.

Changes in the channels of distribution and retailer–supplier relationships

As the large multiple-store retail organizations have emerged, so there have been major changes in the nature of the supply chain, which is represented diagrammatically in Figure 4.3. There are three main aspects to these changes.

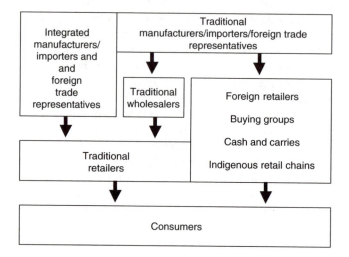

Figure 4.3 Channels of distribution in Greece in the mid-1990s.
Source: Boutsouki and Bennison (1997).

First, the position of traditional wholesalers was undermined as the big retailers sourced directly from their suppliers, and as large cash-and-carry operations were established. The Dutch company Makro led the way with the latter, while the Greek company Metro was also very active. By 1999, there were 85 cash-and-carry warehouses in the country, owned by about 11 main companies. Their quick success in the Greek market is testified by the fact that within a year of opening, the two Makro units in Athens had over 100,000 registered users. Indeed, because Makro allows cardholders and people accompanying them to buy for personal consumption, they also function as supermarkets for those allowed to use them.

Second, there was a reversal of the traditional power relationship between suppliers and retailers, with the latter now in the dominant position. The critical stage was reached quickly in 1993 when Promodes Continent and Marinopoulos, the largest indigenous Greek retailer, joined together in a purchasing alliance, and quickly went head-to-head with major companies such as Pepsi Max, refusing to stock products until they obtained larger discounts and extended credit. One quantitative measure of the shift in power was seen in the lengthening period of credit extended to retailers, which went from 67.3 days in 1991 to 110.2 in 1995 (*Self Service Review*, 1994; *Retailing and Wholesaling*, 1996). However, the initially aggressive relationships that occurred appear to have been tempered rel-atively quickly as mutual interest became obvious. A survey of retailers and suppliers in 1995 (Boutsouki and Bennison, 1997) showed that long-term relationships were being established and partnerships formed. The growth of retailer own-label merchandise, new product development and the use of IT were three important elements in this.

Third, the formation of buying groups by some of the more enterprising small- and medium-sized retailers took place as a defensive reaction to the growing competition from the largest companies. The first such groups were Elomas and Asteras, founded in 1993, and by 1996 there were a further three. Although intended primarily to strengthen the retailers' negotiating position with suppliers, the groups began to take on a wider role in training and marketing activities. However, they remain dwarfed in comparison to the groupings formed by the large companies, which can have nearly 10 times their turnover.

The introduction of modern retail management

The introduction and diffusion of the philosophy and practice of modern retail management in Greece has come very largely from foreign retailers. Such modern retail management has taken many forms, but amongst the most obvious signs of this have been the rapid introduction of EPOS, the use of own label, and the very substantial growth of retailer advertising and promotion, including the use of loyalty cards. However, this development has also highlighted a weakness in the availability of modern retail management skills in the country. 'Knowledge' was identified a number of years ago as a major issue for the sector by one of its leading commentators (Michaelidis, 1993), but it was not until 2000 that any specialist postgraduate course in retail management became available in Greece. A major issue is, as elsewhere, the perceived low status of retailing as a career, especially in a society where there is a heavy emphasis on 'professional' or civil service careers. There is also a problem in indigenous family-owned Greek firms of the operation of a 'glass ceiling' for employees who are not members of the family. This does not encourage such companies to invest in potentially able employees beyond the level of basic shopfloor and selling skills.

Other sectors

The highly visible scale and speed of change occurring in the grocery sector, and its everyday impact on the shopping behaviour of Greeks, inevitably makes it the focus of most commentary on changes in Greek retailing. However, in other sectors too the process of change started in the early 1990s, and the traditional retailers of clothing, shoes, household goods etc. have increasingly found themselves under the same competitive pressure as their counterparts in the grocery sector, even if the timescale has been slightly more elongated. In this process, the activities of foreign retailers have been even more conspicuous than in the grocery sector, as companies recognized the opportunities that existed in Greece, and the potential for capitalizing on their marketing and management expertise. In addition, however, towards the end of the last decade, the growing prominence of a number of Greek-owned chains has become a notable feature of the retail landscape.

By far the greatest number of international retailers has entered the clothing/fashion sector, following the pioneering lead of Benetton which entered the country in the early 1980s, and franchising has been used as the principal mode of entry. Important presence was also established in department/variety stores, fast food and household goods by the middle of the 1990s, and have continued to be built upon. At the moment, non-food stores operating under foreign fascias are still concentrated in the main shopping areas of Athens and other major cities, but their high degree of differentiation ensures that their current profile and potential impact are disproportionate to their numbers, which are yet relatively small compared to the local traders.

The most significant developments in the non-food sector to date are discussed further below.

The introduction of new large formats

Most notable among these were the setting up in Greece of large freestanding stores of over 2,500 sq. m. floorspace selling a combination of DIY, household and electrical goods. The leading company has been Praktiker, a joint venture company set up by the German firm Asko and Shelman, a Greek manufacturer of timber products. There are currently (2001) six, although the original ambitious growth plans for up to 36 stores appear to have been substantially scaled back. A second German company, Groetzen, set up two stores, but withdrew in 1998 following the bankruptcy of the parent company in Germany. Carrefour and other hypermarkets also sell electrical and other household goods alongside their food and grocery offer. The most significant recent development has been the entry of IKEA, which opened its first store in Thessaloniki in September 2001 using a unit vacated by Carrefour/Continent. There are plans for at least another five stores in the country.

The involvement of foreign retailers in the department store sector

A small number of Greek-owned department stores has been a feature of shopping provision in Athens and Thessaloniki for many years, although hardly anywhere else, and until the advent of the hypermarkets, they were by far the largest retail outlets in the country. Located in the heart of the central shopping areas of the two main cities, they typically have between 1,000 and 5,000 sq. m. of floorspace, spread over several floors, and most were originally rather cramped and dowdy in appearance. However, since 1990 they have embraced participation with foreign retailers in various ways in order to improve their operations and position in the market as competition from both specialist chains and new large-scale retail formats has increased. The most important relationships have been franchising agreements between the UK companies of Marks & Spencer and British Home Stores with Marinopoulos SA and Klaoudatos SA, respectively. The latter relationship has been described in detail elsewhere (Boutsouki and Bennison, 1999). In both cases, stores were fitted out and merchandised as in the United Kingdom, and concentrate on clothing and household textiles. Marks & Spencer stores, until the withdrawal of the company from Continental Europe at the end of 2001, also included cosmetics and toiletries. The two other main

department store companies – Lambropoulos Bros. and Minion – have also pursued relationships with foreign retailers, but in different ways. In the case of the
former, a large number of concessions with fashion retailers and manufacturers
have been obtained, and the 'shops within a shop' format has been implemented.
In the case of the latter, a commercial agreement was made with Galleries
Lafayette that gave Minion the right to sell the French company's exclusive own-
brand products, and also gave them access to technical and managerial advice.
However, the store went into bankruptcy in 1998, was reopened in 1999 following government intervention, and may now be completely redeveloped.

Franchising of specialist retailers

International retailers have been very active in developing franchises within the
Greek market, especially in fashion, luxury goods and fast food. Benetton and
Body Shop led the way in the 1980s, but since 1991 the number of companies with
a presence in Greece has grown rapidly. Franchising is particularly appropriate in
Greece since it allows the franchiser to become established in a country whose language and culture are not widely understood outside (despite the tourism) and it
capitalizes on the inclination of Greeks to individual entrepreneurship.

Important fashion retailers with a growing presence in the Greek market include
Zara, Stefanel, Max Mara, Kookai and Levi Strauss. For fashion-conscious Greek
women, these international retailers have invigorated a rather stale domestic provision, and form the benchmark which domestic competition needs to match.
While most Greek clothing retailers find that difficult, there are examples of success. Miss Raxevsky, Anna Riska and Rococca, for example, have a growing presence, even if they may not yet be known outside of Greece. In the fast food sector,
the arrival of McDonalds, Pizza Hut, Wendys and Kentucky Fried Chicken in the
early 1990s was perhaps rather belated, but had been hindered by the earlier price
controls on food. Since then they have expanded very rapidly, and are now to be
found in many provincial towns and along major roads as well as in Athens and
Thessaloniki. There are also some successful Greek-owned companies in the sector which have followed similar aggressive growth strategies through franchising –
Goodys burger restaurants is the most widely known.

Growth of specialist Greek chains

While the clothing/fashion and luxury goods sectors have been dominated by
international retailers, the electrical goods sector is one where indigenous retail
chains have developed a very strong presence, especially since about 1996. The
fact that no major international retailer in this sector has so far successfully
entered the market may be a factor here, but companies such as Germanos,
Kotsovolos and Korasidis have expanded aggressively, and by 2000 were accounting for over half of the market. Indeed, such is their strength that they have also
started to look abroad for further growth. Germanos, for example, announced
plans in 2001 to enter Cyprus, Romania, Bulgaria, Poland, Turkey and FYROM.

Retail location and planning

The great changes in the structure of retailing in Greece since the early 1990s, described in the previous sections, have had inevitable consequences on retail location patterns in the country. The release of the sector from many of the operational restrictions that had impeded competition and development is complemented by a relatively relaxed land use planning regime that does not seek to restrict the amount or distribution of new floorspace to any significant extent. However, the freedom that this gives retailers and developers is limited by the small scale and fragmented nature of land and property ownership, which makes the development of larger formats in particular a more difficult process than in many countries.

The traditional small-scale retail sector operates mainly from premises located in town centres, along streets and scattered throughout residential areas, usually on the ground floor (or sometimes basement) of office or residential blocks. Most of these are leased. Small freestanding units can be found in areas of lower housing density, and in villages. Cafes or restaurants typically occupy the largest units. On-street locations are complemented in larger cities by covered arcades (*stoas*), which usually form part of office blocks, and by covered permanent markets selling fresh food (especially meat and fish). Periodic markets selling fruit, vegetables and cheap clothing and household goods are a feature of all towns, while itinerant traders can be found in the suburbs and throughout rural areas.

A particular feature of the traditional Greek retail landscape is the kiosk (*peripteron*), selling newspapers, confectionery, ice creams, drinks, tobacco, telephone cards, bus tickets etc. In 1999, there were approximately 13,500 throughout the country, and they play an important role in town centres, suburbs and tourist areas as the local convenience outlet. They were originally established to provide a living for disabled ex-servicemen, and they are still run by the Ministry of National Defence who issue licences for their operation.

The traditional pattern, where small shops are located in close proximity to their customers, has resulted in a hierarchy of settlements and centres that approximates very closely to a classical central place system (Bennison, 1979b, 1980). It has emerged without the existence of an interventionist system of land use planning. As described earlier, the role of government in Greek retailing has been confined to issues relating to competition and the protection of customers, employees and producers from exploitation. The economic significance of retailing has never been realized by central government, which provided much assistance for the industrial and agricultural sectors in the postwar period, but failed to appreciate the importance of an efficient system of distribution to link these sectors with consumers (Coutsoumaris, 1963; Bennison, 1995).

Until 1995 the only controls that applied to the size and location of shops were those that applied to all buildings. Responsibility for policy resides with the Town Planning Service of the Ministry for Planning, Settlement and the Environment, and its remit is concerned with the size and physical structure of buildings in towns rather than their use except where there is a clear 'nuisance' factor such as an industrial plant, and with the development of physical infrastructure such as street pedestrianization. The construction of new buildings for shops takes place within the same regulatory framework as for any other kind. The basic feature of this is the definition by the Town Planning Service of a 'City Planning Area' in each town, which corresponds to the contiguous built-up area. This is sub-divided into zones that specify the maximum ground area and height of buildings, and the minimum space between them. Licences are issued for new buildings on the basis that the proposed development conforms to the zonal restrictions for its plot, and that its design meets the legal requirements for earthquake resistance.

Outside of the City Planning Area, a new building must occupy only 20 per cent of the building plot to ensure that infrastructural provision is not impeded. This minimal control has led to the development of quite extensive ribbon developments along major arterial roads, especially those leading out from Athens. In these locations, larger showroom-based retailers (e.g. furniture, cars) can be found intermingled with petrol stations, restaurants, warehouses, factories, offices and housing. These are also the locations where medium and larger supermarkets are found, while the hypermarkets and other very large formats tend to be located on 'green field' sites at the edge of the densest built up areas, usually adjacent to a major road.

The very considerable freedom that this system gave retailers to develop essentially wherever they liked was changed in 1995 only with respect to large supermarkets, following pressures from small traders. The rationale for the decision was based on the issue of competition rather than the environment. Controls were introduced on the maximum size of supermarket to be permitted in particular areas: for example, units no larger than 1,000 sq. m. were permitted in towns with a population of less than 30,000; 2,000 sq. m. was the limit in places with a population between 30,000 and 100,000; but there are no limits in Athens, Thessaloniki and other places larger than 100,000. This control seems unlikely to have significantly impeded the development of large formats given that many would not be viable in smaller settlements in any case.

Modern supermarkets are mainly built as solus freestanding units, with associated car parking (although there are no government controls on how much or how little is provided). However, in suburban areas, units appropriate for neighbourhood supermarket operations are being provided on the ground floors of apartment or office blocks, typically with little *ad hoc* parking provision.

New multi-unit retail developments are also an increasingly common feature of the Greek retail landscape. These basically take one of two forms. First, there are smaller developments within existing town centres, usually with only small units occupied by indigenous independent operators, and not all of them are retail. Most of these are found in the Athens area – for example, the Hermion centre in Kifisia (4,500 sq. m.), and the City Plaza in Glyfada (5,000 sq. m.). However, a development in Thessaloniki, opened in 1998, provides a more recent example. Built on the site of a former tobacco warehouse fronting the main shopping street in the city, the Plateia centre was opened in 1998. It has about 20,000 sq. m. of floorspace, but most of that is taken up with a multiplex cinema and offices (occupants include the US consulate). On the ground and first floor levels there are about 20 relatively small shop units arranged around an open central space occupied by a mixture of retailing and services.

The second type of multi-unit schemes are those in edge- or out-of-town locations, and are by far the more significant new development in Greek retailing. Although some of the hypermarkets built in the last ten years are solus units, others, especially Continent/Carrefour, incorporate a mall of up to 20–30 smaller units, mainly in retail use. As well as being found in Athens and Thessaloniki, such developments have also taken place in some of the largest provincial centres such as Larissa and Herakleion. They typically provide about 10–15,000 sq. m. of floorspace.

The opening of the new airport at Spata in 2001, the associated motorway, and the other major infrastructural investments taking place for the 2004 Olympics, have provided major development opportunities in the Athens region. The Cambas Vineyard centre in Mesogia Valley is scheduled to open in 2004, and will provide 80,000 sq. m. of floorspace, making it the largest such scheme in Greece. In addition, large new developments are in the pipeline in the southern and western parts of the conurbation.

The combination of leisure with retailing in large off-centre developments is also an increasingly common feature. The first was a multiplex cinema built adjacent to the Continent development on the south side of Thessaloniki. However, the largest to date is the Village Entertainment Park at Rendis in west Athens. A 20-screen cinema is complemented with 45 retail units, many of them occupied by major international retailers such as Stefanel, Lacoste, Virgin, Reebok and Nike. There are also a number of restaurants and fast food outlets, including Planet Hollywood. During its first year it was expected to attract more than 3 million visitors – equivalent to 75 per cent of the population of the conurbation (FPDSavills, 2000).

Land and property

The structural and organizational changes that have been transforming the Greek retail scene since the early 1990s are clearly physically manifest in the large modern stores and centres described in the previous section. With relatively few planning constraints on the development of new floorspace, it might be expected that these changes would continue relatively unhindered. However, retailers and developers are now faced with a structural impediment from the nature of land and property ownership in the country as they seek to build and run operations for which the existing stock of retail property is unsuitable because of the small size of units.

The most important feature of land and property ownership is its highly fragmented nature. This originated in the first half of the twentieth century when land reform redistributed large estates to peasant farmers as a response to the problems produced by the refugees from Turkey after 1923. Individuals were given several non-contiguous plots so that differing qualities of land were evenly distributed. The fragmentation was then further exacerbated by the inheritance practice that sees property divided equally between heirs, and by the dowry system in which the exchange of land or property formed an important component. The consequence is that much open land (including on the edge-of-towns) is divided into small plots, although these are not necessarily divided by fences etc. Similarly, buildings, especially apartment and office blocks, are often in multiple ownership, in part because of a system known as *antiparochi*, whereby developers will acquire land from owners by offering them shops or flats in a new high rise building. Both land and buildings are often rented out, and this is an important source of supplementary income for many Greeks. Attachment to property is deep in the national psyche, and the practice of passing property to the next generation is embedded in modern Greek society – another manifestation of the individuality and self-reliance of people.

The problem for modern retailers and developers wishing to expand is, therefore, essentially that of assembling sites and properties of sufficient size. For the operation of smaller formats, this may result in less than optimum performance since a company may have to operate from more than one unit in any particular area. For example, Germanos, the electrical retailer, has at least three units in the main shopping street in Thessaloniki. It also provides a powerful additional incentive to franchising.

For those who develop or operate large retail formats, the issue is less easily resolved, and sites of appropriate size are eagerly sought. It is clear that a number of companies such as Praktiker have not been able to expand as rapidly as they would wish because of this. However, infrastructure development by the government which requires compulsory purchase – such as that associated with road building and airport development – is a potentially important avenue for achieving the goal.

As in the retail sector, the indigenous real estate industry is very fragmented, with individuals operating generally small independent agencies serving local communities. Indeed, it is very common for property sales to be transacted privately. One simple indication is the generic red-on-white 'For Sale' or 'To Rent' signs seen all over Greece, with nothing but a telephone number written below. The absence of a more developed property sector has been attributed to the perceived economic risks, the lack of buildings and portfolios of institutional quality, and high transaction costs (FPDSavills, 2000). However, as also in retailing, international agencies, consultants and developers have been establishing a presence, especially in Athens. New legislation regulating mutual property funds and property investment companies is expected to provide a boost to the sector, and it has generated interest amongst both construction companies and financial institutions, including pension funds (FPDSavills, 2000). The expectation would therefore be for the emergence of a sector that is much better equipped with resources and expertise to meet the demands of retailers in the country as confidence in the market increases.

Conclusions

The last decade of the twentieth century saw more changes in retailing in Greece than at any other time in the long history of the country. Within a remarkably short period of time, a traditional system of small-scale, domestic, independent retailers has had a modern system of multiple-shop retail companies – many of them international organizations operating large formats – superimposed upon it. The consequences have already been far reaching. But the revolution is far from over, and the next 10 years are likely to see continuing rapid change in the Greek retail system as modern methods of retail management diffuse across all sectors and down the urban hierarchy, and as the influences of globalization and information technology grow ever stronger.

The reasons for the transformation of retailing in Greece are not particular to this country, and are to be found in most other countries where sustained economic growth has taken place. With rising disposable incomes has come an increasing demand for goods and services, and concomitant with that a growing demand for retail floorspace. Greece stands out, however, in terms of the speed with which this change has taken place. For almost forty years the demand for floorspace was channelled into an increasing proliferation of small retailers while the multiple-shop retailing enterprise remained a rarity. The reasons for this lay in substantial measure in the very tight legislative controls on retailing that constrained both price competition and operational flexibility in terms of the employment of labour and shop opening hours. It was the removal of these constraints in the early 1990s that led to the rapid changes. The pressures from consumers for lower prices and wider ranges on the one hand, and from international retailers seeking to enter the country on the other, were suddenly brought together in a relationship that was both synergistic and symbiotic.

As elsewhere in the European Union, the food/grocery sector was where the developments were most rapid and far-reaching, but the non-food sectors have not been immune to very substantial changes as well – especially clothing/fashion, electrical/household goods and fast food. Ten years on, the food sector is dominated by a small number of companies operating supermarkets and hypermarkets, while the main shopping streets of Greek towns are gradually accommodating branches of a growing number of nationwide retail chains. The role of international retailers in this process has been critical, not only in exposing the Greek market to modern retail environments, but also in providing both a model and assistance for a relatively small number of enterprising indigenous companies.

The implications of these changes for all the constituent members of the retail system have inevitably been considerable. The success of the large companies and new formats is testified by their sales and market shares. Awareness and responsiveness to price is probably the most important change in the consumer, but there is also undoubtedly a much greater appreciation of retail service in terms of the range and quality of goods, of convenience, and of the service encounter.

The success of the new retailers in attracting customers means inevitably that independent small retailers and their intermediate wholesale suppliers have experienced the consequential losses. The absence of any subsequent systematic census comparable to that of 1988 makes it difficult to assess the actual decline in numbers. But such evidence that exists points to rather dramatic falls in store numbers, particularly of retailers in the Food sector. A report by the National Statistical Service, for example, indicated a decline in shop numbers of 13.4 per cent between 1988 and 1994 (cited in *Financial Times*, 2000), and the president of the Union of Greek Commercial Associations was quoted in 1997 as saying that 40,000 small businesses had closed in the previous 4 years, and only 17,000 had opened (*Financial Times*, 1997). Less visible has been the associated decline in the traditional wholesale sector, whose role has disappeared with the advent of direct deliveries from producers to retailers, and of large cash-and-carry operations.

The competitive pressures from the large companies have led small retailers to form buying groups, as well as to lobby for changes in the law. Moreover, rather than necessarily going out of business altogether, there is anecdotal and unsystematic observational evidence to suggest that a substantial number of traders formerly in the food sector are switching to the sale of other types of goods, particularly if they own their property. This is an important factor in the use of franchising by many larger companies in non-food sectors as a key element of their growth strategies, which compensates for the difficulties posed by the absence of sufficient and appropriate vacant retail premises in the market.

The changes in the Greek retail trades have also had a significant impact on the manufacturing sector of the country. Almost as much as in retailing, small family-owned manufacturing enterprises were the norm, and they have struggled to meet the quality of product and service demanded by modern retailers. McDonalds, for example, was unable to source any of its materials from inside Greece in their early years there, while British Home Stores quickly abandoned the use of Greek suppliers when it found that its products had also made their way to street vendors selling outside the store at a much lower price within a day of their introduction (Boutsouki and Bennison, 1999). The textile and clothing industry has perhaps been hardest hit as the demand for imported fashion has replaced the more workaday items that it produced. Suppliers have had to learn to come to terms with the new environment, and those that have done this are reaping the advantage as mutually beneficial long-term relationships with retailers have developed.

The area where the least impact from the changes seems to have occurred is that of government/public policy. Since the liberalization of regulation in 1991–1992 that triggered the process, and apart from the size limits introduced on supermarkets in certain localities in 1995, there has been very little obvious consideration of the implications of the changes. Nowhere in Greece are the kinds of debate occurring that so engage government, planners, retailers, developers and consumers in countries such as the United Kingdom. The novelty of the developments and their widespread popularity and acceptance by consumers have meant that issues regarding their social and environmental impact do not appear to reach the consciousness of most Greeks, who often seem to be concerned only with the material benefits of urban life. Whether debates about the future of town centres, the problems of traffic generation around large stores, or access by disadvantaged consumers ever become an active concern of government to the extent that a tighter regime for new retail development is introduced is a moot point.

Neither should the resilience of the small-scale, independent retailer in the face of adverse circumstances be underestimated. As well as competition from the large retailers, these small organizations have also been hit by much tighter fiscal controls that have markedly reduced the potential for tax avoidance that had been endemic in the country. However, especially in smaller population settlements and on the islands, social tradition and cohesion is a definite force for inertia in retailing, while the related issue of land and property ownership will clearly continue to act as a major hindrance to modern retail development throughout Greece.

Looking forward to the next 10 years, there is no doubt that change will continue, subject only to the constraints just noted and, perhaps, the wider political situation in the Balkans. There are still important retail sectors where the processes of concentration and polarization have not even started – jewellery, shoes, specialist food, books and stationary, for example – and many places where the only sign of the new retailing system is a supermarket. The stabilization of the Greek economy with its entry into the Euro, the development of equity financing, and the expectations of consumers, amongst other factors, will undoubtedly continue to drive development in an essentially free market. The country will also not be isolated from the wider global trends in retailing. The emergence of giant companies (how long before Wal-Mart enters Greece?), and the impact of new information and communication technologies upon both consumer and business, are two factors that should be monitored as closely here as elsewhere.

References

Bennison, D. (1979a) 'The sectoral and spatial structure of retail trade in Greece, 1951–1969', *Balkan Studies*, 20: 443–65.
Bennison, D. (1979b) 'The structural characteristics of the central place system of West Thessaly', *Greek Review of Social Research*, 35: 111–27.
Bennison, D. (1980) 'Patterns of consumer movements in West Thessaly', *Greek Review of Social Research*, 38: 73–86.
Bennison, D. (1995) 'Retail planning in Greece', in Davies, R. L. (ed.), *Retail Planning Policies in Western Europe*, Routledge, London.
Bennison, D. and Boutsouki, C. (1995) 'Greek retailing in transition', *International Journal of Retail and Distribution Management*, 3 (Part 1): 24–43.
Bistis, G. (2000) *Greek retailing, 1999–2000*, unpublished presentation, AC Nielsen, Athens.
Boutsouki, C. and Bennison, D. (1997) 'The evolution of retailer–supplier relationships in the Greek food sector', *Proceedings of the Ninth International Conference on Research in the Distributive Trades*, Leuven, Belgium.
Boutsouki, C. and Bennison, D. (1999) 'The impact of foreign involvement on the Greek department store sector: The BhS – Klaoudatos experience', in Dawson, J. and Dupuis, M. (eds), *Cases in European Retailing*, Blackwell, Oxford.

Coutsoumaris, G. (1963) *The Morphology of Greek Industry*, Centre of Planning and Economic Research, Athens.

Financial Times (1997) 'Big chains shake up the market', in Survey – Greece '97, *Financial Times*, 25 November 1997, p. 4.

Financial Times (2000) *European Retailing 2000+: Greece*, Financial Times Retail and Consumer, London.

FPDSavills (2000) *Athens: The Commercial Property Market*, FPDSavills, London.

Michaelidis, D. (1992) *Employment, Work and Training in Greek Retailing*, Report for the Force Programme, Foundation of Economic and Industrial Research, Athens.

Michaelidis, D. (1993) 'Letter from the editor', *Self Service Review*, November 1993, 206: 7.

Michaelidis Publications (1999) *Panorama of Greek Supermarkets*, Athens.

Preston, L. E. (1968) *Consumer Goods Marketing in a Developing Economy*, Centre of Planning and Economic Research, Athens.

Retailing and Wholesaling (1996) 'Greek food retailers', Michaelidis Publications, Athens.

Self Service Review (1994) 'Credit conditions are getting worse', 211: 24.

5 Italy

Luca Zanderighi

Introduction

Following the pattern of the remainder of the individual-country chapters in this study, this analysis of retailing in Italy commences with a detailed overview of recent trends and the current position of the retail sector in the Italian economy. This is followed by a survey of developments in retailing in Italy over the last three decades of the twentieth century, which was essentially the period over which the 'modernization' of Italian retailing occurred. An analysis is provided of the various associative forms of food retailing, which played a particularly important role in the development of modern retailing in Italy. The fifth section of this chapter looks in some detail at the impact of the relevant legislation on the development of retailing in Italy since 1970, including the most recent legislation and the likely changes in retailing trends following this. The chapter then offers an overview of the principal retail forms in Italy and some of their constituent organizations, and this individual-country study is brought to an end with some conclusions on particular features of Italian retailing and their impact upon consumers.

Retailing in the Italian economy

The Italian economy is driven by the service sector, which generates the highest percentage of value added. In 2000, the contribution of market services (including Distributive Trades, business services etc.) to value added was 58.6 per cent compared with 25.4 per cent for industry, 13.3 per cent for non-market or public services and 2.7 per cent for agriculture. The gap between market services as a whole and industry is steadily widening. In 1990, industry still accounted for 30.9 per cent and market services for 50.6 per cent of value added. There was also an increase in the share of non-market services offered by the public sector from 12.8 per cent in 1980 to 13.3 per cent in 2000. The shift towards services is also reflected in the employment figures, and data on employment in the Distributive Trades are set out in Figure 5.4.

The share of Italian gross domestic product (GDP) accounted for by the Distributive Trades sector alone has, however, has remained almost constant, expanding over the past thirty years from roughly 11 to 12 per cent. The trend depicted in Figure 5.1 shows a Distributive Trades share of GDP heavily influenced by the overall business cycle until the end of the 1970s. The second oil shock was, however, even less felt by the sector in relative terms because of the interplay of two factors. First, the anticyclical resilience of the large proportion of small independent shopkeepers, and, second, the development of more modern forms of retail taking place in the 1980s and above all in the 1990s which triggered an endogenous expansion.

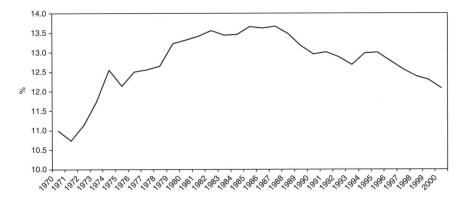

Figure 5.1 Italian Distributive Trades: share of value added (current prices).

Household consumption as a proportion of GDP in Italy has fluctuated over the past thirty years within a relatively narrow margin, between 58 and 61 per cent. The share of the traded part of this consumption (i.e. those goods normally distributed via the retail trade, and excluding services and the consumption of utilities such as electricity, water etc.) as a proportion of total household consumption has steadily decreased over the twenty years since 1980. As illustrated in Figure 5.2, this proportion fell from 68 per cent in that year to 54 per cent in 2000 as household expenditure on services increased in relative terms.

The disaggregation of total household consumption by area of expenditure shows the decrease in the proportion of Food relative to Total Consumption of slightly more than half from one-third in 1970 to 14.6 per cent in 2000 (see Figure 5.3). Overall this suggests a catching up from the relative backwardness of the consumption structure in Italy. However, this trend is still differentiated geographically, and some evidence on this is brought out later in Table 5.2 and in Figure 5.8.

By contrast, the share of services in household consumption increased steadily. For example, the non-traded proportion of total consumption rose from 37.4 per cent in 1986 to 45.5 per cent in 2000. This has occurred as the expected consequence of overall changes in the pattern of consumption, and it is also reflected in changes in the national pattern of production, from manufacturing to services, and among the latter in particular services related to leisure time.

Parallel to the growth of the share of the Distributive Trades' value added in GDP, employment in this sector expanded from 13.0 per cent in 1975 to 15.6 per cent of the employment in the national economy in 2000. Within this, the

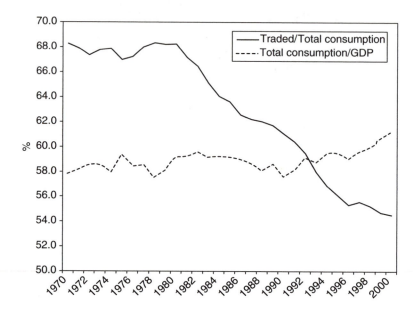

Figure 5.2 Total household and traded consumption.

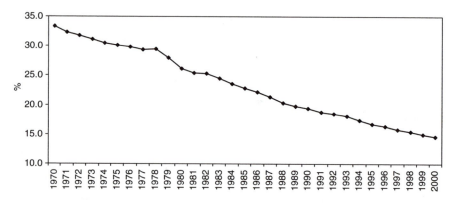

Figure 5.3 Food relative to total consumption.

distributive sector in the Italian economy is characterized by a disproportionate number of small retail outlets, run as family business, with low levels of employ-ment per outlet. Figure 5.4 shows the aggregate position with regard to employ-ment in the Distributive Trades. The proportion of employment in the Distributive Trades rose from just under 12 per cent in 1971 to a peak of a little over 16 per cent in 1988, since when it has stabilized at around 15.5 per cent at the present time (2000).

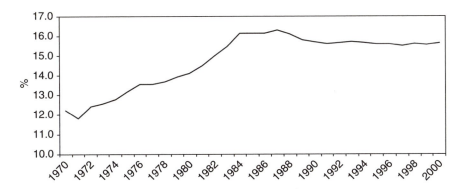

Figure 5.4 Italian Distributive Trades: share of total employment.

Within this picture of total employment in the Distributive Trades, until 1990 the share of employees, as opposed to the self-employed, within the total employment in this sector remained at around 41–45 per cent. In the last ten years, however, there has been a substantial increase in multiple-shop and other large-scale retail organizations, mainly in food retailing, and this has significantly affected the composition of employment in the sector. However, in no other country at a similar stage of economic development is the share of self-employment so high, and this is possibly the most peculiar feature of the Distributive Trades in Italy.

This high share of self-employment, although it has been gradually decreasing in recent years, becomes even more evident if we examine separately the three main components of distributive trades; data relating separately to retailing, wholesale and intermediaries, and Auto-Motor Distributive Trade (including petrol stations) are set out in Figure 5.5. In retailing, the current (2000) share of self-employment is a little more than one-half (52 per cent), although this has fallen from 63 per cent since 1992, during which time there has been a growth in the number of employees. In the wholesale and intermediaries and in the Auto-Motor Distributive Trades, the change in the ratio of self-employment to total employment has been rather less marked, and the current (2000) share of self-employed is lower at 38 per cent in each case.

A simple aggregated analysis of the Distributive Trade sector in the Italian economy would, however, mask the profound changes in the sector brought about by the rapid modernization of retailing over the last two decades of the twentieth century in particular.

The 1980s and 1990s were marked by:

- an increase in the number of self-service outlets, especially food retailing;
- the opening of large-scale retail outlets in the form of supermarkets, superstores and hypermarkets, as well as the establishment of shopping centres;
- a progressive concentration of retailer buying groups and voluntary chains; and
- an increase in the number of franchised outlets in non-food retailing.

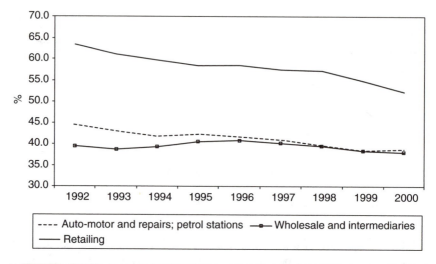

Figure 5.5 Employment: share of self-employed.

This transformation of the Italian distribution system, which occurred later than those of other economies within the European Union covered in this study, was often hindered by administrative entry barriers and other forms of government control of retailing. These are discussed in some detail below, and they continued almost until 1998. It was the large-scale food retailers who were most affected by these entry barriers, which favoured small independent entrepreneurs rather than large multiple-shop retail organizations. The result of this situation is that even today in Italy modern, large-scale retailers still account for a low share of total retail sales.

The transformation of the Italian retailing from 1970

An analysis of the transformation of Italian retailing during the 1970s and 1980s is a useful starting point, as over that period the distributive system began to take on the particular features of its present-day appearance. The overall picture emerging from the comparison of 1991 Census results with the corresponding data from the previous 1981 and 1971 Censuses is of a process of modernization, occurring albeit at a relatively slow pace. This transformation can be summarized as follows:

- an overall increase in number of retail outlets;
- a transformation in terms of the size of individual retail organizations, with a relative increase in the number of large-scale businesses, in terms of establishments (retail outlets), number of employees and of sales area;
- an increase in the number of shops organized on a self-service basis; and
- diffusion of vertical integration allowed by different forms of association and cooperative forms of ownership.

This transformation took place in the context of protective barriers to entry created by the system of required government authorization in retailing which had the effect of slowing down the growth of large, mass-market stores while it favoured the development and modernization of small, local, independent entrepreneurs against large multiple-shop retailers.

Table 5.1 shows the breakdown of the Italian retail sector into its three main sub-sectors: specialized food (mainly fresh products), non-specialized food (mainly packaged grocery products) and non-food outlets. Data are provided for the growth in store numbers in each of these three categories over the two decades 1971–1981 and 1981–1991, and for store numbers in 1991.

Table 5.1 Number and trend of outlets by sub-sectors (1971–1991)

	Number in 1991	*Growth*	
		1981–1991	*1971–1981*
Specialized food retailing	189,633	−33.9	2.4
Non-specialized food retailing	88,257	12.7	−34.7
Non-food retailing	644,758	9.8	25.5
Total[a]	922,648	−4.6	6.7

Source: Istat.

Note
a Excluding auto and motor distribution.

In the 1970s, large self-service stores gained ground first in the non-specialized food area of packaged groceries. However, the extent of the reduction in the number of small non-specialized grocery shops of a little more than one-third (34.7 per cent) is surprisingly large if compared to the parallel increase of large stores. This can be explained by the fact that the entry of these large stores prevented the large number of marginal small-scale shopkeepers from increasing their profits and maintaining the growth in their incomes relative to trend of average earnings in the economy. Specialized or predominantly fresh food retailing was much less affected by this entry of supermarkets, and this may be explained by the shopping habits of consumers which are rooted in frequent purchases that require a high density of stores and a level of service which was only provided by small, local specialized stores. However, during the 1980s, there occurred an increasing development of large stores, and the resulting intensity of competition had the effect of reducing the number of specialized food stores by one-third.

Thus a slow and partial modernization of the Italian retailing systems began in the 1970s and took further shape during the 1980s. But it was only in the 1990s that the often relatively imperceptible movements within almost 900,000 retail businesses became more apparent. Although it will only be when the data of the 2001 Census are available that the real extent of this transformation will be revealed, the growth of large stores recorded by official sources allows for some ongoing consideration. The total number of outlets (comprising both stores and itinerant trade) decreased slightly from 922,648 units in 1991 to 799,937 in 1996.

The decrease of small food stores continued, and more than 50,000 outlets left the market. In contrast with experience in previous decades, when the numbers of non-food retailers hardly decreased at all, during the 1990s, almost 10,000 of such outlets left the market each year. In particular, the development of large specialized stores in several sectors – such as DIY, furniture, consumer electronic goods, sports products – and the general slackening of consumer demand in non-food areas during the early 1990s brought about a considerable reduction in the numbers of small stores also in these sectors.

The overall transformation of retailing in Italy over the last twenty years can be seen in an even clearer way by looking at a measure of the standard of service provided to customers, using as a very rough indicator of this the number of outlets per 1,000 inhabitants. Data on this for the years 1981, 1991 and 1996 are set out in Table 5.2, and from this one can see that while this index remained relatively unchanged over the period 1981–1996 as a whole in the case of non-food outlets, there was a reduction in the case of food retailing from 6.2 outlets in 1981 to 4.0 in 1996.

Table 5.2 Number of outlets per 1,000 inhabitants in Italy (1981–1996)

	Food			Non-food		
	1981	*1991*	*1996*	*1981*	*1991*	*1996*
North-west	5.7	4.4	3.4	7.2	7.9	7.1
North-east	5.8	4.3	3.4	7.8	8.6	8.1
Central	6.1	4.7	4.0	8.1	9.3	8.6
South	6.8	5.5	4.8	7.3	8.0	7.9
Italy	6.2	4.8	4.0	7.5	8.3	7.7

Source: Author estimates.

Figure 5.6 illustrates the evolution of large stores in Italy from 1971 to 2000, distinguishing among supermarkets, hypermarkets and department stores. This last category includes both department stores and variety stores, that is, it includes all stores of more than 400 sq. m. of sales area having at least five departments.

As Figure 5.6 shows, supermarkets increased in number relatively slowly. Over the period 1971–1982, the average annual number of net new supermarket openings was 87. During the remainder of the 1980s, the annual average rose to 144. However, the annual average for the 1990s was 339, with a marked increase in the latter half of this decade, rising to a figure of 690 for 1999. The later development of hypermarkets was even more rapid. These outlets were almost non-existent in Italy until the early 1980s, with annual store openings in this category ranging from 0 to 3 during the period 1974–1983. These figures increased slightly from then until 1987, and the average figure for the period 1988–1999 was 22. These comparative trends can be explained by the lowering of administrative barriers and by new favourable attitude of regional authorities with respect to hypermarkets located inside shopping centres.

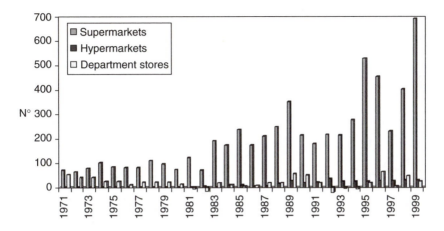

Figure 5.6 Large stores net growth.

The trend in respect of large non-food stores is quite different. While their numbers increased substantially during the 1970s, from 498 units in 1970 to 775 in 1980, the data in Figure 5.6 show a clear reduction in the number of annual net new openings during the latter part of the 1970s. These new openings fluctuated somewhat during the next decade. In 1990 there were 50 net new openings, but in 1992 there were 22 net closures, and the overall effect of this was that the total number of stores shows a net increase of 162 in the 1980s and of 146 in the 1990s. The expansion in terms of square metres of sales area was even smaller: 250,000 sq. m. in the 1980s and 375,000 sq. m. in the 1990s against 820,000 sq. m. in the 1970s, and this was accompanied by a modest increase of the average size of stores from 1,669 sq. m. in 1990 to 1,790 sq. m in 1999.

As already noted, for a period, small specialized shops were able to compete successfully against non-specialized stores. The standard of services provided by large stores – measured in terms of square metres of sales area per 1,000 inhabitants – offers a more immediate picture of the degree of modernization reached by Italian retailing system. The sales area of supermarkets more than doubled in the last decade reaching 99 sq. m. per 1,000 inhabitants in 1999, and the trends in this respect with regard to all three categories of retail organization over the period 1971–1999 are set out in Figure 5.7.

Although significant progress has occurred, this standard is still far from those available to consumers in the other comparable European countries. With respect to hypermarkets, the index shows an even faster increase than in respect of super-markets and department stores, with the index more than doubling between 1992 and 1999. However, the difference with respect to comparable countries is also larger. As for department stores, the index shows more clearly than the data relating to the number of stores how slow the diffusion was of this particular retail

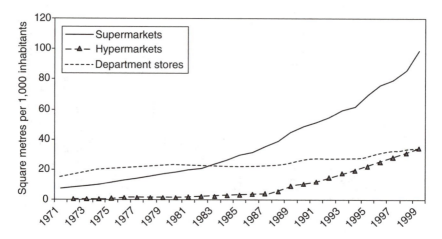

Figure 5.7 Large stores: square metres per 1,000 inhabitants.

format. The level of provision for this category of stores was virtually constant from 1973 to 1988, although from the following year until 1999 there was a rise of just over one-third.

Total sales and relative market shares is another way to look at the same trends. Modern retail formats (supermarkets, hypermarkets and department stores) accounted for 22.3 per cent of retail sales in Italy in 1999, up from less than 10 per cent in 1989. Considering only the food sector, the combined market share of supermarkets and hypermarkets was just over 30 per cent. Department stores accounted for a very small proportion of retail sales: just below 3 per cent in 1999, excluding food turnover. This is linked to consumption patterns and to difficulties experienced by department stores in positioning themselves *vis-à-vis* specialty stores and hypermarkets.

In addition to traditional types of non-specialized large stores, the last ten years have witnessed a noticeable development of large specialized non-food stores. Ambitious local entrepreneurs and integrated foreign groups such as Castorama, Ikea, Virgin Fnac, GrandOptical, Mediaworld, Decathlon, Leroy Merlin have opened a large number of outlets in Italy, and Table 5.3 sets out the current (2000) position in this respect in the four main product areas.

Unfortunately the available statistics do not account separately for this type of retail format and only the data from the 2001 Census will make it possible to evaluate the extent of their growth and development.

The mechanism for the authorization of new stores, administered at a local level in Italy, has led to widely different patterns of retail development in the different regions of the country. On the one hand, differences are less marked if one looks at the overall density of stores. On the other hand, if we consider the supermarket store format, which epitomizes the modern form of distribution in Italy, the regional differences are much more marked. Thus, the figure for square metres

Table 5.3 Large-scale retail specialists in Italy (2000)

	Turnover (billion lire)	*Outlets* (number)	*Sales area* ('000 Sq. m.)
Furniture			
Ikea	652[a]	6	93,500
Mercatone Zeta	782	15	25,000
Mercatone Uno	956[a]	66	324,000
Sport goods			
Decathlon	n.a.	4	16,500
Giacomelli	299[a]	62	61,850
Longoni	168[a]	13	2,500
Cisalfa	386[a]	46	40,000
DIY			
Bricocenter	423[a]	41	n.a.
Obi	265	25	85,000
Castorama	234[a]	10	64,000
Big Mat	200	42	n.a.
Consumer electronics			
Media World	1046[a]	23	n.a.

Source: Largo consumo, company account.

Note
a Excluding VAT.

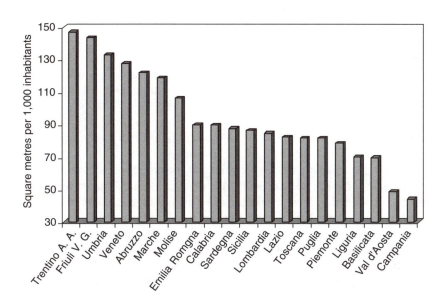

Figure 5.8 Supermarkets: square metres per 1,000 inhabitants by region (1999).

of supermarket sales area per 1,000 inhabitants in 1999, set out in Figure 5.8, varied between 147 in Trentino A. A. and 44 in Campania, and although it is true that the presence of large stores decreases from northern to southern Italy, there are a number of exceptions. For example, Marche and Abruzzi, two central regions, show a density of supermarkets (118.5 and 121.8 per 1,000 inhabitants, respectively) that is higher than most northern regions.

The role of associative forms in Italian food retailing

Buying groups and voluntary chains were prime movers in the modernization of Italian retailing, the supermarket being their preferred store format. These organizations succeeded in expanding their supermarket share in the 1980s and the 1990s and this can be chiefly attributed to the Law 426/71 and its amendments, discussed below, that favoured them. Regional differences in the pattern of food consumption and the relatively large number of local small- and medium-sized manufacturers are also important factors in the development of associative forms of retailing, whereby members are better able to adjust store assortments to fit the needs of local demand more easily than can the large-scale multiple-shop retail organizations.

Buying groups and voluntary chains are characterized by a three-level organizational structure, as follows:

1 Central organization
   • purchases products on domestic and international markets
   • promotes the corporate identity of the group
   • provides member firms with marketing services.
2 Local or regional distribution centres
   • have a financial stake in the central body
   • purchase products from regional manufacturers
   • provide administrative (purchase order processing), logistical (inventory management and transport) and distribution support (delivery to retailers).
3 Member firms
   • with or without financial stake in the regional distribution centres.

Concentration among these organizations at regional and multi-regional level has increased in the last decade owing to competition. Smaller local cooperatives either merged together or were taken over by central organizations in an attempt to cut costs. Conad, the largest buying group in Italy, radically cut down the number of local cooperatives from 38 in 1990 to 11 in 2000. Buying groups and voluntary chains have developed their networks by establishing their own outlets (forward integration) and by associating retailers to the group through franchising and similar contracts. In particular, during the recent period common marketing and other corporate policies developed by the central body were readily implemented by member retailers, and in general, the increasing and more intensive competition for market shares has helped central bodies to convince members that a coherent group image is indispensable to compete successfully against large-scale, multiple-shop retail operators.

The impact of government legislation

Law 426/71 and its effects on the evolution of Italian retailing

Retail planning regulations in Italy have been by far one of the most restrictive in Europe. From 1971, and the enactment of Law 426/71, all forms of retail development in Italy have been subject to a set of controls that have significantly influenced the development and structure of this sector of the economy.

The main objective of this Law was to soften the impact of the entry of large stores on existing independent retailers. Its impact on the industry has been considerable, and a general appreciation of its content is a necessary preliminary to an understanding of the development of the Italian retailing system. The Law was divided into sections concerning three main issues:

• Trade Registry
• Retail Development Plan
• Administrative permission.

The Trade Registry was meant to discourage the entry of small independent retailers into the sector. Every individual or company who wanted to establish a retailing establishment was subject to registration with the Chamber of Commerce of the district where he was resident or where the organization had its legal seat. In order to register, the shopkeeper had to fulfil a number of requirements and to pass an examination.

The Retail Development Plan was the main provision of the Law. Municipalities were required to formulate a plan for the rational development of the retailing system over their territory. This plan had to be prepared independently from the existence of standard town planning instruments (master plan), and the procedure can be summarized as follows. Municipalities had to determine the amount of sales area needed to serve actual and expected demand for each product category. On the basis of estimated demand, each municipality had to prepare a Retail Development Plan, dividing its territory into a certain number of areas, and providing a detailed indication of the retail selling space available for each shop type within each area. In respect of this Plan, retail outlets were not defined in terms of their distributive formats but as shops allowed to sell merchandise only within one or more product lists defined by the Law. New shops were required to fit into the Retail Master Plan, and a new shop could be opened only if there was space available in the sub-area where the shop was to be located.

Third, administrative permission issued by the mayor of the relevant municipality was required under the Law for the enlarging of stores and for transferring stores among merchandise categories. The application should contain information concerning the site, the dimensions of the store, the description of the activity to be undertaken and evidence of the registration at the relevant Chamber of Commerce. Permissions to trade were granted on the basis of the Retail Master Plan. A permit from the Regional Government was also required in respect of stores of more than 1,500 sq. m., and if the population of the municipality was less than 10,000 inhabitants, this requirement for a permit applied to all stores exceeding 400 sq. m. of sales area. If the mayor did not decide upon an application for administrative permission within 90 days, this should be regarded as a rejection of the application.

In order to promote the modernization of retailing, a number of amendments were made to Law 426/71: they consisted in Laws and Ministry Decrees which provided for some automatic approval concerning expansion of existing stores.

The data on the structure of the Italian retail system analyzed above are evidences of the impact of Law 426 on the development of large stores in Italy. The impact has, however, been different across space, between shop types and different retail organizations, and over time. Across space, the Law has had a more serious impact in the areas where large stores would have had stronger negative social effects. Between shop types and retail organizations, food retailing was more affected by the Law than non-food retailing, and associative retailing organizations fared better than other multiple-shop organizations. Finally, over time, in the areas where the diffusion of modern retailing was accomplished more rapidly, the Law was on occasions an incentive to new store openings.

Differences across space

The Retail Development Plan involved municipalities, and thus exposed the planning process to local interests and circumstances. This was intended to guarantee a flexible management of barriers to retailing entry, depending upon the social impact of new stores in the different areas of the country. Where the economy was weaker, local authorities could be stricter in awarding permission for new, large-scale retail developments than in areas where shopkeepers excluded from the market could more easily find alternative jobs. This is one of the main reasons behind the different speed of diffusion of supermarkets and hypermarkets in the different Italian regions as already seen from Figure 5.8.

Differences across shop type

The diffusion of large stores was slowed down especially in the food retailing: during the 1970s in respect of supermarkets, and during the 1980s and the 1990s with regard to hypermarkets. This may be attributed to the fact that it was in the food retail sector that the new large-scale retailers were more likely to have a significant adverse impact upon smaller traditional retailers. By contrast, large non-food stores – department stores and variety stores – were much less affected by the application of Law 426/71, and it should be noted, therefore, that the slow development of department stores and variety stores cannot be attributed to the authorization mechanism of the Law. These retail formats, and other types of

large stores specializing in narrower lines of merchandise, did not develop until
the end of the 1980s for reasons to be found in the general structure of the Italian
economy. On the supply side, Italian industry was – and still is to some extent –
characterized by small firms. Manufacturing industry market concentration in
such sectors as clothing, furniture, textiles, footwear and other similar consumer
goods was never high. Thus, the shift from the search for manufacturing
economies of scale to product differentiation which started in the 1970s suited
Italian industry very well, allowing small- and medium-sized firms to survive and
develop, occupying market niches. On the demand side, in areas such as clothing,
furniture and household items, consumers were never accustomed to standardized
products. These items were traditionally provided by small firms, while mass-
produced goods in these product categories were normally exported.

Differences across retail organizations

The authorization mechanism introduced by Law 426/71 acted as a barrier to
entry with different degree of strictness between different types of retail organizations. Local interest groups or lobbies had their own impact on decision making. Thus, local entrepreneurs were able to overcome the opposition by local
shopkeepers better than large companies without local ties. Also, for members of
cooperatives, buying groups and voluntary chains, which were closer to local
authorities, it was easier to obtain authorization than it was for other multiple-
shop organizations. Due to this discrimination, multiples lost market share. Thus,
while in 1977 the multiple-shop organizations' share of supermarkets sales area
was almost one-half, 20 years later it was reduced to less than 40 per cent. By
contrast, buying groups and voluntary chains grew faster, owing to the explicit
priority given to their conversion of existing small shops to supermarket outlets.

Differences through time

The ample discretion given to municipalities in deciding about new retail licences
was also reflected in changing attitudes through time. Where, in any local area,
the entry of large stores was achieved, leading to a sharp reduction in the number
of small shops, the defence of these latter ceased to be a relevant aim for local
authorities. Their attitude towards large-scale retailing changed, and the establishment of such outlets came to be seen as a positive contribution to the local
economy which – especially for small municipalities – could be considerable.
When this happened, the effects of the Law were the opposite to the preceding situation. Authorizations for retail development were easily granted and nearby
municipalities competed among each other to attract large stores.

Social factors behind the retail regulatory framework in Italy

The Italian distribution system has always been heavily affected by regulations,
their main aim being to protect small retailers. The anticompetitive implications
are obvious, but the problems that a total liberalization of entry into the retail

sector posed at the time have also to be acknowledged. When Law 426/71 was enacted in 1971, it was thought necessary to balance the interests of the consumer with the social cost of possible widespread bankruptcies among small shopkeepers. Consumers would have benefited from the diffusion of large stores such as supermarkets offering lower prices and the opportunity to concentrate purchases. However, without some form of restraint, a large number of small independent retailers, especially in the food sector, would have been deprived of their jobs. Given the already high level of unemployment and the economic and social characteristics of marginal shopkeepers, they would have had serious difficulties in finding a different occupation. In the condition of social unrest existing in Italy in the 1970s, it was considered inappropriate to undermine through a total liberalization of entry into the retail market, a politically stable group such as small independent retailers. The solution devised with Law 426/71 was to leave each municipality, and to a lesser extent each regional authority, to set the degree of retail trade liberalization acceptable in the light of local conditions. Thus, barriers to retail entry under Law 426/71 were the results of the interplay of local economic circumstances, possibly conflicting interests at a local level, and the effectiveness of local lobbies.

During the 1980s and the 1990s – two decades of social stability and sustained economic growth – it would have been possible to change the regulatory framework, liberalizing entry to the retail sector. However, the flexibility of Law 426/71 partially allowed for such a reduction of entry barriers as local authorities became less worried about the costs of bankruptcies among existing small retailers and thus less obliging in response to their lobbying. Moreover, at this time, the pressure from large retailers to change the Law also eased substantially. This change of attitude may be explained by the fact that possibly the Law gave these larger scale retail organizations a more certain framework within which to plan their own expansion at this time, and this may have been preferred to the uncertainty created by a sudden change of regime that a liberalization of entry into retail markets would have implied.

Although over time entry into the retail trades has tended to become easier than before, there are exceptions concerning large hypermarkets and specialized stores. Such forms of retailing are rarely allowed unless they are included within shopping centres. A number of regional authorities have stated explicitly in their planning documents their opposition to the development of very large free-standing stores, favouring instead the development of shopping centres. This opposition to free-standing stores is justified in terms of negative externalities on traffic and on the balance of activities between town centres and peripheral areas. It is argued that the uncontrolled geographical diffusion of large stores would lead to a reduction in the viability of town or city centres, especially those of the large number of medium-sized towns existing in Italy.

As already noted, barriers to entry were particularly strong in respect of food retailing. They affected both inter-type competition and intra-type competition, that is, both competition between different store formats such as traditional retailers and supermarkets, and competition among traditional retailers themselves and among supermarket groups. Different shop types provide different retail products and levels of retail service. Barriers to entry generally prevent any alteration in the mix of retail types available to consumers, ration the supply of some of the service, reduce consumers' welfare and allow for stable rents. New large stores – first supermarkets, then hypermarkets – were in position to obtain such rents. The slow diffusion of supermarkets reduced inter-type competition in food retailing in Italy until the mid-1980s. From then on the rate of new openings increased substantially. In the 1980s and 1990s, barriers to entry applied to hypermarkets, this time sheltering supermarkets instead of traditional food stores.

Intra-type – that is, competition among retailers operating the same store format – was also reduced as a result of entry barriers. Especially in food retailing, where retail services play a significant strategic role, intra-type competition increases as the trading areas of similar stores of different firms overlap. This competition is therefore reduced when new stores are not able to access locations giving access to consumer areas unserved by other stores. The slowdown of entry due to the application of Law 426/71 led to a postponement of such intra-type competition.

However, some of the potential rents were dissipated. Economies of scale could be exploited only partially in most centralized functions performed for the advantage of the entire network of stores (i.e. sourcing, marketing and central warehousing). Moreover, difficulties in obtaining authorizations for new stores led to acceptance of stores of sub-optimal size and of second-best locations. Some firms also tried to obtain authorizations in new areas in order to establish bridgeheads then to develop a local network of stores. This proved to be very difficult, leading to logistics inefficiencies as isolated stores had to be stocked from warehouses located in distant places. At present, with new regulations, regional councils have expressed conservative views about large stores. Entry is easier for supermarkets but more difficult for hypermarkets. In the past, multiples, especially large ones, were discriminated against relative to other types of retail organizations. The effect of this can easily be seen in their loss of market share. At present, this asymmetric effect of barriers to entry with respect to different types retail organizations is encouraging expanding multiple-shop retailers to grow through acquisitions of local chains. Similarly, foreign chains operating in Italy, such as the French Carrefour and Auchan, but excluding the German hard-discounter Lidl, have preferred to open hypermarkets through joint venture with an Italian partner.

The anticompetitive effects of Law 426/71 on non-food retailing were less marked. Until the mid-1980s, when the pressure to open large specialized stores started to increase, the growth of non-food consumption and the vitality of small-scale retailing allowed for more stores and lively competition. Small, specialized shops were very successful in competing with large ones, especially with department stores and variety stores. These latter forms of retailing were never very profitable in Italy and there is, therefore, no evidence that regulations constrained entry and, even less, that existing stores might have obtained rents due to barriers of entry.

During the 1990s, the market for large retail shops specializing in single product categories matured. This type of retail organization, however, found it difficult to obtain planning permission, although probably less difficult than it used to be for supermarkets and hypermarkets. Unfortunately, the present lack of data concerning the diffusion of large specialized stores makes it impossible to evaluate the relevance of barriers to entry arising though the application of Law 426/71.

The new Retail Planning Regulation

Although a number of amendments were made to Law 426/71 in order to grant some degree of freedom to retail groups, this law remained in place until April 1998, when new and more liberal regulations were introduced. Essentially, the new Regulation aims to streamline the process for establishing new retail outlets with the ultimate goal of modernizing Italy's fragmented retail market. More freedom has been given to each municipality for determining local planning issues, and greater authority has been given to regional bodies for larger, strategic level developments and for setting the planning criteria to be used at a local level.

The most important changes have been made in the following areas:

- Administrative approval
- Trade Registry
- Trading hours
- Product list restrictions
- Role of regional administrations.

Change in criteria for administrative approval

The new Regulation makes it more straightforward for retailers to get permission (licence) to open a store. Under the new system, stores are given permission based on their size rather than their product list. Retailers do not need to obtain a licence if they are planning to open a store of less than 250 sq. m. in a town of more than 10,000 inhabitants or a store of less than 150 sq. m. in a town of fewer than 10,000 inhabitants. Instead, they only need to inform the mayor that they are planning to open the store. However, licences have to be obtained from the town council for new outlets between 150 and 1,500 sq. m. in towns fewer than 10,000 people, and for shops between 250 and 2,500 sq. m. in towns of more than 10,000 people.

The regional authority has overriding control over the development of large stores, and administrative licences for these formats and shopping centres have to be obtained from the local council with the authorization of the regional authority. This Regulation covers stores with a sales area of more than 2,500 sq. m. in towns with more than 10,000 inhabitants or more than 1,500 sq. m. in towns of fewer than 10,000. The application has to be analyzed and approved by three administrative levels – region, provincial and local council – which all participate in the debate.

Abolition of Trade Registry

The Trade Registry, which used to be kept by the Chamber of Commerce, has been abolished. Shopkeepers no longer have to be included in this Registry, thus making it easier for them to start a business.

Deregulation of trading hours

Store operators are able to determine the hours between 7 a.m. and 10 p.m. when they are to be open, up to a maximum of 13 h a day. Beyond this, more flexibility is given in towns which are centres for tourism and art. It is up to the local council to decide Sunday opening regulations and mid-week store closures after consultation with local entrepreneurs and consumer representatives. Stores are allowed to open on Sundays over the holiday periods and for a maximum of eight other Sundays during the year.

Removal of restrictions on product lists

As mentioned above, restrictions have been removed which prevented shops from selling goods from more than one product list. Each outlet is now able to sell a wider range of goods, with the separate product categories reduced to just two: food and non-food. The removal of these restrictions is particularly advantageous for small retailers who are able to sell a wider range of merchandise within these broader headings.

More power of regional administrations

The 1998 Regulation gives greater authority to the regional administrations for determining retail development strategy. These administrations have the responsibility for setting general guidelines for retail development, such as the amount and location of retail space in their region, and for establishing urban planning criteria to be used in local plans. During the last two years (1999–2000), the regions have drawn up these guidelines, in consultation with representatives from the local council, consumer and retail associations. General guidelines for retail development are been formulated taking into account their implications on different types of settlements. The various types of settlements and issues for consideration are as follows:

- In metropolitan areas, the impact on the retail system of the central area should be taken into account when considering the development of large stores or out-of-town shopping centres.
- Planners should try to achieve a balanced development pattern in areas of interconnected towns, which form a continuous market place.
- An emphasis should be placed on the preservation in centres which are important for their history or art.
- In small towns, consideration should be given to ways of improving their infrastructure in order to bolster economic and social development.

Impact of the new Regulation

As the regional administrations have had only about one or two years to prepare their guidelines and retail development criteria, evidence of the impact of the Regulation to date is fairly limited, particularly as during this period all planning decisions on large stores and shopping centres have been frozen. However, smaller retailers have been able to take immediate advantage of the new Regulation which enabled them to extend their floorspace and expand their product range. Conversely, in order to promote modernization in retailing, small family-run shops are given financial subsidies if they decide to cease operating. As far as it is possible to judge today, regional councils have expressed conservative views that might undermine the impact of this much-needed reform of retailing, with the consequence of a 'freeze' on enlarging existing stores or on large new openings in the next years.

Leading retail groups in Italy

The development of major retail organizations in Italy was significantly affected by the application of Law 426/71. Large-scale retailers are few in number, they are generally small in scale compared with those of similar European countries, and they trade mainly in mass markets and in food. Chains of specialized non-food stores are rare – with the exception of franchised outlets, although these have increased during recent years. Even so, the retail sector in Italy has been subject to a degree of consolidation and concentration in recent years, much of it shaped by the influence of foreign entrants to the market, either organically, through partnerships or through acquisition. In the last decade, leading Italian retail organizations have focused their efforts on opening large stores and on modernizing existing networks to gain market share and reduce operating expenses. Even foreign retailers are discovering new market opportunities in Italy, as seen in the acquisition of Gs by Carrefour and by the partnership of the French Auchan with La Rinascente. Table 5.4 summarizes the current (1999) position regarding the major stores in the four retail-organization categories of multiples, voluntary chains, buying groups and consumer cooperatives.

Multiples

There are five major multiple-shop retailers operating in Italy. La Rinascente, controlled by Fiat and operating now in both the food and non-food sectors, is the most diversified retail group. It initially developed in the non-food sector through department and variety stores, and then entered into the food market, operating both supermarkets and hypermarkets. During the 1980s, the company diversified into specialized retailing, with a do-it-yourself (DIY), a furniture and an electrical chain. In the 1990s, however, it returned to refocus on its core business. In 1997, La Rinascente entered into a partnership with Auchan, involving the merger of the two companies' grocery and DIY activities.

Table 5.4 Major food retail organizations in Italy (1999)

	Turnover (billion lire)	Outlets (number)	Sales area ('000 Sq. m.)
Multiples			
La Rinascente-Auchan	9.132[a]	439	1,025
Carrefour-Gs	7.545[a]	n.a.	643
Esselunga	5.289[a]	106	195
Pam	3.888[a]	379	364
Finiper	2.479[a]	18	163
Voluntary chains			
Mdo[b]	8,200	3,532	1,168
Selex	8,100	1,799	1,000
Interdis	7,800	3,235	1,370
Sisa	6,000	689	387
Despar	4.825[a]	1,876	602
Buying groups			
Conad	6,914[a]	2,891	1,114
Crai	4,500[a]	5,000	882
Consumer cooperatives			
Coop Italia	15,685	1,320	1,075

Source: Largo consumo, company account.

Notes
a Excluding VAT.
b Estimated.

In the food sector, the French Carrefour has consolidated itself as one of Italy's largest retailers following the merger with Promodes in 1999 and the acquisition of Gruppo Gs. The Carrefour-Gs group, now entirely controlled by Carrefour, operates both supermarkets and hypermarkets, and in 1999, the turnover amounted to 7,545 billion lire. On the other hand, Esselunga and Pam are both supermarket specialists, while Finiper is a hypermarket specialist. These last three are private companies trading in Northern Italy. There are also some smaller local chains that could, within the next few years, be the main targets for further acquisitions by larger retailers.

One of the most significant events in the non-food sector was the break up of the Standa group. The limited food activities were sold off separately, and Gruppo Coin acquired 270 variety stores, which are being converted to Coin and Oviesse stores. Gruppo Coin has also developed significant international links, acquiring the Kaufhalle chain in Germany as well as establishing a joint venture with Marbert of Germany to operate Limone perfumery counters in its department stores. It has also entered into a partnership to develop Fnac stores in Italy.

Voluntary chains

The major voluntary chains are all involved in food retailing. They are controlled by wholesalers and operate both owned and associated stores. Their network of stores includes all types of food outlets, but during the 1990s, they increased their network of large stores, including hypermarkets. In respect of large stores, there was an increasing tendency both to expand through outlets already directly owned by wholesalers, and also to acquire new, large-scale members. The recent trend has been for voluntary chains to develop a common trading name for their different retail formats, and to move towards common operating procedures across the chain. A number of smaller voluntary chains were also developed in the non-food sector, especially in the electrical and pharmaceutical sectors.

Buying groups

Conad and Crai are the two largest buying groups operating in Italy. With total sales of 6,914 and 4,500 billion lire, respectively in 1999, they rank in the top ten retail organizations in Italy. During the last decade, Conad, in particular, has implemented a policy of centralization through several mergers of local cooperatives, and has concentrated on small supermarkets.

Cooperatives

Coop Italia is by far the most important cooperative organization and, in terms of total sales, the largest retail organization in the country. During the last two decades, it too has centralized rapidly through several mergers of local cooperatives. Although the group still operates a number of smaller stores, it is concentrated on large supermarkets and hypermarkets.

Franchising

Although it is difficult to assign different economic content to the two contracts, in Italy a distinction is made between franchising and *concessione,* a very similar type of selective distribution contract. The former arrangement has a very well-established legal tradition, while the latter is not recognized under Italian law as a specific contractual formula. Statistics relating to retail-format franchising in Italy do not include *concessione* and therefore they underestimate the extent of retail franchising as it is more broadly understood, making comparison with other countries difficult. It is therefore difficult to record precisely the extent of existing contracts establishing vertical relationships, which can be subsumed into franchising. The number of franchisors and their franchisees existing in Italy in 1999 is set out in Table 5.5. These data provide an estimate including only franchising systems proper as defined in Italian law, excluding *concessione,* and therefore underestimate the diffusion of other contractual forms having a similar economic meaning. Franchising systems defined in this narrow sense involve 536 franchisors and 28,127 franchisees.

Motor car dealerships and petrol retail outlets are among the most important sectors where *concessione* contracts are used. There are no data concerning other types of vertical agreements, even though they are widespread. Exclusive territories

Table 5.5 Franchising in Italy (1999)

	Number of franchisors	Number of franchisees	Turnover (billion lire)
Specialized food	28	2,198	2,368
Mass retailing	19	2,840	7,776
Household goods	36	897	840
Footwear, clothing, textiles	125	4,942	2,724
Other non-food retailing	80	3,268	2,387
Catering and hotels	31	756	870
Services	211	12,579	5,085
Other (including manufacturing)	6	647	207
Total	536	28,127	22,257

Source: Assofranchising.

and exclusive dealings are common in a number of sectors (cosmetics, clothing) and are often a substitute for franchising when the product portfolio of the manufacturer is too small to allow for a viable retail assortment.

Conclusions

Faced with the constraints imposed by the current retail regulatory environment and the relative sluggishness of consumer demand, retailers in Italy are developing their strategies with reference to a number of key factors.

In the food sector, with limited possibilities of growth in the number of supermarket and hypermarket stores, promotion of customer loyalty has become a major challenge. Increasingly, strong competition in the domestic market leads to a search for and the utilization, of all of the possibilities for economies of scale. Bulk buying and the contingent concentration of the number of chains in the market are seen as being essential stages on the road to increased profits, and despite the increased competitiveness, the growth of the Italian market justifies the setting up of development projects from European retailers.

With regard to retailers' competitive strategies, the current intense competition, the density of stores and the relatively uniform nature of the range of goods offered have led to a change in retailers' strategies from one of depending on price-related special offers – a large range of items sold at attractive prices – to one focused on demand – providing a pleasant shopping experience, ambience, convenience and services. Marketing teams have been developed within the major retail chains, reinforcing the customer-oriented focus of stores.

The need to promote customer loyalty helps to explain some of the important changes in Italian retailing, including (a) the development of the concept of a 'pleasant shopping experience', (b) increasingly sophisticated consumer communication on the part of retailers, (c) the adoption by retailers of store and other credit cards, and (d) an increasing proportion of sales under retailer's private labels. Thus, shopping in enjoyable surroundings and saving time are two preoccupations around which the retailers are developing marketing strategies. First of all, at the level of store organization, one sees the development of merchandising concepts for food and non-food items within large stores that reflect a concern with fully adapting the presentation of goods on offer to customers' needs. Reorganization of the sales area – regrouping and presentation of items – is intended to optimize time spent and enhance the customers' enjoyment of the shopping experience. Second, the attention devoted by retailers to the in-store environment reflects that fact that while shopping, price and product choice are no longer the sole determinants in attracting customers. Customer services provided, as well as in-store decoration and lighting, also represent essential elements in a retailer's offering.

Under the heading of customer communication, catalogues now form part of retailers' normal array of marketing tools and are no longer used only by mail-order companies. These are usually organized by theme and are produced specially for promotional activities undertaken by the chains. In addition, these retail chains organize theme-based promotional activities. Apart from the traditional 'anniversaries', numerous theme-based promotional activities are organized throughout the year, and these activities are used by retailers to promote innovative product offerings and to improve the image of the retail groups, who are recognized as the creators of these events.

Discount cards and personal credit cards, introduced in the second half of 1980s, have now been adopted by nearly all the chains. There are currently more than 8 million discount or frequent-shopper cards in Italy. These provide specific rebates for customers, offer higher credit limits, and also offer loyalty discounts. Even though their usage rates remain limited in terms of revenues, the development strategy in this area consists of negotiating partnerships to enable the range of services on offer to be broadened and to share the costs associated with card management.

Finally, with regard to the development of retailer private label products, these private brand products, launched in the 1980s, have gradually been adopted by all food retailers. They were initially developed as an alternative to branded products, and then at times as a response to the lowest prices of the hard-discount retailers. They have recently become more attractive due to the increasing competition and they are now seen as a significant factor in winning loyal customers, and the share of private-label sales within all hypermarket and supermarket sales is currently 10.6 per cent.

In these various ways, retailers in Italy – both indigenous firms and those for whom Italy is part of their strategy of growth and geographical diversification – are responding, within the constraints of government legislation in this sector, to a more competitive market and the particular needs of the consumer.

Suggested reading

Autorità Garante della Concorrenza e del Mercato (1993) *Regolamentazione Della Distribuzione Commerciale e Concorrenza*, Edizione Speciale, suppl. al 'Bollettino', 1, anno III, Roma.

Bertozzi, P. (1991) 'Vent'anni di disciplina del commercio', *Commercio, Rivista di Economia e Politica Commerciale*, 13(43): 93–102.

Bertozzi, P. (1995) 'Intervento pubblico e apertura delle grandi superfici: le principali esperienze europee', *Commercio, Rivista di Economia e Politica Commerciale*, 17(55): 93–102.

Main, O., Zanderighi, L. and Zaninotto, E. (1990) *Strategie e strutture organizzative nel commercio associato*, Egea, Milan.

Pellegrini, L. (1990) *Economia Della Distribuzione Commerciale*, Egea, Milan.

Pellegrini, L. (1996) *La Distribuzione Commerciale in Italia*, Il Mulino, Bologna.

Pellegrini, L. (2001) *Il Commercio in Italia*, Il Mulino, Bologna.

Spranzi, A. (1991) *La Distribuzione Commerciale: Economia del Commercio e Politica Commerciale*, Franco Angeli, Milan.

Zanderighi, L. (1990) *Piccole e Medie Imprese e Sviluppo Commerciale*, Egea, Milan.

Zanderighi, L. (1998) *Come Cambia il Commercio. Modificazioni Strutturali e Dinamica Occupazionale*, Istat, Rome.

Zanderighi, L. (1998) 'Il sistema distributivo al dettaglio in Italia: cambiamenti in atto e prospettive', in Bertinetti, G., Farinet, A., Nova, A. and Zanderighi, L. (eds), *Il Sistema Italia: Sviluppo o Declino*, Etas Libri, Milan.

6 Spain

Marta Frasquet, Irene Gil and Alejandro Mollá

Introduction

This chapter analyses the Spanish retail sector, whose process of modernization began somewhat later than that of other European countries. Therefore, the first section, which deals with the evolution of the structure of the sector, distinguishes two phases of development: the era of traditional retailing, and the era of mass distribution. Modern retail structures did not consolidate in Spain until the 1980s, and an analysis of recent changes in the sector and a description of the present situation are dealt with in the second section. In this part, the authors provide statistics both for the sector as a whole and for the most important retail formats individually.

The third section of the chapter focuses on the analysis of some particular features of Spanish distribution channels, including the wholesale trade and franchising. Section four then provides an analysis of the legislative background to Spanish retailing structures and activities. This analysis is divided into two parts: covering the regulation of retail activity, and the measures for the promotion of business. The chapter ends with the drawing of some conclusions, and these are focused around the fact that modern retail structures have an important impact upon Spanish retailing, and that while many of the features of Spanish retailing are similar to those of the remainder of Europe, it also contains some unique features, including the survival of a number of aspects of traditional retailing.

The development of retailing in Spain until the 1980s

The Spanish market has been characterized for decades by particular historical circumstances which, until the 1970s, created a subsistence level retailing scenario. Political events earlier in the twentieth century – such as the Spanish Civil War and the international embargo following the Second World War in the 1930s and 1940s, together with a military dictatorship for a period of more than thirty years until 1978 – resulted in very limited development in the Spanish retailing structure until the end of the 1960s. Hence, the development of Spanish retailing over the last century can be divided into two main periods. The first stage, identified as the era of traditional retailing, lasted until the late 1960s, while the second began with the outset of the era of mass distribution.

The era of traditional retailing

The development of this period can be divided into three main phases (Casares and Rebollo, 2000). The first stage stretched from the turn of the twentieth century to the year 1936 when the Spanish Civil War broke out. These years were characterized by a shift from a self-sufficient economy to a market economy, although the demographic characteristics of Spain, with its basically rural population, constituted what was virtually a guild structure in retailing and wholesaling with specialized establishments dedicated mainly to the sale of foodstuffs. A second phase took place during the period of the Spanish Civil War (1936–1939) and the postwar period (1939–1949). These years were characterized by a strict rationing policy and considerable intervention in trade with a high level of state control. It was against this background that the CAT (Transport and Supply Bureau) was established in 1939. Its mission was to promote the production required for supplying the country, to improve the earnings of farm workers, and regulate the market by organizing the purchase and subsequent distribution of surpluses.

The 1950s was the decade in which traditional, specialist retailing was consolidated. This coincided with a certain liberalization process in foreign trade, the onset of which may be dated from the late 1950s. This was the era when private enterprise began to take over some of the CAT's activities, whilst the CAT focused its operations on reforming certain traditional retail structures which had by then become obsolete. As a result, Operation Supermarket got under way in 1959. It promoted the introduction of this type of retail outlet throughout Spain and created the public-sector company MERCASA (Limited Company of Central Markets), designed to facilitate the operations of retail networks of perishable products through creating a network of foodstuff units known as central municipal markets (Marrero, 2000).

From the 1960s onwards greater economic growth occurred which brought about certain changes in retailing – changes which accelerated in the 1970s following the creation of IRESCO, the Retailing Reform Institute, in 1973, and which marked the start of the era of mass distribution.

The scenario facing IRESCO highlighted a chronic problem in the structure of Spanish retailing, which was unable to cope with a modern, developed economy. Several traits that characterized the structure of Spanish retailing at that time were:

- a high density of retail outlets, particularly in the food trade, which reflected a pronounced and high concentration of small retail outlets: many of these retail outlets were small in terms of both average floor space and number of employees;

- a dearth of supermarkets;
- limited growth in self-service types of sales: traditional full-service retailing was a characteristic of 71.3 per cent of all food sales and 94.7 per cent in non-food products; and
- the prevalence of family businesses with insufficient specific professional training and a lack of awareness about the need to modernize, in addition to considerable obstacles to obtaining the financing needed to implement such modernization.

It was against this background, and at a time of considerable political upheaval marked by the end of the military dictatorship regime and the onset of a period of democracy in Spain, that a stage of profound transformation began for both the demand and supply sides of this sector, involving a considerable metamorphosis in the landscape of retailing in Spain as it moved towards the era of mass distribution.

The era of mass distribution

The 1970s saw the opening of the first retail establishments that belonged to the period of mass distribution. The first hypermarket was opened in 1973, and 1978 saw the implementation of a programme of reform designed to modernize retail structures, which had the backing of Spain's first constitutional government, and which initiated an accelerated process of change and innovation.

The new retail scenario that came into being during the 1980s was clearly portrayed in the survey conducted by the IRESCO in 1983 of the structural characteristics of Spanish domestic retailing. The principal features of this were:

- the gradual reduction in size of the foodstuffs subsector in favour of other subsectors;
- the existence of considerable inequalities from one region to another, which indicated imbalances in retail structures on a geographic level;
- an insufficient level of horizontal links and the very low profile of retail trade association movements;
- the small size of retail outlets in terms of both sales area and number of employees per establishment; and
- the low level of training in the sector, although increased awareness of the need for greater professionalism was observed.

The year 1985 constituted a significant landmark in this modernization process of Spanish retailing structures, in the form of an Order in Council (Real Decreto 1985/1985 dated August 28), which abolished the IRESCO and transferred its powers to the self-governing or Autonomous Regions (Comunidades Autónomas). From that point in time on, the Autonomous Regions became responsible for the reform of retailing, and have defined the present-day shape and form of this sector in Spain.

Current structural trends in retailing

From 1985 until the present time, the growth in this sector has been characterized by the entry into the Spanish market of the leading European retail distribution groups as a result of globalization. This has led to the modernization of competitive structures at the wholesaler level, in response to the increasing involvement in distribution channels of other intermediaries who are assuming its functions and implementing a complete overhaul necessary to achieve greater professionalism. This has coincided with an evolution in the relationships between manufacturers and distributors in which cooperation consisting of developing both vertical and horizontal links has been one way of increasing market competitiveness.

There have also been changes in the socio-demographic structure of the Spanish population which have deeply affected not only consumer patterns but also habits concerning how, where, when, how much and what is required to meet consumer wishes and needs (Gil *et al.*, 1994).

Structural variables

In the last two decades, Spanish society has undergone significant changes related to population growth, with a fall in the average size of families, an increase in one-parent households, an increasingly ageing population and the gradual incorporation of women into the workforce. All of these, together with urban growth and increased consumer purchasing power, have led to a number of new purchasing and consumption patterns in Spanish consumers. One indicator that highlights these changes is the distribution of consumer expenditure. Table 6.1 shows the breakdown of expenditure of Spanish consumers and reveals the tendency towards a gradual reduction in the amount spent on food, drink and tobacco and an increase in the expenditure on other items.

Lying behind these trends, since 1993 the Spanish economy has undergone considerable growth following a long period of crisis. The service sector now

Table 6.1 The Spanish consumer: breakdown of expenditure

	Food, drink and tobacco	*Apparel*	*Housing, heating and electricity*	*Furnitures, household wares and home services*	*Total (thousand of million pesetas)*
1992	24.21	9.27	22.95	6.49	30,803.37
1993	23.60	8.31	24.48	6.23	31,669.27
1994	23.88	7.70	25.51	6.00	32,752.55
1995	24.03	7.44	26.03	6.09	34,054.12
1996	24.00	7.51	25.87	5.80	35,099.29
1997[a]	20.36	6.66	29.85	4.66	36,302.68
1998	21.96	7.28	26.92	4.87	35,129.77

Source: INE. *Encuesta continua de presupuestos familiares* (2001).

Note
a It should be noted that the definition of the expenditure structure changed this year.

Table 6.2 Components of Spanish GNP (thousands of million pesetas)

	1993	%	1994	%	1995	%	1996	%	1997	%	1998	%
GNP at market prices	60,942.6	100.00	64,789.2	100.00	69,760.8	100.00	75,571.8	100.00	77,786.2	100.00	82,650.3	100.00
Agriculture and fishing	2,163.2	3.54	2,136.3	3.29	2,077.9	2.97	2,547.7	3.46	2,446.9	3.14	2,448.8	2.96
Manufacturing industry	19,382.2	31.79	20,524.1	31.67	22,393.9	32.10	22,976.7	31.23	24,315.8	31.25	26,027.3	31.49
Services	35,943.2	58.96	38,264.3	59.05	41,237.2	59.11	43,677.1	59.36	46,271.3	59.48	48,974.9	59.26
For selling purposes	27,212.2	44.64	29,286.5	45.20	31,642.2	45.35	33,593.4	45.66	35,926.0	46.18	38,132.5	46.14
Not for selling purposes	8,731.0	14.32	8,978.8	13.85	9,595.0	13.75	10,083.7	13.70	10,345.3	13.29	10,842.3	13.12
VAT	3,331.6	5.46	3,732.6	5.76	3,911.0	5.60	4,248.9	5.77	4,619.2	5.93	5,048.8	6.11
Net tax to imports	132.3	0.21	132.0	0.20	140.7	0.20	121.3	0.16	133.0	0.17	150.5	0.18

Source: INE. *Contabilidad Nacional*, febrero (1999).

predominates in the Spanish economy, as revealed by the analysis of the proportion it contributes to gross national product (GNP) which has increased in recent years to 59 per cent (see Table 6.2), a predominance to which retailing contributes significantly.

The retailing sector generates a considerable proportion of the gross national product (GNP). In Spain, gross added value (GAV) totals 74,296,629 million pesetas, with the GAV of services amounting to 48,482,006 million. The GAV of retail services in particular amounts to 9,677,008 million pesetas, that is, 13.02 per cent of the total GAV.

With regard to the socio-economic variable of employment in this sector, Table 6.3 shows its evolution since 1993, and gives the mean figures of the total labour force, numbers in employment and wage earners taken from the data gathered by the labour force survey. In 1998, Spain had a workforce of 2,436,500 in commerce as a whole, which represents a rate of employment of 89.5 per cent and a rate of wage earners of 62.6 per cent. The first of these figures simply relates to the proportion of the 'workforce' of any sector (i.e. both employed and unemployed) that is currently in employment. The second provides a basis for examining trends in self-employment, a matter which is taken up in respect of all of the EU economies in the final chapter of this study. In Spain, the retailing sector employed 1,347,800 people in 1998, of which 54.86 per cent were wage earners and the remainder self-employed.

Looking at the first basic data in our analysis of the nature of retailing structure, that is, the number of retail outlets (see Table 6.4), according to information provided by the Department of Interior Commerce (Dirección General de Comercio Interior), the total number of retail outlets registered in Spain in 1997 was, according to the most recent information, 590,190.

The data in Table 6.4 show an average of 14.57 retail outlets per thousand inhabitants and a floor space of 1.37 sq. m. per inhabitant, which represent 822,489 business licences distributed amongst the business sectors shown in Figure 6.1. The number of food outlet permits accounts for 37.5 per cent of all business permits, with a reduction in recent years in the number of retail outlets

Table 6.3 Employment in the retailing sector

	Workforce in commerce	Employment in commerce	% of employment in commerce	Employment in retailing	Wage earners in retailing	% of wage earners in retailing
1993	2,346.7	2,035.8	86.76	1,276.3	608.1	47.63
1994	2,377.3	2,022.8	85.09	1,285.2	637.5	49.60
1995	2,359.9	2,017.3	85.47	1,286.3	651.3	50.63
1996	2,369.8	2,064.2	87.20	1,302.2	676.7	51.94
1997	2,390.8	2,123.8	88.83	1,314.8	716.1	54.46
1998	2,436.5	2,179.5	89.45	1,347.8	739.5	54.86

Source: Dirección General de Comercio Interior (1998).

Table 6.4 Number of retail outlets

Number of licences				Outlets		Area	
1991		*1997*		*No.*	*Outlets/ 1,000 inhab*	*Sq. m.*	*Sq. m./ 1,000 inhab.*
Total	*Food*	*Total*	*Food*				
906,777	311,055	822,489	308,805	590,190	14.57	55,496,054	1.37

Source: Dirección General de Comercio Interior (1998).

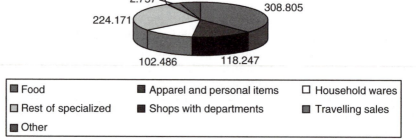

Food · 308.805
Apparel and personal items · 118.247
Household wares · 102.486
Rest of specialized · 224.171
Shops with departments · 2.757
Travelling sales · 24.318
Other · 41.705

■ Food	■ Apparel and personal items	□ Household wares
□ Rest of specialized	■ Shops with departments	▨ Travelling sales
■ Other		

Figure 6.1 Number of business licences by sector.

Table 6.5 The retail economy: breakdown by activity

	1997		1998	
	Number	*%*	*Number*	*%*
Food	215,002	35.9	204,096	34.6
Apparel and personal items	112,266	18.8	114,191	19.3
Drugstores and pharmaceutical products	37,674	6.3	35,781	6.1
Household wares	92,663	15.5	94,251	16.0
Vehicles, accessories and carburants	23,609	3.9	23,148	3.9
Rest of specialized	93,112	15.6	94,707	16.0
Shops with departments	24,115	4.0	24,016	4.1
Large supermarkets (more than 1,000 sq. m.)	986		1,067	
Hypermarkets (2,500–4,999 sq. m.)	146		155	
Hypermarkets (more than 5,000 sq. m.)	186		198	
Department stores	46		46	
Other	22,790		22,550	
Total	598,441	100	590,190	100

Source: Dección General de Comercio Interior (1997, 1998).

selling food in favour of those selling household and personal items, as can be seen in Table 6.5.

Retail formats

When considering the Spanish retail structure from the viewpoint of types of business, the *supermarket* emerges as the self-service format that has the greatest floor area and highest growth rates in the last decade (see Table 6.6). The average floor space of these outlets is 822 sq. m., and they are generally situated in preferential town centre sites.

Hypermarkets (see Table 6.7), with their preferential sites in shopping centres where they act as anchor outlets, have also undergone considerable growth. By 1985 there were already 59 branches of French hypermarket chains in Spain and since then, this has been the retail format which has grown most. Between 1985 and 1995 in particular, the increase in the number of outlets was calculated to be 278 per cent. Although in recent years this growth has begun to slow down, there has, nonetheless, been a slight increase in average hypermarket size and a reduction in the market or geographic areas of that are attractive for this retail format.

Table 6.6 Evolution of supermarkets

	Supermarkets in Spain 1994–1998				
	1994	*1995*	*1996*	*1997*	*1998*
Number of establishment	3,238	3,462	3,630	3,941	4,159
Total sales area (sq. m.)	2,570,980	2,755,000	2,888,656	3,198,865	3,418,484
Mean sales area (sq. m.)	794	796	809	812	822
Mean number of employees	12.8	12.9	13.1	13.0	13.2
Mean number of cashiers	4.7	4.7	4.9	4.4	4.5
Sales/establ./year (million pesetas)	412	419	426	420	433
Sales/sq. m./yera (pesetas)	490,000	526,315	529,000	517,440	526,549

Source: Dirección General de Comercio Interior (1998).

Table 6.7 Evolution of hypermarkets

	Hypermarkets in Spain 1973–1998								
	1973	*1976*	*1980*	*1985*	*1990*	*1995*	*1996*	*1997*	*1998*
Number of establishments	1	13	29	59	110	223	236	256	267
Total sales area (sq. m.)	11,107	75,460	201,226	428,120	840,065	1,725,255	1,836,467	2,018,130	2,138,557
Mean sales area (sq. m.)	11,107	5,805	6,939	7,256	7,637	7,735	7,782	7,883	8,009

Source: Dirección General de Comercio Interior (1998).

Table 6.8 Food retailer groups and companies in Spain

Ranking 1999	Company/Group	1999 Sales	1998 Sales
1	Carrefour	1,593,587	1,484,547
	CC Continente	610,852	570,188
	CC Pryca	532,927	524,766
	Dia	356,088	313,767
	Grup Supeco-Maxor	76,820	59,431
	Puntocash	16,900	16,395
2	Grupo Eroski	639,919	519,510
3	El Corte Inglés	481,814	418,283
	Hipercor	353,056	307,033
	El Corte Inglés (supermarkets)	125,000	110,000
	Gespevesa	3,758	1,250
4	Auchan	465,488	429,365
	Alcampo	365,200	330,500
	Supermarkets Sabeco	100,288	98,865
5	Mercadona	420,556	336,195

Source: Alimarket (2000).

The latter phenomenon has been due to the increase in both inter- and intra-sector competition caused by the growth of discount stores and supermarkets.

The leader in food distribution in Spain is the Carrefour group, followed by the two Spanish groups Eroski and El Corte Inglés (see Table 6.8).

With regard *discount stores*, this has been one of the formats that has undergone the greatest growth, to the detriment of traditional retail outlets. The undeniable leader is Día which accounts for over 80 per cent of all such outlets, that is, a total of 1,725. Of these, 1,300 belong to the chain itself and the other 426 are franchises. This is followed in the market by the German group Lidl. The traditional discount model in Spain has been one of soft discounts in which the campaign strategy or philosophy focuses on creating a cheap, low-price image across the entire range of merchandise, whilst offering fewer services in order to affect the quality of the products as little as possible, and projecting a more austere image and presentation of the outlet. There has, however, been a shift towards hard discount in recent years, in order to compete with the German companies that are rapidly being implanted in Spain, by means of a far more aggressive pricing policy and a plethora of promotions and special offers.

There is no doubt that at the present time the *department store* has reached maturity in its life cycle in Spain. The heyday of this format occurred in the 1970s during the growth phase of the three most representative firms, El Corte Inglés, Galerías Preciados and Simago, as they expanded throughout Spain. However, over the period 1985–1993 they grew by a mere 15 per cent, in sharp contrast to the high growth rates of other retailing formulae such as supermarkets and hypermarkets. In 1995, El Corte Inglés bought Galerías Preciados, and since then has maintained a clearly dominant position on the Spanish retailing scene. This combined operation endowed El Corte Inglés with outlets in more capital cities of Spanish provinces, whilst increasing the number of its stores in the centres of other major cities. This situation led to an increase in the product range of this department store, converting it into a multi-specialist outlet. The most recent strategic development of El Corte Englés has been the acquisition of the stores that earlier belonged to Marks & Spencer, following this group's decision at the end of 2001 to withdraw from Continental Europe (Table 6.9).

Table 6.9 Evolution of El Corte Inglés

	1992	1993	1994	1995	1996	1997	1998
Revenues (millions pesetas)							
Group	994,469	984,623	1,015,566	1,084,382	1,199,075	1,296,174	1,435,000
Department stores only	779,954	727,127	761,743	796,264	8,720,611	933,032	1,075,000
No. of department stores	20	20	20	49	51	n.a.	n.a.
No. of employees	51,710	48,018	48,402	51,307	57,276	n.a.	59,356
Net profits (million pesetas)	31,377	32,330	33,580	30,928	31,038	40,080	48,979
Total sales area (sq. m.)	483,140	483,140	483,140	772,618	780,060	n.a.	n.a.
Mean sales area (sq. m.)	24,157	24,157	24,157	15,768	15,295	n.a.	n.a.

Source: Dirección General de Comercio Interior (1997, 1998).

Planned shopping centres (see Table 6.10 and Figure 6.2) have, in a short space of time, become one of the most successful formulae in Spanish retailing. According to the statistics of the AECC (the Spanish Shopping Centre Council), there are almost 400 shopping centres in Spain. Forecasts suggest that growth will continue, albeit at a slower rate. The predominant shopping centre model is based

Table 6.10 Shopping centres by type

Type of shopping centre	No.	%	GLA	%	Units	%	Parking	%
Regional, GLA bigger than 40,000 sq. m.	31	7.8	1,808,397	27.4	4,565	19.7	82,690	19.8
Big, GLA between 15,001 and 40,000 sq. m.	78	19.6	1,940,444	29.4	6,230	28.2	122,118	29.2
Small, GLA between 4,001 and 15,000 sq. m.	106	26.6	853,943	13.0	6,494	29.7	34,278	8.2
Hypermarket-based	108	27.1	1,243,262	18.9	2,240	10.3	132,202	31.6
Shopping arcade, GLA smaller than 4,000 sq. m.	49	12.3	114,370	1.7	1,756	8.0	2,876	0.7
Retail park	14	3.5	484,567	7.4	533	2.4	32,699	7.8
Theme parks: manufacturers and leisure	12	3.0	155,752	2.3	363	1.7	11,710	2.8
Total	398	100.0	6,600,735	100.0	22,181	100.0	418,573	100.0

Source: AECC (2001).

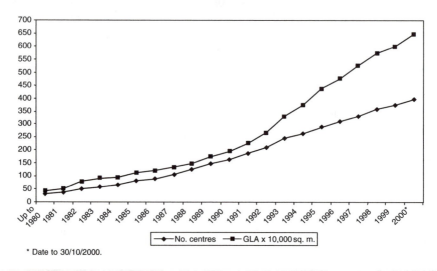

* Date to 30/10/2000.

Figure 6.2 Shopping centre openings.
Source: Derived from data of the AECC (2000).

on an anchor hypermarket complemented by a shopping arcade consisting of small shops, which together constitute what is known as GES (large shopping facilities). There are 108 of this type of shopping centres with a combined shopping floor space of 1,243,262 gross leasable area (GLA).

Particular issues

Following the analysis of the development and growth of retailing structures in Spain, this section addresses the more noteworthy aspects which characterize Spanish retailing as opposed to retailing elsewhere in Europe. First, we will address the role of municipal markets and shopping districts insofar as they represent what has been and continues to be traditional Spanish retailing. We will then highlight the changes taking place in the distribution channel such as the increased power of retailers, the role of franchises, and the concentration of wholesalers.

Retail municipal markets

Retail municipal markets are a phenomenon that has characterized the evolution of Spanish retailing in recent years. These were established by the local municipalities, that in most of cities is both the landowner and is also responsible for the management of their markets. Furthermore, it must be remembered that although almost two-thirds of present-day municipal markets were inaugurated between 1950 and the late 1980s, they nonetheless continue to constitute the basis of the distribution of perishable foodstuffs in most Spanish cities. These markets are a spatial cluster of general foodstuff retailers enabling supply to be concentrated by grouping together establishments providing buyers with perishable products (fruits, vegetables, meat, cold meats, sausages, other meat products, fresh and frozen fish etc.) and which are complemented in some cases by other non-perishable products (nuts and dried fruit, cleaning materials, cosmetics, other household products, stationery etc.).

Retail municipal markets are at the same time the centre of a wider shopping area, in which traditional outlets are located, characterized by the proximity and complementary nature of their supply. However, their present-day role in city retailing supply is undoubtedly quite different from their original role due to the intense competition from other types of outlets, mainly supermarkets, which have gradually increased their market share. The total number of retail municipal markets in towns of more than 10,000 inhabitants was 837 according to the 1988 census of the Dirección General de Comercio Interior. This represents 21.78 establishments per million inhabitants, and shows the wide coverage provided by these markets. Although no censuses have been conducted subsequently, the number of markets may be considered to have remained virtually unchanged (Casares and Rebollo, 1997).

The most typical location of these municipal markets is in towns of fewer than 50,000 inhabitants that are not provincial capitals, and more than half of the retail markets are in such locations. The others are located in provincial capitals, particularly in capitals of between 200,000 and 1,000,000 inhabitants. The geographical distribution of these retail markets is, however, very irregular. They are located mainly in coastal areas such as the regions of Catalonia, Comunidad Valenciana, Murcia, Andalucía and Galicia, which confirms the importance of perishable goods, particularly fresh fish, in the development of such establishments, and likewise the cultural element in their growth.

The management of 85.8 per cent of all municipal markets is conducted by the municipality itself – a reflection of the origins of these establishments which were basically designed to be markets supplying basic produce promoted by public initiatives. The management of 8.1 per cent is by means of a concession to an association of traders, with a lower percentage (6.1 per cent) managed by a concession to private individuals.

The role played by retail municipal markets in achieving a minimum level of shopping facilities in towns or areas established recently or having fewer shopping facilities is reflected in the expansion in the number of these markets in response to growth in demand and the tendency for the population to become increasingly urbanized. There is, however, a series of characteristics such as the sales area, the space among outlets for the circulation of shoppers, and the shopping mix which reflects the failure of this type of retail outlet to adapt to the new conditions and characteristics of demand and buying habits. Hence, to enable retail municipal markets to continue to be the regular shopping centres they used to be, they must develop retailing policies in line with the demand and competitive situation of other types of retail outlets and must study the consumer segments that are related to them.

The individual characteristics of retail municipal markets mean they are thought of as a specific type of outlet on the Spanish retail scene. And yet, these very characteristics are the source of 'their opportunities and threats, their pros and cons' (Rebollo, 1999):

- Municipal markets are characterized as specialized outlets, not only because of the type of product sold but also because of their particular consumer shopping characteristics of daily, low-unit-value purchases.
- The high level of specialization in these markets, their town location and serious parking problems, means that they are perceived to be neighbourhood shopping outlets.
- Municipal markets are laid out in sections or 'departments', with many establishments in each 'department'. This extends the choice available to consumers whilst also increasing the degree of existing competition both among departments within the municipal market and with retailers outwith the market.
- The social and economic diversification that has taken place in Spain has changed shopping habits. Municipal markets are therefore no longer attractive outlets to those in certain consumer segments who prefer to shop in larger quantities for a far wider range of products, less often and more quickly. Hence they prefer other types of retail establishments.
- Presently, MERCASA is carrying out a programme for the reorganization and redesign of municipal markets. This includes viability studies, market research, marketing activities and training of traders.

Shopping districts

Although traditional retailing in Spain has enjoyed considerable interia, it has in recent years undergone radical changes in city centres. In some Spanish towns, the concentration of shops with a variety of choice, pedestrianized streets with leisure activities and restaurant facilities, has caused clusters of spontaneous shopping centres to spring up in city centres, albeit without any centralized type of management. This urban and shopping transformation of traditional city centres undoubtedly represents a challenge to the cornerstone of both the traditional and specialized retailing which are so important in Spain, although the drop in traditional food outlets highlighted in Table 6.11 must also be recognized (AC Nielsen, 2000).

The CNC (Spanish Retail Confederation) has undertaken a project consisting of the creation of a national network to integrate all the retailing models developed within the concept of shopping districts with a view to revitalizing shopping areas in town centres.

This management approach implies considerable involvement by both traders and also the local authorities. It consists of associating the establishments involved within a specified area of the city under a shared market image and with the joint management of external factors related not only to retailing activities but

Table 6.11 Changes in the number of foodstuff retail outlets in Spain (1995–2000)

Type of establishment	1995	1996	1997	1998	1999	2000
Traditional	57,758	56,178	54,266	48,607	44,374	41,239
Self service <100 sq. m.	14,434	14,115	13,947	13,672	13,474	13,209
Self service 100–399 sq. m.	7,212	7,371	7,530	7,686	7,963	8,252
Self service 400–999 sq. m.	2,413	2,557	2,820	2,967	3,159	3,332
Self service 1000–2499 sq. m.	614	694	784	831	904	981
Hypermarkets	221	242	268	285	298	306
Total	82,652	81,157	79,675	74,048	76,172	67,319

Source: AC Nielsen (2000).

also with a wide variety of services for consumers, including leisure and cultural opportunities. This also obliges town centre traders to adopt professional management, to maintain their competitive edge and to attempt to win customers back.

Such initiatives can obviously create opportunities for traditional retailing due, amongst other things, to the shopping appeal of traditional agglomerations in the centres of towns, districts or areas; the ease of access by public and private transport to shopping districts in general and to town centres in particular; the possibility of developing public areas with combined and individual management inside cities; and to the possibility of including shopping districts on tourist and cultural routes around the city.

Such initiatives can, however, be seen to include certain threats. Weaknesses may surface such as the lack of awareness by city authorities of the potential of transforming clusters of shops into real shopping districts within their cities; the lack of laws and regulations governing on-going, joint projects implemented by the street traders in any given cluster and the local authorities, to avoid mistrust and criticism from other traders; the possibility of traditional clusters losing market share to new shopping centres on the town outskirts; and the difficulty in achieving association membership rates of more than 50 per cent of the establishments (Ministerio de Economía y Hacienda, 1998).

Changes and relationships in the distribution channels

One of the main features in the changes occurring in Spanish retailing is the new power balance within marketing channels which has led to conflicts in the relationships between manufacturers and distributors and which has also stimulated verticalization processes (Casares and Rebollo, 2000). These relationships are created by retailers when negotiating with suppliers, and are the origin of the retailer in-house management of certain manufacturer activities. The example of retailers' brands is a clear forerunner of such processes. Retailer branding has increased in recent years and now plays an important role in the different product lines in shops, with the ensuing reduction in space for products with the manufacturer's brand, and an implied cut-back in manufacturers' margins. The main areas of contention are the buying price, buying terms, delivery and ordering conditions, credit or deferred payment and inventory policies (Casares *et al.*, 1999). The market share of retailer brands in Spain is increasingly significantly, reaching an average of 19 per cent in the food sector in 1999. This proportion is higher in cleaning materials, where in some product categories the own-brand market share exceeds 90 per cent.

The changes that have taken place in Spanish retailing have particularly affected the relationships between manufacturers and distributors, and have shifted greater negotiating power onto distributors. Manufacturers have traditionally controlled channels, although recent years have seen a shift in the decision-taking power of distribution towards the retail sector. However, there are notable differences in the balance of power in the channels among product groups and sectors, although small- and medium-sized producers are often completely dependent on distributors.

One study of the marketing channels of consumer goods in Spain (Cruz Roche, 1999) which analyses power relations in the distribution channel in a sample of major distribution companies, highlighted deferred payment as a considerable problem in business, particularly amongst food retailers. This practice is an expression of the market power of distributors over producers, as the former extend payment periods more than is needed to finance the marketing process (see Table 6.12). The average number of days taken to pay suppliers in 1996 varied between 138 and 30 days, with 14 of the companies analysed exceeding the

Table 6.12 Changes in the average days deferred payment period per company (1992–1997)

	1992	1993	1994	1995	1996	1997	Var. 1996–1997 (%)
Pryca	132.51	132.49	124.24	128.93	130.89	130.7	−0.15
Continente	143.54	140.6	121.24	127.1	116.4	125.4	7.73
Alcampo	107.11	104.1	99.28	101.77	105	112.33	6.98
Eroski	n.a.	n.a.	118.88	111.65	117.8	125.58	6.60
Mercadona	107.01	104.3	97.28	88.09	74	69.79	−5.69
Gallega Distrib.	80.07	76.65	67.71	69.26	70.83	n.a.	n.a.
Dialco	110.47	n.a.	115.67	136.81	111.64	n.a.	n.a.
Ecore	78.85	89.75	89.51	81.04	80.09	76.16	−4.91
Superm. Alcosto	87.15	121.44	92.14	130.69	104.19	113.85	9.27
Simago	108.19	103.39	118.13	114.7	104.17	93.70	−10.05
Enaco	71.74	77.26	77.76	66.4	54.79	50.5	−7.83
Hilario Osorio	96.3	89.73	93.59	86.88	81.08	88.44	9.08
Superm. Claudio	89.96	69.83	66.59	67.87	62.23	70.61	13.47
Makro	112.51	98.61	107.34	108.7	111.47	98.67	−11.48
Ecovol	96.69	107.16	93.48	384.34	123.8	120.27	−2.85
Miquel Aliment.	62.14	77.01	78.6	88.02	72.43	63.56	−12.25

Source: Cruz Roche (1999), using data from IBD, Anuario Financiero de Distribución (1997, 1998).

Table 6.13 Distribution companies payment and collection period differences according to turnover, in days

	Distribution companies with turnover of less than 1,000 million pesetas[a]			Distribution companies with turnover of more than 25,000 million pesetas[b]			Total distribution companies[c]		
	1995	1996	1997	1995	1996	1997	1995	1996	1997
Payments to suppliers	10.70	6.40	5.36	101.24	92.12	96.17	75.36	66.96	85.02
Collected from customers	5.92	6.40	1.65	11.95	8.70	7.42	11.58	19.87	14.46
Difference	4.78	0.00	3.71	89.29	83.42	88.75	63.78	47.09	70.56

Source: Casares *et al.* (1999), using data from CABSA (Alimarket, 1999).

Notes
a Based on the yearly accounts of 1,384 companies.
b Based on the yearly accounts of 18 companies.
c Based on the yearly account of 1,839 companies.

longest traditional period in business practice, that is, an average of more than 90 days to make payment.

Studies carried out after the Spanish retail regulations of 1996 governing this area suggest that these regulations have made no difference. Table 6.13, for example, provides information from another study of differences in payment and collection periods according to the turnover of a sample of 1,839 distribution companies in the period 1995–1997. This information reveals that the differences between collection and payment times continue to increase, and that the size of the companies affects the payment period (Casares *et al.*, 1999).

Data on the main distributor companies show the double benefit of deferred payment. Not only does such deferred payment provide a means of financing distributor growth without an explicit cost, but also putting financial surpluses on the capital market is a basic element in the profitability of companies (Cruz Roche, 1999). However, the analyses carried out show the link between the average days of deferment in payment to suppliers and gross margin to be tenuous. One would expect, in a negotiation context, longer payment periods to be compensated by higher purchase prices, and vice versa. However, empirical evidence seems to sustain the premise that the two concepts are negotiated independently, or that the length of payment period is presupposed to be a characteristic assumed by those involved.

It is clear that distribution groups must deal with a range of financial activities such as financing for suppliers, managing liquid assets, financing for customers, and dealing with other financial products (credit cards, insurance etc.) arising from all these activities. In other words, they deal with liquid asset management in addition to the diversification derived from taking on functions that used to be handled by finance companies (Casares *et al.*, 1999).

Table 6.14 Growth of franchises in Spain

	1994	1997	2000 (Up to June)
No of brand names	349	514	651
No of establishments	5,130	9,282	17,381
Employees	37,008	66,933	127,867

Source: Instituto Nacional de Empleo (2000).

Franchises

It was in the 1980s that franchises began to assume an importance in Spain, becoming a highly dynamic sector that affected both the retailing and production sides of the business world to a considerable extent. Franchises are still far from widely established, being a new phenomenon with recently established chains. The growth of this sector in recent years has been revealed by analyses of different directories and particularly the recent survey conducted by the INEM (Spanish Employment Bureau) (2000). This survey showed that the number of franchise outlets increased by 238.8 per cent from 1994 to 2000, with an increase of 245.5 per cent in their employees (see Table 6.14). According to the Asociación Española de Franquiciadores (AEF) – Spanish Association of Franchisers – the number of franchise outlets increased by 11.4 per cent in 2000, reaching 25,950 outlets.

The franchise sector in Spain is growing particularly internally, that is, increasingly wide networks are appearing. Hence, whilst the average number of outlets per franchise brand was 14.7 in 1994, it was 18.1 in 1997 and 26.7 by mid-2000, demonstrating the growth in the size of networks (Instituto Nacional de Empleo, 2000). This can also be explained by the approach of franchisees to expanding their networks: trying to be more meticulous and making them as solid as possible. Franchises are particularly important in Spain in sectors such as specialized shops, with 17.9 per cent of brand names, and apparel and accessories, with 11 per cent of franchisors. These sectors also contain the greatest number of establishments, and have been characterized by the greatest growth in franchising in recent years.

With regard to the presence of Spanish franchise networks in international markets, 10 per cent of such companies are active abroad: Portugal being the first destination, followed by France and Latin America. It is interesting that 74.4 per cent of the franchise brands or retailers operating in Spain are of Spanish nationality, a proportion that increases slightly to 78.6 per cent of franchise outlets or shops (Barroso, 1999). Although the presence of foreign companies in Spain is significant, due largely to the favourable situation for franchising business in Spain, national firms are expanding at a greater rate than foreign ones.

The wholesale trade

With regard to the role of wholesalers in the Spanish retailing system, their number fell during the 1990s, judging by the reduction of some 41,000 wholesaler licences to 209,700 in 1998, as opposed to more than 250,700 in the early 1990s. The two activities that account for the greatest number of wholesalers are first, raw material and foodstuff wholesalers (25.9 per cent) and sales intermediaries (24.9 per cent), followed by hardware wholesalers (18.9 per cent) (Rebollo, 2000).

Wholesaling evolutionary trends point towards a greater concentration of increasingly large companies strengthening their positions to obtain greater international presence. Such trends also point towards vertical integration strategies which involve opening branches and developing links by means of associations in the form of voluntary chains or buying groups, resulting in increasingly complex companies. In certain channels, this will result in the disappearance of the separately identified wholesaler, particularly in the form of independent wholesalers. However, although it is understood that wholesalers, particularly independent ones, may disappear, the function they play will of course be adopted by other intermediaries in the channel. The wholesalers that survive will undoubtedly be more actively involved in marketing strategies.

Retail legislative environment

Spain is regarded as a 'late starter' in the European process of modernization of retail structures. This is the cause of a more rapid evolutionary process in Spain, characterized by the internationalization of retailing. As Dawson (1993) recognizes, retail internationalization has exerted significant pressure on the retail structure of Southern Europe. Moreover, large European retail companies have been able to expand in Spain quite easily, as Spanish retailers were, in the 1980s, weak competitors and there was no public policy deterring the growth process of large firms.

As a consequence, the dualism of the Spanish retail sector has intensified, resulting in the coexistence of a reduced number of large retail companies and a significant number of small-scale traditional retailers. Therefore, it has become necessary to establish some 'rules of the game' in order to guarantee fair competition among retailers and high level of efficiency in the distribution system. In effect, a deficit of public policy regarding the retail sector relative to European neighbouring countries has existed in Spain up to 1995. Awareness of this situation has lain behind the drive to harmonize Spanish public policy in this regard with that of countries with more advanced retail structures (Cruz and Rebollo, 1995; Allúe, 1996).

The importance of independent and small-scale retailers for the vitality of the traditional city centres is another of the main reasons for government intervention in the retail sector. Also, as Cruz and Rebollo (1995) indicate, the situation of power that large retail firms have been enjoying for several years has not had positive effects, in the sense that retailer productivity earnings have not been passed to consumers, employment has not improved, and competitiveness in the manufacturing sectors has not increased.

Also, as Casares (1994) points out, the increased public policy intervention in the retail sector can be interpreted as a consequence of changes in the negotiating power of the various pressure groups involved. Associations of large retail firms have always been powerful and the interests of their members have been cohesive, in contrast to traditional retailers associations. This imbalance is changing as the latter have been growing in number and negotiating power, improving the defensive capacity of small-scale retailers. In addition, consumer organizations have proliferated in recent years. They have become more active, and the activities of these pressure groups have also triggered government intervention in the retail sector.

The basic objective of Spanish domestic trade policy is twofold: to assure the population of supply and to reduce the costs of distribution. As a prerequisite for the attainment of these, but also as an objective in itself, policy is further directed to achieve a structural balance within the retail sector (Marrero, 2000). With the aim of attaining these objectives, Spanish public policy intervention in the retail sector operates in two directions: restrictions on certain market behaviours, and promotion of business initiatives (Cruz and Rebollo, 1995).

Regulation of retail activity

The year 1996 is regarded as a landmark in the regulation of the Spanish retail sector because of the enactment of the Leyes de Ordenación del Comercio Minorista (Laws of Retail Trade Regulation), which are the Law 7/1996 and the complementary Organic Law 2/1996. This is a shift of posture, as the state had previously opted for non-intervention in the sector since 1984 and had given the regional authorities freedom to regulate the terms of the retailing activities (Carrasco, 1996). Both of the 1996 laws are in fact part of a single legislative act that complies with the constitutional precept (art. 51.3) of regulating domestic commerce.

One important feature is that in Spain different levels of authority share the responsibilities for domestic commerce: state, regional and local. At present, all the Autonomous Regions have acquired, in a series of steps from 1979 to 1998, absolute authority on domestic trade (legislation, execution and law development). This does not, however, prevent the state from maintaining complete authority on certain matters (listed by the art. 149 of the Constitution) that have a direct impact on domestic trade, thus limiting policy making autonomy of the regional authorities. Regional legislative autonomy is also limited by some other constitutional precepts, such as: the freedom for establishing a business (art. 39), the legislative resonsibilities of the state to provide for collective needs and harmonize regional and sectoral development (art. 131), and the freedom of circulation of people and goods (art. 139). The implication of the different levels of legislative authority in Spain is that the impact of the application of the law will

Table 6.15 The Law of Retail Trade Regulation 7/1996

Aspects	Regulated matters	Reference
Establishment of large retailers[a]	• Obligatory licence given by the regional government that should take into account the existent retail supply and the potential impacts of the proposal	Título I, Capítulo I, Artículo 6.1, 6.2, 6.3 y 6.4
	• Report of the Court for Fair Competition as a prerequisite for the licence	Título I, Capítulo I, Artículo 6.2
Sales at loss	• Prohibition to sell under the acquisition price as per invoice, deducing discounts but not payments for services nor gifts from suppliers	Título I, Capítulo II, Artículo 14.1, 14.2, 14.3, 14.4.
	• Exceptions: price reductions to reach the prices of a competitor with capacity to affect the own sales, clearance sales, and perishables close to expiry date	Título I, Capítulo II, Artículo 14.1.
Payment to suppliers	• The date of payment must be recorded in a document	Título I, Capítulo IV, Artículo 17.2
	• If the payment is deferred more than 60 days, a bill of exchange must be presented	Título I, Capítulo IV, Artículo 17.3
	• If the payment is deferred more than 120 days, the supplier has the right to ask for bank guarantee or credit insurance	
Sales promotions	• Requirement of obligatory information about the price and quality of the promoted goods	Título II
	• Only two periods of seasonal sales per year, whose minimum duration should be of one week and maximum of two months	Título II, Capítulo II, Artículo 25.1 y 25.2
	• The regional governments should fix the definite dates for seasonal sales	
Non-store retailing	• The firms engaged in non-store retailing must have an authorization from the Ministry and must register at a special office	Título III, Capítulo II, Artículo 38.2
Franchising regime	• The franchisor must register in an office specially created for this purpose by the Autonomous Regions	Título III, Capítulo VI, Artículo 62.2
	• The franchisor must provide some specific information to the franchise-holder before signing the contract	Título III, Capítulo VI, Artículo 62.3

Note

a The Law says that it is the responsibility of the Autonomous Regions to set the criteria to charac-terize an outlet as a large retailer, but that in any case the retail oulets with a sales area larger than 2,500 sq. m. should be considered as such.

vary somewhat. Thus, in some respects national laws apply generally only in the absence of regional legislation, in other areas of law national legislation prevails over regional authority and its impact is therefore nationally uniform.

The objectives of the Law 7/1996, according to its preamble, are as follows:

- to establish the rules of the game in the retail sector,
- to regulate new retail formats,
- to correct the imbalance between large-scale and small-scale retailers, and
- to preserve the free and fair competition.

Following the text of the Law, the attainment of these objectives will be 'the most effective means of preserving the interest of the consumer'.

Among the aspects regulated in the Law 7/1996 the following may be highlighted: the opening of large-scale establishments, sales at loss, the payment to suppliers, sales promotions, non-store retailing (embracing e-commerce and more traditional mail-order selling), and the franchising regime. The main points regulated in relation to these aspects are detailed in Table 6.15.

With regard to the regulation of these aspects of the retail sector, the Law should be understood as a legal framework that sets the basic conditions and minimum requirements from which the regional authorities or participants in the sector must regulate in detail the different commercial practices. This means that some sections of the Law are of direct application, while others merit further detailed regulation, either by the state or the regional authorities. Also, the Law lists the sections that are of direct application, and these include all matters covered in Table 6.15 with the exception of non-store retailing. In this sense, and regarding the opening of large establishments, the regional policy on this issue has tended to demand a licence to start business for every retail outlet of more than 2.500 sq. m. and also to the hard discount shops regardless of their size. In relation to the regulation of the periods allowed for seasonal sales, the most common position is to establish the maximum period allowed by the Law, although the specific dates vary among communities.

The Organic Law 2/1996, complementing the Law 7/1996, has the single objective of regulating the shopping hours. In this way, art. 2 provides that shopping hours would be unrestricted, but art. 3 postpones the application of this measure until the state and regional governments decide upon this matter, and not before 1 January 2001. Thus, this article sets a transitional period during which otherwise to improve the competitive position of traditional retailers, with the aid of the so-called Plan Marco de Modernización del Comercio Interior (Draft Plan for the Modernization of Interior Trade) which is referred to in the following section.

However, although the state government has not negotiated with the regional governments the freedom of shopping hours, it has promulgated an Order in Council (Real Decreto Ley 6/2000 dated 23 June) that amends some aspects of the Law 2/1996, opening a route to a greater liberalization. This regulation provides, first, that absolute freedom of shopping hours is postponed until further agreement of regulation between the central and regional governments, and not before January 2005. Until this takes place, the regional governments are responsible for regulation of shopping hours, always respecting the minima established by the Order in Council. These minima are 90 weekly hours of opening, nine Sundays or public holidays of opening in the year 2001, which will increase annually by one until twelve Sundays or public holidays in 2004. There are some exceptions. Some types of shop enjoy complete freedom in shopping hours: bakeries, take-away shops, fuel stations, florists, convenience shops, shops in transport stations and tourist areas, and shops whose sales area is smaller than 300 sq. m. provided they do not belong to a retail chain.

There has been a profound debate in Spain about the appropriateness of liberalizing shopping hours. The majority opinion argues that the measure will benefit the large retail firms, and will thus provoke the disappearance of many traditional retailers. This, it is argued, will cause a loss of vitality of city centres and will intensify the dualism of the Spanish retail sector. However, the Autonomous Regions had two options: either to adopt as maximum shopping hours the minima established by the order in Council, or to expand shopping hours from the minima, that is, setting a maxima higher than nine Sundays in 2001 and 90 weekly hours. Within these possibilities, most of the Autonomous Regions have adopted a restrictive posture and have chosen the former option. The autonomous Region of Madrid is an exception, with a slightly more liberal attitude towards shopping hours.

We believe that state intervention in the retail sector by means of the above-mentioned regulation is appropriate in the Spanish context, taking into account the existing legal vacuum in which the process of modernization of the retail structures was taking place. It is felt that with regard to these regulations, the state has tried to protect smaller retailers from full competition with larger firms. Public policy intervention in the market in this way slows or reduces the extent of structural change in the retail sector (Pilat, 1997). The rationale behind this kind of intervention is that the small retailers provide a range of social services in addition to economic ones. Therefore, as the Law declares, 'the actions undertaken will be in the benefit of the consumer'. On the other hand, these norms have been the target of harsh criticism that denounce their interventionist character, raises questions with regard to their impact in promoting free competition and achieving a balance among large and small retailers, and highlights the implementation and control costs of the rules (Carrasco, 1996; Arévalo, 1996). In this sense, apart from the matter of the shopping hours, the opening of large establishments has been one of the most controversial aspects. Some experts argue that this measure may be responsible for restricting intra-type competition and creating monopoly positions for some shops (Casares and Rebollo, 1996).

Measures for the promotion of business initiatives

The promotion of business initiatives is organized by means of the so-called 'Draft Plan for the Modernization of Domestic Trade' which is designed by the

Table 6.16 Draft plan for the modernization of domestic trade

	Fields of action	Main specific measures
Improvement of the Environment	Labour	• Promotion of early retirements
	Fiscal	• Reform of taxes affecting retail trade
	Regulation of commerce	• Promulgation of a Law of Retail Trade Regulation
	Information and diffusion of the EU actions	• Facilitate the access to EU helps for retailers
General programmes	Training	• Training to shopkeepers on business management • Postgraduate education programmes on retailing
	Information on the retail sector	• Structural reports • Reports on current issues • Retail databases • Observatory of the Retail Trade
	Diffusion of innovations	• R&D centres for commercial technologies • Conferences, seminars and round tables
Specific programmes	Business cooperation	• Promotion of retail associations • Improvement of distribution channels structures
	Geographical administration of retail supply	• Adaptation of retail supply to the population needs • Administration of the opening of large-scale establishments
	Help to independent retailers	• Improvement of retailer competitiveness, by means of: – Specialization and modernization of shops – Improvement of business management – Implementation of innovations

Department of Interior Commerce of the Ministry of Economy (Ministerio de Comercio y Turismo, 1995). The justification for this Plan is the necessity for a guide to the process of retail modernization which in Spain began at the end of the 1980s. Overall, the Plan consists of a series of measures designed to improve the competitiveness and efficiency of the small-scale retailers, since they are a key element of the social structure of cities and contribute to the variety of the retail supply.

The Plan is developed from 1995 up to 2000, and coordinates actions in three different fields: Improvement of the Environment, General Programmes and Specific Programmes. The particular actions and measures within these three broad fields can be seen in Table 6.16. Improvement of the Environment includes a series of measures with the objective of improving the general conditions that surround the retail firms, but are not specific to them. This field embraces a programme for Regulation of Commerce that includes as the most important action the regulation of the retail sector, which refers to the laws analysed in the preceding section.

The distinction between general and specific programmes lies in the former being carried out directly by the Department of Interior Commerce, financed by the state, and with nationwide scope, while the specific programmes are implemented by means of agreements with the Autonomous Regions and are jointly financed by the state and the Autonomous Regions. Another difference is that all retail firms can benefit from the general programmes, independently of their participation in a specific programme, while the specific programmes are designed for the specific firms or associations that request them, adapting the actions to their particular needs.

It should be noted that the General Programmes include within their fields of action development of Information on Retail Structures in the form of the creation of a Monitor of Retail Structures (Observatorio de la Distribución Comercial). This follows similar initiatives undertaken in other European countries. According to the Department of Interior Commerce (1998), the Monitor is meant to be a meeting point for a range of different participants in the retail sector with the different governments. In this sense, Casares (1997) asserts that the essential functions of the Monitor are three: to generate information about the sector, to reconcile differing interests and to design sectoral policies. In these ways, the Monitor has acted as an organ of information, as well as a consultative body.

The Monitor works in plenary meetings and in specific commissions. The constituents of these bodies are representatives of the different governments, of large and small retailers, of the universities, of the industries connected with the sector, and of other public bodies with some connection with commerce. This variety of members is meant to guarantee the representation of all the interests, although it may lead to increased difficulty for decision taking. The specific commissions are the following: Monitoring of the Law of Retail Trade Regulation, Town Planning,

Table 6.17 Evolution of the state help in the Specific Programmes of the Draft Plan for the Modernization of Domestic Trade

Programmes	1995	1996	1997	1998
Business co-operation	7.20	11.30	14.30	43.86
Geographical administration of retail trade	0.15	26.70	44.50	44.79
Help to independent retailers	92.65	62.00	41.20	11.35
Total	100.00	100.00	100.00	100.00

Source: Dirección General de Comercio Interior (1998).

Training, Environment and Administration, SMEs versus big companies, Monitoring of the Euro, and Individual Studies.

The Specific Programmes are co-financed between the state and the regional governments. In the first two years of application of the Plan, the programmes were financed 30 per cent by the Ministry and 70 per cent by the autonomous region. But the reform of the Plan that came into force in 1997 changed the financing of the system. In order to accomplish the priority objectives, a different amount is granted by the state, depending on the programme. In this way, priority is given to the programme of Business Co-operation, whose actions receive from the state 40 per cent of the help granted by the Autonomous Region, whereas 20 per cent is granted for the programme Help to the Independent Retailers, and 30 per cent for the programme Geographical Administration of Retail Supply. The 1997 reform also introduces the possibility of financing up to half of the special actions proposed by the interested parties that are regarded as being particularly innovative or as having beneficial effects on other actions. With the same objective of more effective resource allocation, a minimum of 30 per cent of the total aid from the state is allocated for the programme of Geographical Administration of Retail Supply and 10 per cent for the programme of Business Co-operation. As can be seen in Table 6.17, these proportions have been broadly achieved in the year 1998.

Conclusions

The purpose of this chapter has been to outline the characteristics of retailing in Spain. This was begun by presenting the background to the present-day retailing system, which was then described in the second section. On the basis of this general description, the third section provided an in-depth analysis of the more individual aspects of Spanish retailing before ending with an analysis of the setting in which retail businesses operate, with particular emphasis on the nature and effect of government legislation and assistance in this sector.

Generally speaking it may be concluded, as with all of the individual countries covered in this study, that the Spanish retail sector has certain particularities in comparison with other EU economies. These include especially the later modernization of retail networks in Spain, and the continuing importance which 'traditional' retail outlets still have. However, as a direct result of this relative delay in the development of Spanish retailing, the transformation of retail structures has been highly accelerated and characterized in some trades by the arrival of foreign firms. Hence, one particular trait of present-day retailing in Spain is its obviously international nature. The fact that traditional outlets continue to exist is, moreover, also due to the delay in the modernization process, since the inevitable fall in the market share of traditional outlets has been stemmed partly by the increased awareness of the public authorities as regards the problems involved. The authorities have seen the impact which the modernization of the retail sector has had upon old city centres in other economies and have taken measures to palliate such effects.

The following are the main conclusions to be drawn from this analysis of retailing in Spain:

- Spanish retailing has undergone radical changes over the last twenty-five years, resulting in a complete overhaul of retailing structures at an accelerated rate of change. Between the late 1970s and the present day, this sector has been subject to constant change and modernization which have created retail structures now largely similar to those of other European countries.
- Despite the survival and modernization of the traditional Spanish retail trade – particularly in the food and household goods subsectors – the concentration of retailing into large business organizations has been the most significant development. As a result, the top ten firms in food distribution now account for 53.3 per cent of total turnover. This trend was caused by the arrival *en masse* of European groups due to the globalization of markets. Hence, five of the top ten distribution companies are foreign (Carrefour, Auchan, Ahold, Unigro and Makro) and they account for 39.5 per cent of the total sales. The Carrefour group deserves special mention since it alone has a market share of 22.5 per cent. It can be deduced from these figures that power in distribution channels is shifting towards the retailers, and this trend is being reinforced by the importance of own brands. All this is an indication too of the unstoppable tendency of vertical integration, in one form or another, in distribution channels.
- The Spanish retail sector is nonetheless highly fragmented and dominated, in terms of numbers of employees, by small- and medium-sized businesses. Overall, 63.5 per cent of Spanish retail outlets have only one or two employees, and only 16.7 per cent have five or more employees. With regard to sales area, the average size of a store in Spain is 94 sq. m. However, as we have pointed out, current trends in Spanish retailing reflect a dramatic modernization of retailing structures. The outcome is that businesses of different sizes and management styles exist side by side, with both a small number of family businesses and other highly professionalized ones.
- The continuing importance of traditional retail outlets in Spain is, however, demonstrated by the fact that two-thirds of retailers are not constituted as companies, which mixes personal and corporate assets and makes it difficult to manage their businesses in a more professional manner. Association and cooperation strategies among retailers are increasingly being adopted, but there is still room for growth since only 21.1 per cent of Spanish retail outlets belong to any type of chain, franchise, purchasing group or cooperative. This statistic highlights the current importance of independent Spanish shopkeepers, despite the steady drop in their market share. In their awareness of the need to increase their competitiveness, this type of trader is moving beyond the traditional image towards a more management-oriented outlook, and becoming more flexible and able to plan ahead and respond to the changing environment.

Considering the Spanish retail structure in terms of types of outlet, the following trends can be seen:

- Supermarkets are the self-service outlets with the greatest floor space and considerable growth in the last decade. They have become more competitive in recent years in comparison with other types of outlets (hypermarkets and discount stores) thanks to the increase in the size of leading market chains and the increased importance of buying groups.
- The hypermarket format is characterized by the leadership of the Carrefour brand. In the last decade, this format has undergone significant growth in floor space, although in recent years, the number of new stores being opened has slowed down, mainly due to legal obstacles concerning the creation of major retail outlets, but also because of the saturation of shopping areas.
- One tendency in the Spanish market has been the increasing importance of the price variable in the distribution of products used and consumed frequently. This has encouraged the growth of discount outlets, mainly Día and Lidl.
- Department stores continue to be highly popular and are something of an idiosyncrasy of the Spanish retail trade. This can be explained largely by the strategy implemented by El Corte Inglés, a company which constitutes a benchmark of business excellence. The fact that their outlets are located in city centres has contributed to a considerable extent to boosting trade in these geographic areas. Indeed, one frequently finds that El Corte Inglés acts as an anchor outlet in these shopping areas, defining an emerging retail formula which is the town or open shopping district.
- Shopping districts have been actively promoted by the public authorities and retail associations in recent years, using the programmes implemented in other European countries as an example. They enable greater competitiveness in city centres which are affected by the competition of suburban shopping centres which otherwise have the advantages of accessibility, car-park facilities and efficient shopping trips.
- The concentration of floor space of retail outlets in planned shopping centres has increased considerably since the mid-1980s in parallel with the expansion of hypermarkets. As a result, the predominant type of shopping centre in Spain is the type organized around a hypermarket. Regional shopping centres have, however, assumed a more important role in recent years since they allow shopping to be combined with leisure activities in response to the new purchasing patterns of Spanish consumers. The reason for this change of habit lies within the Spanish society itself, with women joining the workforce in large numbers and a considerable increase in purchasing power.
- Within the scope of planned concentrations of floor space, special mention must be made of retail municipal markets. This deep-rooted type of retail outlet continues to play an important role in the distribution of perishable products and is attempting to adapt to new consumption and purchasing habits.

- Changes in Spanish society also provide the foundations for the growth of electronic trade – a sales channel that can be considered to be in a consolidated, introductory phase with high potential growth rates.

In short, it may be said that, despite having begun the transformation process somewhat later than in most other European countries, the degree of development and modernization in the Spanish retail sector is now on a par with them.

References

AC Nielsen (2000) *Anuario Evolución 2000*. AC Nielsen Company. Madrid.

Alimarket (1999) 'Distribución alimentaria Guía de las 500 primeras empresas'. *Alimarket*.

Alimarket (2000) Especial distribución alimentaria. No 133.

Allúe, A. (1996) 'Legitimidad de la Ley de Ordenación del Comercio Minorista'. *Distribución y Consumo*, 27: 27–9.

Arévalo, J. (1996) 'Ley de Ordenación del Comercio y empresa comercial'. *Distribución y Consumo*, 27: 37–9.

Barroso, R. (1999) 'Franquicias. Un sólido sistema para la expansión de una marca'. *Distribución y Consumo*, 45: 60–9.

Carrasco, A. (1996) 'Ley de Ordenación del Comercio Minorista. Juicio crítico de una reforma', *Distribución y Consumo*, 27: 40–5.

Casares, J. (1994) 'Regulación pública, intereses sectoriales y calidad de vida', *Distribución y Consumo*, 17: 10–18.

Casares, J. (1997) 'Observatorio de la distribución comercial', *Distribución y Consumo*, 35: 109–11.

Casares, J. and Rebollo, A. (1996) 'Innovación y adaptación en distribución comercial. Ideas nuevas en 'odres' viejos', *Distribución y Consumo*, 27: 7–23.

Casares, J. and Rebollo, A. (1997) 'Mercados minoristas tradicionales. Situación actual y alternativas de actuación', *Distribución y Consumo*, 32: 75–113.

Casares, J. and Rebollo, A. (2000) *Distribución Comercial*, 2ª edn, Civitas, Madrid.

Casares, J., Martín, V. J. and Aranda, E. (1999) 'Vértigo en la distribución comercial. Concentración, competencia, empleo y relaciones con proveedores', *Distribución y Consumo*, 49: 5–25.

Cruz Roche, I. (ed.) (1999) *Los Canales de Distribución de Productos de Gran Consumo. Concentración y Competencia*, Pirámide, Madrid.

Cruz, I. and Rebollo, A. (1995) 'Plan Marco de modernización del Comercio Interior'. *Distribución y Consumo*, 22: 46–55.

Dawson, J. A. (1993) 'The internationalization of retailing', in Bromley, R. D. F. and Thomas, C. J. (eds): *Retail Change: Contemporary Issues*, UCL Press, London.

Dirección General de Comercio Interior (1997) *La Distribución Comercial en España. Informe 1997*. Madrid.

Dirección General de Comercio Interior (1998) *La Distribución Comercial en España. Informe 1998*. Madrid.

Gil, I., Mollá, A. and Rovira, A. (1994) 'Distribución y consumo en la Comunidad Valenciana: respuestas para un nuevo escenario'. *Distribución y Consumo*, 15: 46–67.

Instituto Nacional de Empleo (2000) *La Franquicia: Fórmula de Desarrollo Empresarial y Potenciación Empresarial*, INEM, Madrid.

Marrero, J. L. (2000) 'Comercio y Administración Pública. Veinticinco años de cambio'. *Distribución y Consumo*, 50: 163–9.

Ministerio de Comercio y Turismo (1995) *Plan Marco de Modernización del Comercio Interior*, Madrid.

Ministerio de Economía y Hacienda (1998) *Centros Comerciales Abiertos*, Madrid.

Pilat, D. (1997) *Regulation and Performance in the Distribution Sector*, OECD, Economics Department Working Papers 180.

Rebollo, A. (1999) 'La planificación estratégica en los mercados minoristas', *Distribución y Consumo*, 44: 29–37.

Rebollo, A. (2000) 'Geografía comercial de España. Distribución regional de la oferta y la demanda de servicios comerciales', *Distribución y Consumo*, 50: 123–60.

Websites

www.aedecc.es
www.ine.es

7   United Kingdom

Stewart Howe

Introduction and background

This chapter on the United Kingdom follows the pattern of others in comprising a historical background to contemporary retailing, a discussion of some particular features of UK retailing, a consideration of structural features of retailing and the influence upon these of government legislation, and conclusions on the efficiency of retailing and the impact upon this of government action.

The early history of retailing

Retailing in the United Kingdom, in a form that we might vaguely recognize it today, began to take shape in the reign of Elizabeth I (1595–1603). During this period, at least in London and for the benefit of the wealthy, retailing began to appear as something separate from production, and something fixed and permanent as opposed to itinerant and periodic (see Howe, 1992: chapter 2).

The 'industrial revolution' in the United Kingdom at the beginning of the nineteenth century resulted in some further development in this respect, principally as a result of rising levels of income, new manufacturing processes, and a growing and increasingly urbanized population. A number of writers have, however cautioned against exaggerating the extent of change in retailing that accompanied developments in manufacture at this time. One of the most noted authors in the field suggested that 'The wholesale and retail trades in Britain in the middle of the nineteenth century were examples of those trades that still bore the marks of the old system rather than of the new. ... The distributive system as a whole still bore the marks of a pre-industrial economy' (Jefferys, 1954: 1, 5). Alexander (1970: 11–12) too emphasized of this period that 'the extent of change must not be exaggerated'. At this time, most food products including ready-cooked foods, were sold in markets or bakeries. In clothing and footwear too there was normally direct contact between the craftsman tailor and shoemaker and his customers; and here one also has to bear in mind that much clothing, both underwear and outerwear, was still made at home.

Retailing developments at the end of the nineteenth century

It was not in fact until the end of the nineteenth century that a recognizably separate retail trade emerged. This further development too was based upon the advent of new products and processes such as refrigeration that brought meat from Australia and South America, continued urbanization of the population, and a generally rising standard of living particularly among the working class population with its relatively homogeneous demand for basic foodstuffs including tea, sugar, butter, eggs and bacon (see Fraser, 1981). At this time also there were the early signs of a change in the organizational and structural form of retailing, as the later nineteenth century developments in the economic and demographic environment began to result in the displacing of the traditional, single-outlet, fixed-shop retailers by larger scale, multiple-shop enterprises. In addition to the larger scale developments along these lines in the grocery and provisions trade in the hands of such firms as Lipton, Maypole and Home & Colonial Stores (see Mackay, 1998), this pattern of the emergence of multiple-shop retailers also came to be applied to chemists goods (Chapman, 1974), books and newspapers (Wilson, 1985), and clothing and footwear.

Three other new forms of retailing occurred in the United Kingdom that were to become significant by the early decades of the twentieth century. The consumer Co-operative movement was founded in 1844 and emerged strongly in the latter half of the nineteenth century, having a membership of more than 10,000 by 1880 (Birchall, 1994: 45). It was an early example, in its way, of a multiple-shop organization, and was also characterized by considerable vertical integration, having its own tea plantations in Ceylon, a fleet of ships and a number of factories involved in both food processing and non-food manufacturers such as clothing and footwear. Jefferys (1954: 58) estimated that in 1900, the Co-operative Societies' total retail market share was 6–7 per cent, and that in food and household items its market share approached 10 per cent.

Also to emerge in the middle of the nineteenth century were the department stores, catering for a more middle-class demand in the clothing and other retail sectors, sold originally at keen prices from shops which boasted new facilities such as restaurants and passenger lifts. These commenced as large shops – Selfridge's employing 5,000 staff – and the names of many others such as Harvey Nichols and Harrods survive today (Pound, 1960).

Competition across the retail sector was added to in the years before 1914 and into the inter-war period by the arrival of the variety store chains: multiple-shop organizations with a wide range of merchandise sold at low prices. The US Woolworth entered the United Kingdom in 1909, and this was joined by British Home Stores, by Littlewoods which opened its first retail stores in 1937 (Clegg, 1993), and of course Marks & Spencer which was originally founded in 1884 (Briggs, 1984).

UK retailing in the first half of the twentieth century

By the early years of the twentieth century, UK retailing had changed significantly in shape and scale from the third quarter of the previous century, and had begun to take a shape and structure that would be clearly recognized today. In particular, the major types of retail organization – ranging from single-outlet family business to large-scale multiple outlets – were in place. The multiple-shop grocery chain Lipton, for example, had 245 branches across the UK in 1910 (Davis, 1966: 283). In addition, the various forms of retail organization such as (consumer) Co-operative Societies, department stores, variety store chains and multiple-shop retailers as well as single-outlet family businesses were in place. Large-scale retail organizations were increasingly professionally managed, and in the early decades of the twentieth century, there was a clear trend to amalgamations among the largest of these. In the grocery sector, such amalgamations led to Home & Colonial Stores having more than 3,000 outlets (Mathias, 1967: 38–9), Boots the Chemist increased its number of outlets from 200 in 1900 to 1,180 in 1938 (Levy, 1948: 185), and Debenhams, United Drapery Stores and the John Lewis Partnership emerged as the largest department store groups.

As emphasized before, however, with regard to trends in retailing, the effect of such amalgamations on the overall retailing scene should not be exaggerated. In 1930 there were still an estimated 500,000–600,000 'unit' retailers, that is, where a retail organization comprised only one shop, and these accounted for some two-thirds of total retail sales (Braithwaite and Dobbs, 1932: 239). And although the number of these and their proportion of the retail trade had fallen off quite considerably by the time of the first UK Census of Distribution in 1950, they still amounted in that year to some 450,000 shops (84 per cent of the total number of these) and accounted for 53 per cent of total retail sales (Ross, 1955: 19–21).

UK retailing structure and forms since 1950

Data on retail distribution

The years following the Second World War are an appropriate point in time from which to examine UK retailing as it is today. By the early 1950s, war-time restrictions – including rationing and building controls – had come to an end; and since 1950 we have the advantage of the data in successive Census of Distribution reports on which to base an analysis of trends in the pattern of retailing.

Although these data are not entirely satisfactory so far as consistency is concerned, successive census reports provide a reasonably consistent national picture of the development of the retail trades for the second half of the twentieth century. The data presented in full in Table 7.1 show the overall size of the retail sector in terms of the number of shops (establishments), retail economic output relative to gross domestic product (GDP), and the total number of employees in the sector. From these we can see that shops numbers rose to a postwar peak of 577,307 in 1961. From this point a fairly steady decline commenced until 1988, when the figure for that year was more than 40 per cent below the 1961 total. The 1988 figure was followed by totals slightly above this for the next three years; but a steady decline continued thereafter through the 1990s to produce a figure of 289,996 in 1994 although succeeded by a slightly surprising rise to 320,622 for 1996. In contrast to data on shop numbers, retail employment has remained remarkably constant. This figure peaked at 2.85 million in 1971; and having fallen to 2.4 million

Table 7.1 The retail sector in the UK economy

	Establishments[a] (No.)	Sales[b] (£ million)	Value added/ GDP (%)	Employment ('000)
1950	531,143	4,923	7.8	2,265
1957	573,988	7,798	8.3	2,569
1961	577,307	8,919	8.1	2,524
1966	504,412	11,132	8.1	2,556
1971	509,818	16,949	8.4	2,853
1977	387,588	39,056	7.3	2,442
1980	368,253	59,757	7.1	2,408
1982	356,590	70,167	7.1	2,258
1984	349,728	82,794	7.2	2,317
1986	343,387	97,296	7.6	2,334
1987	345,467	104,627	7.5	2,319
1988	338,248	114,705	7.4	2,347
1989	350,015	123,556	7.2	2,463
1990	348,920	132,704	7.4	2,468
1991	342,321	132,544	7.8	2,367
1992	318,751	137,526	7.6	2,324
1993	305,827	148,529		2,337
1994	289,996	156,649		2,379
1995		185,222	8.3	
1996	320,622	201,951	8.9	2,188
1997		207,489	8.4	
1998		220,998	8.8	

Sources: *Reports of the Census of Distribution, Business Monitor SDA 25 Retailing, Retail Sector Review*, Central Statistical Office *Economic Trends* and *Annual Abstract of Statistics*, all HMSO, London.

Notes
The third data column in this table relates retail value added less taxes to expenditure-based GDP at factor cost, which is also a value-added measure, except that for the years 1950–1971 inclusive prior to the introduction of VAT neither the numerator nor the denominator in this proportion is net of tax.
a That is, retail outlets.
b Including value added tax (VAT).

at the end of that decade, the figure remains at just under 2.2 million in 1996. Similarly, with regard to the contribution of retailing to the total of economic activity, the ratio of retail value added (less taxes) to GDP at factor prices (i.e. also excluding the impact of taxes) rose to a post-1945 peak of 8.4 per cent in 1971. It fell off to 7.5 per cent in 1987 but has more recently risen to 8.8 per cent.

Table 7.2 provides an initial insight into the size structure of UK retailing by breaking down the total number of shops or retail establishments into those which were part of 'independent' organizations (including both those shops which were owned by 'single-outlet' retailers and those outlets which were part of multiple-shop organizations having up to nine branches), multiple-shop organizations with 10+ branches, and Co-operative Society outlets. What is immediately apparent is the remarkable stability of independent retailers in terms of their proportion of retail outlets: their proportion of the total number of retail outlets having declined only from 85 per cent in 1950 to more than three-quarters in 1996. Moreover, within this category, the physical presence of the 'unit' retailer, where a retail organization has only one shop, has also continued to dominate the retail scene. In 1950 there were 376,446 of such shops, comprising 71 per cent of the total number of retail outlets. By 1980, while the number shops had fallen off considerably, the proportion of outlets within Independent retail businesses had fallen only to 82 per cent, and the proportion of unit retailers within the total was still 61 per cent. Between 1980 and 1996, the reduction in the total number of shops was 13 per cent, but within this reduced total of 320,622 retail outlets, independent shop organizations accounted for 77 per cent of outlets and unit retailers for 57 per cent, thus continuing the physical dominance of the UK shopping environment on the part of single-shop retail businesses or relatively small-scale retail organizations with fewer than 10 outlets. The other obvious statistic from Table 7.2 is the massive decline in the number of consumer Co-operative Society outlets: from 26,458 or 5 per cent of the total in 1950 through 8,197 or 2 per cent in 1980 to 2,818 outlets in 1994 amounting to 1 per cent of the total number of shops in the United Kingdom.

Table 7.2 Retail establishments by organization structure

	Total (No.)	Independents[a] (No.)	Multiples[b] (No.)	Co-operatives (No.)
1950	529,684	448,999	54,227	26,458
1957	574,218	482,606	61,027	30,585
1961	544,873	434,063	81,618[c]	29,396
1966	504,046	404,312	71,536	28,198
1971	471,396	392,354	62,535	16,480
1977	387,588	309,770	66,897	10,921
1980	368,253	302,123	57,933	8,197
1982	356,590	293,382	56,555	6,653
1984	349,728	288,935	55,224	5,569
1986	343,386	283,030	55,497	4,859
1987	345,468	282,762	58,015	4,691
1988	338,248	274,348	59,630	4,270
1989	350,015	283,495	62,313	4,207
1990	348,920	280,901	63,934	4,085
1991	342,321	271,214	67,128	3,979
1992	318,751	253,910	61,258	3,583
1993	305,827	237,859	64,485	3,483
1994	289,996	224,689	62,489	2,818
1996	320,622	246,366	74,256	n.a.

Sources: *Reports of the Census of Distribution, Business Monitor SDA 25 Retailing*, and *Retail Sector Reports*, all HMSO, London.

Notes
a Including retail organizations with 1–9 outlets.
b Organizations having 10+ retail establishments or outlets each.
c Organizations having 5+ retail establishments or outlets each.

However, the data in Table 7.2 increasingly through time overstate the significance of smaller scale retail businesses and correspondingly understate the growing importance of the multiple-shop retail organization. When, as in Table 7.3, we
examine the proportions of retail sales accounted for by different size categories
of retail organization, a rather different picture emerges. Although in 1950 independent retail organizations accounted for 85 per cent of the number of retail outlets, their proportion of total retail sales was only 65 per cent; and within this size
category, the single-outlet retailer, despite accounting for 71 per cent of shop
numbers, was responsible for only 48 per cent of total retail sales. Correspondingly,
in 1950 multiple-shop retail organizations (each with ten or more outlets), while
having only 10 per cent of retail outlets, were responsible for 23 per cent of total
sales. By 1980, the concentration of total retail sales into the hands of multiple-
shop organizations had risen to 47 per cent, even while they accounted for only
16 per cent of retail outlets; and by 1996, while the proportion of retail outlets
within these large-scale retail organizations had risen only to 23 per cent, they
accounted in that year for 67 per cent of total retail sales. Even these data understate
somewhat the level of retail market concentration in the hands of very large-scale
organizations. If we consider retail organizations each with 100+ outlets, then in

Table 7.3 Total retail market shares by retail organization structure

	Independents[a] (%)	Multiples[b] (%)	Co-operatives (%)
1950	65	23	12
1957	63	25	12
1961	52	36[c]	12
1966	58	33	9
1971	55	37	7
1977	48	45	7
1980	46	47	7
1982	44	50	6
1984	43	52	5
1986	41	54	5
1987	40	55	5
1988	39	57	4
1989	39	57	4
1990	39	57	4
1991	37	59	4
1992	36	61	3
1993	35	62	3
1994	32	66	2
1996	33	67	n.a.

Sources: *Reports of the Census of Distribution, Business Monitor SDA 25
Retailing, and Retail Sector Reports*, all HMSO, London.

Notes
a Including retail organizations with 1–9 outlets.
b Organizations having 10+ retail establishments or outlets each.
c Organizations having 5+ retail establishments or outlets each.
n.a. = not available.

1987, there were 130 of these, with a combined total of 43,696 outlets and a total retail market share of 47 per cent. In 1990, the 125 such organizations had a total of 47,061 branches and a retail market share marginally up at 48 per cent; and by 1996, the corresponding figures were 156 organizations with 49,203 outlets and a market share then of 54 per cent. As in the case of other comparisons with Table 7.2, the data in Table 7.3 show even more forcefully the declining position of the Co-operative Society branches from a combined retail market share of 12 per cent even in 1961 to half of that proportion two decades later, and to a figure of 2 per cent in 1994.

Four features stand out in this aggregated statistical picture of UK retailing. First, within the greatly reduced number of shops, whose total fell by 40 per cent from a postwar peak in 1961 to 1996, the smaller scale, independent retail organ- ization is still today the dominant physical feature of retailing, representing more than three-quarters of the total number of shops. Indeed, within this category, there were in 1996 still 181,880 single-outlet retailers in the United Kingdom, account- ing for more than half of all retail outlets. Second, independent retail organizations have, however, suffered a significant loss in their share of retail trade during the second half of the twentieth century. This proportion fell from 65 per cent in 1950 to 46 per cent in 1980 and to 33 per cent in 1996, and the decline indicates both the cost competitiveness of multiple-shop retail organizations and the extent to which they have been able to attract an increasing proportion of shoppers with a wider range of goods. Third, from enterprise or business decision-making unit data, it is clear that there is at the present time, a trend towards increased concen- tration of economic power in the retail sector. In 1950, those multiple-shop organ- izations that accounted for 23 per cent of total retail sales yet comprised nearly 2,000 business organizations; and even in 1961, when their market share had risen to about one-third, there were still 1,300 separate business organizations in this size category. However, the picture painted by Jefferys and Knee ([1962]: 24) in that year of 'the existence of a vast number of individual entrepreneurs ... in retail- ing', and their reference to retailing as 'still a very small scale and human occu- pation', was becoming increasingly less accurate with the growth of large-scale, oligopolistic and professionally managed retail organizations. As we saw above, even within the aggregated census data, it is clear that the largest retail organiza- tions – and the Census of Distribution data even in 1987 had identified a 'top tier' of 24 of such businesses, each with an average of 896 outlets and a combined retail market share of 17.6 per cent – now enjoy considerable market power, and further examples of this within individual markets, and the influence that such structures have on retailer behaviour, are discussed further below. Fourth, it is evident from the data in Tables 7.2 and 7.3 that the Co-operative movement in the UK is no longer the force in retailing that it was at one time. Some of the reasons for this decline are discussed below when we look at changing forms of retailing.

Changing forms of retailing

As we noted above, there has been a very significant change in the role of the *independent retail organization*, and within this the place of the single-unit shop has declined as shop numbers fell from 376,446 in 1950 to 181,880 in 1996, and their share of total retail trade from 48 to 21 per cent over this period. There may, however, be some ground for believing that the rate of decline in the position of the independent shop is slowing down, and that a core of such shops – greater in some trades than others – will remain viable. Three factors may contribute to this survival. First, one response by certain independent retailers to the competitive outcome of the ending of resale price maintenance from the late 1950s was to form voluntary buying groups. These comprise organizations such as Spar, VG and Mace whose retailer members enjoy trade discounts and other services. In particular, discounts are available because of the buying power of the voluntary-group wholesalers *vis-à-vis* manufacturers arising from the larger orders that they can place. This practice has developed most noticeably in the food trades, and as a further development in this area, independent retailers may in effect take over some of their own wholesaling functions by purchasing at cash-and-carry outlets. The largest firms in this sector are Landmark, Nurdin & Peacock, Linfood and Booker McConnell. Cash-and-carry warehouses – a number of which are operated by voluntary group wholesalers – have expanded in terms of their scale and the range of goods carried. Finally, certain features of the pattern of consumer demand may promote the continued survival of independent retailers. This may apply in those areas where the 'corner shop' offers a unique convenience service in terms of location and opening hours; and even in larger centres of population the more specialist retailer in the delicatessen/fishmonger, clothing boutique, wine and spirits shop, or jeweller-cum-watch-repairer trades can survive in the face of competition from large-scale multiple organizations. These arguments led two authors at the beginning of the last decade of the twentieth century to suggest that in the United Kingdom 'small retailers do have, and will continue to have, an important role to play within the retail market-place', emphasizing their contribution to 'convenience' in retailing and also their broader social function (Davies and Harris, 1990: 129). Some support for this view may be found in evidence on the 'polarization' phenomenon which suggests that across all retail trades in the United Kingdom in recent decades, it is the smallest size category of retail organization which has suffered least in competition with the largest multiple-shop retail organizations when compared with the deterioration of the market position of medium-sized retail organizations (see Howe and Dugard, 1993). However, changes in the competitive environment suggest that the 'protection' afforded to small, independent retailers by this polarization phenomenon is declining as, for example, in the food–grocery sector, the grocery supermarkets and their smaller offshoots themselves are offering a number of aspects of convenience for shoppers, and competition for traditional retailers is also coming from petrol-forecourt outlets in this sector. Recent research confirms these impressions, and suggests that in addition to small-scale retailers taking full advantage of available information technology and forming appropriate vertical and horizontal trading alliances, smaller retailers at least in the food and grocery sector may improve their competitive position by securing their position as 'a centre for social and community activity' in their catchment area (Baron *et al.*, 2001: 412).

In contrast to independent retailers, *multiple shop retailing* advanced steadily in the United Kingdom during the second half of the twentieth century. Conditions relating not only to retail costs but also to the pattern of shopper demand continued to favour large-scale retailers over this period. These features included the pre-packaging and national branding of foods and other products, and the ending of building restrictions on retail development from the mid-1950s. Particularly important during the following decade was the gradual withering away of resale price maintenance, which allowed large-scale, cost-efficient retailers to compete openly on price with their smaller competitors. Especially in the context of self-service and supermarket operations, large-scale retailers in the food trades achieve significant savings in labour costs. The largest retailers in particular enjoy considerable advantages in the trade terms given to them by their suppliers: savings which there is clear evidence to suggest that they pass on to their customers in terms of reduced prices. Such large-scale retailers have thus been able to enjoy economies of scale both in their buying power and their store operations, and also in replication of outlets within their expanding store portfolio. They have also been able to capitalize upon a growing homogeneity of demand in many areas, and a general tendency for the British public to prefer a higher quality of product in, for example, grocery retailing in terms of merchandise variety and retailing services. As was set out above in terms of aggregated Census of Distribution statistics, by 1987 a top tier of very large-scale retail organizations had begun to evolve, and by 1990 this source identified five retail businesses each with more than 1,000 outlets, and indeed an average of 1,502. These were concentrated in the Food and the Drink, Confectionery and Tobacco trades, and the corresponding result of these figures is that, for example, by the end of the 1990s in the grocery supermarket sector the three largest retail organizations (Tesco, Sainsbury and Asda) had a combined market share of 54.9 per cent, and the largest five (including also Safeway and Somerfield) had a combined share of 63.6 per cent (Retail Intelligence, 2001: 261)

Despite its inherent advantage as a multiple-shop form of retailing, the *retail Co-operative movement* in the United Kingdom has more recently experienced a significant decline in its fortunes, its share of the total retail trade having fallen from 12 per cent in 1950 to 5.1 per cent in 1991 and 4.2 per cent in 1999 (Retail Intelligence, 2001: 167–78), although the last figure suggests some recovery from the data in Table 7.3 drawn from the Census of Distribution. The distinguishing features of the UK consumer Co-operative movement are that its share capital is provided by a large number of individual consumer subscribers and that these investors are rewarded by a dividend related to their level of store purchases. During the latter part of the nineteenth century, this movement was responsible for major innovations in retailing, including the establishment of multiple branches and backward vertical integration (Birchall, 1994). Again, in the second half of the twentieth century, the Co-operative movement led the way in the development of self-service and the establishment of supermarkets in grocery retailing; and even by 1961, 42 per cent of all UK self-service outlets and 26 per cent of supermarkets were owned by the Co-operatives (Bamfield, 1987). Despite remaining one of the largest retailing organizations in the United Kingdom, the Co-operative movement has experienced relative failure, seen most obviously in data on its market share, leading the Corporate Intelligence Group in 2000 to write of how 'time is running out for the Co-operative Societies' (Retail Intelligence, 2000c: 167). The explanations for this are normally couched in terms of the Co-operative Society's loose overall management structure as a federation of some 46 retail societies (2001) despite the amalgamation of the Co-operative Wholesale Society and the Co-operative Retail Society; the remaining local influence of lay management committees; a product position in the market (including its 'dividend' policy) which is no longer widely popular with consumers; and the movement's lack of success in the convenience-store sector in which it has tried to develop (Retail Intelligence, 2001: 167–78).

Among other specific retail forms in the UK' *department stores*, which grew up in the last quarter of the nineteenth century, based upon rising standards of living among the middle classes and expenditure upon clothing, furnishings etc. in particular, have experienced a reduction in their popularity. The turning point in their expansion in fact occurred in the inter-war period; and in the postwar years consumers tended to move to more specialist popular clothing multiples such as Marks & Spencer (Davis, 1966: 293–4). In some merchandise areas such as clothing and footwear, department stores retained a market share of more than 10 per cent in the 1950s (Stacey and Wilson, 1965: 37, 41), and their overall retail market share remained at around 6 per cent until 1971. By the end of the 1980s, however, the market share of department stores was some 4.5 per cent (Mussanif, 1988: 16). Current (1999) data relating to the almost 600 department stores in the United Kingdom, including 105 owned by the Co-operative movement, suggest that their total retail market share is now around 4.1 per cent (Retail Intelligence, 2001: 179–93). Department store retailing in the United Kingdom is now largely concentrated in the hands of two groups, John Lewis and Debenhams, with respective market shares within this sector of 22.8 and 19.4 per cent (Retail Intelligence, 2001: 179–93); and despite the significance of department stores for shopping-centre developers in their role as 'anchor stores' within these developments, it seems unlikely that there will be any resurgence of the overall popularity of department stores on the part of an increasingly car-borne population of shoppers attracted to more specialist and out-of-town retailers. It should, however, be noted that some of the earlier variety-store chains such as Marks & Spencer, and also the multiple-store group Boots the Chemist, exhibit some of the merchandise range characteristics of traditional department stores, with the result that the official statistics relating to department store trading (which classify department stores within Mixed Goods Retailers, and exclude Marks & Spencer) somewhat overstate the falling away in the popularity of this form of shopping.

Also occupying a very small proportion of UK retail consumer expenditure is *mail order*, with a total retail market share in the late 1980s of little more than 3 per cent (Mussanif, 1988: 16). Within this figure, the traditional agency mail-order system accounted for about 90 per cent of sales, although it was recognized then that the direct-order system was by far the faster growing, and likely to benefit from advances in information technology. As with the Co-operative societies, traditional consumer loyalty to mail order has declined, and the 'free credit' that was once one of its main attractions is now provided by a range of deferred payment arrangements with traditional shop retailers, who also have greater flexibility in their pricing and merchandise range than conventional mail order. There has, however, been something of a resurgence of interest in this area of retailing under the heading of home shopping, described more recently as 'now the sector where virtually every UK retailer has aspirations' (Retail Intelligence, 2000b: 96). This broader heading includes agency and direct mail order, catalogue showrooms, direct selling, and electronic shopping channels, although the first two still account for 56 and 21 per cent, respectively of the total home shopping market. However, in some merchandise areas, home shopping is a fairly significant part of the total retail market (7.4 per cent in the case of non-food retailing); and although, at 3.75 per cent in 2000, the share of total retail sales accounted for by home shopping has yet to show any significant expansion, new technologies and a combination of 'bricks and clicks' may see some revival of this form of retailing in the United Kingdom (see Retail Intelligence, 2001: 286).

Finally, *retail business-format franchising* – one of the best known being Body Shop – retains a place in the United Kingdom (Stern and Stanworth, 1988: 40). Retail franchising grew particularly rapidly in the 1980s when the number of franchisees doubled within a few years (Hall and Dixon, 1988: 10), and the total turnover has continued to grow – from £900 million in 1984 to £8.9 billion in 1999 – leading to a situation in 2000 when there were 35,200 franchise outlets: an increase of 55 per cent since 1994 (see *Financial Times*, 29 June 2000). However, the most recent figures for the UK show a reduction in the total number of franchise units from 31,200 to 30,500 between 2001 and 2002. And the explanation for this is couched in terms of the usual argument that, just as economic recession tends to lead to an increase in those turning to franchising as a form of employment, the currently relatively buoyant UK economy is one where, for franchisors, 'extracting suitable candidates [franchisees] from safe jobs has been the key problem' (see *Financial Times*, 5 June 2002). Nonetheless, the popularity of this business form is likely to continue with the opportunities for self-employment that it provides.

A final characteristic of UK retailing that deserves mention here, because of the overall theme of this study rather than the scale of activity, is that of *internationalization*. With regard to inward foreign direct investment, historical data show that this has always been a limited feature of the UK retail sector, and that while there were some very obvious retailer examples, such as the US Woolworth in the variety store chain sector, this trend was in its early stages manufacturer originated, by such firms as Singer in sewing machines and Hoover in vacuum cleaners, both from the United States. It is estimated that by 1961 less than 4 per cent of UK retailing was accounted for by foreign direct investment (Godley, 2001). Over the last thirty years, however, the pattern of this inward investment has moved to being accounted for almost exclusively by internationalizing retailers rather than manufacturers, to being a feature of a larger number of organizations, including the Mister Minit franchise and Dollond & Aitchison in optician services, and to featuring clothing retailers in particular such as Benetton (Godley, 2002). There is little to suggest that the level of inward investment into

UK retailing has risen significantly, and it is certainly very modest when compared with the proportion of 31 per cent for foreign direct investment in UK manufacturing industry in 1997 (OECD data quoted in *Financial Times*, 29 March 2002). As indicated in the Introduction to this study, UK retailing has only a limited international dimension sofar as outward foreign direct investment is concerned. In the mid-1990s, only 93 UK companies had retail activities overseas, or 13 per cent of those 700 UK retail businesses having sales exceeding £3 million. Within this, of the top ten UK retailers, only four (Tesco, Sainsbury, Marks & Spencer and Kingfisher) had overseas investments, and of the next ten largest, only three had extensive networks abroad (Corporate Intelligence on Retailing, 1996). Marks & Spencer has, of course, now withdrawn from its mainland European operations and from its Brooks Brothers stores in the US; of the grocery supermarket groups, according to the published company accounts, the proportions of overseas sales for Sainsbury (2000) and Tesco (2001) are 15.6 and 8.7 per cent respectively. This leaves Kingfisher, now focused on its B&Q DIY superstores and Comet discount electrical appliances outlets, as the only UK retail group with significant foreign direct investment. Kingfisher's international investment began in 1993 with its acquisition of the French electrical retailer Darty, was added to in 1996 with the purchase of a further French group BUT with its electrical and furniture stores, was particularly extended by the acquisition of the French DIY stores group Castorama in 1998 with its operations also in Germany and Italy, and continued in the same year with the purchase of the German electrical goods chain Wegert. This strategy has created a situation where, according to the company's latest annual report, overseas sales now (2001) account for 43 per cent of Kingfisher's total, and where it may be said to have achieved in the non-food sector the significance in terms of a genuinely European presence of the quite recently combined French Carrefour and Promodès in the food sector.

Manufacturer–retailer relations in the United Kingdom

The conventional relationship between retailers and manufacturers in the United Kingdom has been that of the former being a relatively inert conduit for the passing of the latter's products to final consumers. Market initiatives and power in terms of product design and marketing, choice of distribution channel, trade terms, and indeed until the 1960s, final consumer prices traditionally lay with manufacturers, who were generally much larger and enjoyed greater market concentration than their retailer customers.

An indication of the extent to which this relationship has changed is the way in which the major fast moving consumer goods (FMCG) manufacturers now devote considerable managerial energy and financial resources to winning the battle not only for the 'mindspace' of consumers but also the 'shelfspace' of retailers (Corstjens and Corstjens, 1995: 3). This has produced a market situation for manufacturers where 'the nub of the problem ... is that in most markets retailers do not need all manufacturers to supply them', while 'adequate distribution is a necessary condition for [manufacturer] success' (Randall, 1994: 3).

Historically in the United Kingdom, as the National Board for Prices and Incomes (NBPI) pointed out in its 1971 report on food distribution, the balance of market power had lain with manufacturers (National Board for Prices and Incomes, 1971: chapter 2). However, the expansion of large retail chains which followed on the abolition of food rationing and building controls in the 1950s, and in particular, the increasingly open price competition in many retail markets, resulted in a structural transfer of power from manufacturers to retailers. This created a situation by the 1970s where even major food manufacturers found that their largest ten retail customers accounted for 30–65 per cent of total sales (Howe, 1973: 82), and where the Unilever subsidiary Birds Eye, with a frozen food market share of 47 per cent, admitted to the UK Monopolies and Mergers Commission that its trade discounts to large retailers 'were not created at the initiative of the manufacturer but were *an unavoidable response to the power of the retailer*', and that 'the discounts earned by these retailers exceeded the cost savings in supplying them' (Monopolies and Mergers Commission, 1976: paras 125–6, emphasis added). On two occasions at this time – the Monopolies and Mergers Commission in 1981, and the Office of Fair Trading in 1985 – government inquiries into this situation resulted in limited adverse comment. It was generally found that in the food-grocery market the largest retailers tended to pass on to their customers the enhanced trade terms that they enjoyed. However, the OFT report in particular highlighted the increased buying-power disadvantage of independent grocers compared with multiple-shop retailers, where the advantage of the latter rose from the 10 per cent reported in 1981 to 15.5 per cent in the latter study (Monopolies and Mergers Commission, 1981: appendix 6 para. 8; Office of Fair Trading, 1985: para. 5.15)

In addition to this quantitative evidence, more institutional and qualitative analysis of the power relationship between retailers and manufacturers suggests that the early 1980s was a particularly fraught period for manufacturer–retailer relations in the grocery field, characterized by the use of retailers' power to 'delist' even major brands over disputes regarding trade terms and retailer freedom to set (and in particular, cut) consumer prices (Davies *et al.*, 1985). Moreover, although the following decade was characterized by the development of longer term, more 'relational' negotiations and contracts between manufacturers and their retailer customers, it was noted that there was at the same time a trend for 'major retailers to demand, and get, increased services from manufacturers' (Hogarth-Scott and Parkinson, 1993: 12). This was a period when there was continuous pressure by retailers upon manufacturers for merchandise quality improvements and product innovation (Bowlby and Foord, 1995), and a situation where, as one senior retailer put it, 'We all want partnership as long as it is on our own terms … We have the power to dictate the agenda' (Ogbonna and Wilkinson, 1996: 408).

This changed relationship between retailers and their manufacturer suppliers has come about not simply as a result of the largest retailers taking advantage of disparities in structural market power, the advantage of the latter in the use of information technology or their closeness to the final consumer but also because of trend towards retailers seeing themselves as a brand in their own right (Dawson and Shaw, 1989). This has led to a distinction between the more traditional 'own-label' product which is a product-by-product individual retailer version of a national brand, normally positioned on a price basis, and the 'own brand' which is more frequently a range of merchandise unique to the individual retailer. It is in the latter case where 'the quality of the products and the trust created in the retailer brand came to be perceived as a differential advantage for the store itself. *The brand was making shoppers loyal to the store*' (Corstjens and Corstjens, 1995: 144, original emphasis). One result of this is that the United Kingdom has the highest level of own-brand sales in Europe, ranging from 100 per cent in the unique case of Marks & Spencer, through almost 60 per cent in respect of Sainsbury, to around 40 per cent at Tesco (Davies and Brooks, 1989: 41; McGoldrick, 1990: 342), and in areas such as chilled ready meals, retailer own-brand products account for 90 per cent of the market (Samways, 1995: 15, 66).

A natural extension of the own-brand relationship between retailers and their suppliers, and the 'relational contracting' commented upon above is the increased involvement by retailers themselves in product development. As one author put it, 'procurement of own label products is a powerful method of initiating [product] innovation' (Senker, 1988: 133). Another study noted the contrast in emphasis between manufacturers and retailers, concluding that 'manufacturers are concerned with production costs, [etc.] ... Retailers expressed their concern in marketing terms ... [and] felt that food manufacturers are out of touch with consumer demand which shapes the food market' (Omar, 1995: 13). Marks & Spencer, not surprisingly, provides a number of early examples in this respect (Rees, 1969: 176); but in many newer areas such as convenience foods, the product innovation has come from retailers rather than traditional food processors.

Finally, in terms of retailer–manufacturer relations, while traditional vertical integration of manufacturing and retailing within retail-dominated organizations such as Burton, the men's outfitters, has largely disappeared (Sigsworth, 1990: postscript), more sophisticated trade arrangements, which nonetheless provide retailers with the advantages of such integration without the capital investment and fixed offtake, have grown, based upon the retailers' dominance in such arrangements (Blois, 1972). Marks & Spencer has long been referred to as the 'manufacturer without factories': enjoying what an earlier chairman referred to as 'mutually beneficial relationships – virtually partnerships' with its suppliers (Sieff, 1990: 125). And in a range of its supplier relationships, Tesco, the market leader in the grocery supermarket field, has built up a similar position. In fresh foods, Tesco's sophisticated relationships with farmers led a representative of these in the mid-1990s to complain, however, that 'The power brokers in the modern food economy are the distributors. It isn't a market economy any more, it's a hypermarket economy' (*Financial Times*, 16 November 1995); and more recently, the UK 'Farmers for Action' lobby group has been disrupting food supplies to Tesco by picketing the company's regional distribution depots in protest at inadequate prices being paid to farmers (see *Financial Times*, 9 January 2002). Since beginning to sell petrol in the 1970s through forecourt outlets adjacent to its major superstores, Tesco has increased the degree of vertical integration in its buying arrangements, and has benefited considerably from this in the prices paid to its major oil company suppliers (Pretious, 1995). Similarly, while physical distribution management of products was once very much under the control of manufacturers, UK retailers are now regarded as being 'at the forefront of fostering partnerships with professional distribution companies' (Fernie, 1995a: 144). In grocery distribution, for example, the major multiple retailers channel almost 90 per cent of their products through retailer-controlled distribution arrangements, and they are able to use their buying power to ensure high performance levels and competitive prices from those 'third-party' companies seeking contracts from retailers for warehouse and transport services (Fernie, 1994).

The UK economy is thus characterized by many unique relations between retailers and their manufacturing suppliers. The 'balance of power' in this relationship has changed significantly in the past four decades in favour of the largest retailers, and this trend has been highlighted particularly in the grocery supermarket field. The largest supermarket operators have been able to take advantage of their structural market power, the use of information technology, and generally increasingly sophisticated management to achieve considerable cost savings not just in traditional merchandise purchases but, as we have seen, in newer areas such as fresh produce and petrol, as well as in the area of retailer-dominated physical distribution management. It is, however, debatable whether the development of such retailer–manufacturer relations is beneficial for consumers, and the following section on competition policy within the broader consideration of the influence of government on UK retailing returns to this issue.

UK government policy and retailing

In one form or another the government exerts considerable influence over a number of aspects of retailing in the United Kingdom. The broadest way in which to understand this is to put it in the context of consumer protection. This can be interpreted as a vast range of government action designed to ensure that the final consumer is best served and protected in a whole range of final consumption activities (see Swann, 1979; Smith and Swann, 1979). As a particular example only, shop opening hours are regulated in ways that have implications for both retailing competition and consumer service (Davidson and Ervine, 1992). In this respect the UK retailing environment is particularly liberal, and since 1994 there have been few restrictions on shop opening hours. Across the United Kingdom there is now an increasing incidence of 24-hour grocery supermarket opening in addition to the widespread availability of smaller scale 'convenience stores', and Sunday trading is also both widespread and popular with shoppers (UK Home Department, 1993).

Beyond this, the two principal areas of government intervention in retailing in the United Kingdom – other than an earlier short-lived essentially *ad hoc* attempt through the tax system at increasing service-sector labour efficiency (Reddaway, 1970) – are competition policy and land-use planning regulations. These are dealt with in the following two sub-sections.

UK competition policy and retailing

While there is a lengthy history of government action on monopolies and restrictive trade practices, including individual government reports and case law, the legislation as it stands today stems from the 1948 Monopolies and Restrictive Practices (Inquiry and Control) Act and the 1956 Restrictive Trade Practices Act, and was importantly developed through the 1964 Resale Prices Act and the 1965 Monopolies and Mergers Act (Wilberforce *et al.*, 1965). By the last quarter of the twentieth century, UK competition-policy legislation was covered by four acts: the 1973 Fair Trading Act dealing with mergers and the abuse of monopoly power, the 1976 Resale Prices Act relating to resale prices maintenance, the 1976 Restrictive Trade Practices Act covering restrictive trading agreements, and the 1980 Competition Act dealing with anti-competitive practices (Clarke *et al.*, 1998; chapter 2; Utton, 2000). Some of this legislation had specifically stemmed from general reports by the Monopolies Commission immediately prior to this period (see Monopolies Commission, 1969, 1970 and 1973b). Over this period, the UK approach to dealing with competition and restrictive business practices moved from a 'major reconnaissance of the field' under the Monopolies Commission over the period 1948–1956, through a 'predominantly legalistic approach' by the Restrictive Practices Court 1956–1973, and on to the 'development of an administrative and discretionary procedure' culminating in the 1980 Competition Act. This procedure in turn evolved from an overwhelming concern with the 'form' of restrictive trading agreements or market structures to the 'effects-based' approach derived from the Treaty of Rome and enshrined in the 1998 Competition Act discussed below (see O'Brien, 1982).

There is a considerable literature on UK competition policy theory – some of it stemming from the earlier legislation in this area (e.g. see Department of Prices and Consumer Protection, 1978, 1979; Fulop, 1964a; National Economic Development Office, 1978; Swann *et al.*, 1974) as well as more recently published material to which reference is made below. The purpose of this literature has generally been to set out the traditional economic case in favour of competitiveness in markets as best serving the interests of consumers. However, UK legislation and procedures in this area are characterized by a strain of pragmatism in judging the outcome of uncompetitive market structures or particular forms of anti-competitive behaviour on their merits rather than taking the *per se* approach of US legislation in this field, which assumes, for example, that certain market structures are in themselves detrimental to the interests of consumers (see Monopolies and Mergers Commission, 1981: appendix 2).

The UK Conservative government of the 1980s published a number of consultation papers in the areas of restrictive trade practices and market power which considered moving towards an 'effects based' prohibition of trading agreements, including vertical agreements (Department of Trade and Industry, 1988, 1989, 1992). And in the light of considerable criticism of government policy and procedures of the 1980s in this area (see Hay, 1993), these consultation documents were followed by legislative proposals (see Department of Trade and Industry, 1996a, b), and by a draft parliamentary bill under the succeeding Labour government (Department of Trade and Industry, 1997) which proposed dealing with such matters on a clear effects-based, prohibition approach modelled upon Articles 85 and 86 of The Treaty of Rome. The result of this was the 1998 Competition Act which basically prohibits both anti-competitive agreements and the abuse of dominant market positions (Office of Fair Trading, 1999).

Not content with this significant step forward in its competition-policy legislation, the UK government has recently published a further consultation document in this field (Department of Trade and Industry, 2001). Its latest intention is 'to make enterprise and productivity the cornerstone of the Government's economic reforms (Foreword) and in this context 'to build a world-class competition regime for the UK' (para. 1.9). The government sees this as being achieved by the competition authorities (principally the Office of Fair Trading and the Competition Commission) being the supreme advocate of competition in advising the government on the impact of current legislation and by proactively promoting competition in the economy. In future, the principal reference test by which the OFT will decide whether or not to investigate a market or a particular merger will be whether it 'believes (or has reasonable suspicion) that a market may operate in a manner which adversely affects competition' (para. 6.15). In particular, the recently published parliamentary bill that followed from this consultation document borrows heavily from the US anti-trust model. It provides for the criminalization of cartels, including prison sentences for those who operate them; third-party damages claims are available for those, including consumer groups, who are adversely affected by anti-competitive conduct on the part of companies; a competition-based test is to be applied by the authorities for takeover and merger decisions, and the final decision in this area is to be removed from government ministers; and broader market investigation powers are to be made available to the OFT, including a facility for designated consumer groups to make complaints to the Office (see *Financial Times*, 1 April 2002).

So far as retailing is concerned, UK legislation prior to the 1998 Competition Act essentially gave the government powers to investigate trading practices with a view to coming to a conclusion on their impact upon consumers, and to investigate 'monopoly' situations, defined broadly as where a company had 25 per cent or greater share of its market. The 1964 Resale Prices Act provided to all intents and purposes for the ending of the practice of resale price maintenance on the part of individual manufacturers, although this practice was allowed to continue in the case of books until 1995 (see *Financial Times*, 27 September 1995), and continued until recently to operate in the case of household medicines (Howe, 1973).

Until the passing of the 1998 Competition Act, the major impact of UK competition-policy legislation has been its contribution to the virtual ending of resale price maintenance, associated reports on related manufacturer practices under the headings of *Recommended Resale Prices* and *Refusal to Supply* (Monopolies Commission, 1969, 1970), and general inquiries into manufacturer–retailer relations. There have been few 'merger' reports that have prevented retailers from pursuing this route to corporate expansion.

Thus, although resale price maintenance in the grocery trade had very largely broken down by the end of the 1960s, well ahead of the 1964 Resale Prices Act (Pickering, 1966: 121), the Act itself played a direct role in the ending of the practice in confectionery and footwear, through hearings in the Restrictive Practices Court, and in influencing the voluntary abandonment of the practice by manufacturers in a range of other trades including domestic electrical appliances, cigarettes and tobacco, and gramophone records. Only in two cases did the Court uphold the manufacturers' case for the retention of this practice: books and household medicines. The Net Book Agreement, embodying the practice of resale price maintenance, was abandoned by the Publishers' Association in September 1995, and was finally declared illegal in 1997 (Utton, 2000: 273). With regard to household medicines, the original Restrictive Practices Court decision of 1971 upholding the practice of r.p.m. in this area remained in force until quite recently, although it was periodically flouted by one or two of the major grocery supermarket chains. However, the matter was again brought before the Restrictive Practices Court late in 2000 (*Financial Times*, 19 October 2000), and, despite arguments for the retention of the system of r.p.m. by both drug manufacturers and small-scale pharmacists under the umbrella body of the Community Pharmacy Action Group, the practice was outlawed by the Restrictive Practices Court in May 2001. Not surprisingly, this decision was greeted with a round of price cutting in this trade by the leading UK supermarket groups, and was accompanied by worries regarding the longer term outcome of the decision on behalf of small-scale independent pharmacy outlets (*Financial Times*, 16 and 17 May 2001). While it is too early to indicate the impact that this final ending of r.p.m. in the United Kingdom will have, it clearly leaves the United Kingdom without any restrictive provisions in this respect.

With regard to the impact upon consumers of the balance of power between manufacturers and retailers, although the UK government's National Board for Prices and Incomes noted in 1970 in the case of supermarket distribution of bread that 'It is not self-evidence that the growth of the big retailers is at present helping to keep down the price of bread' (NBPI, 1970: para. 67), its more general conclusion at this time was that 'We do not consider that at the present time the power of the multiple grocers operates to the disadvantage of the consumer' (NBPI, 1971: para. 267). Indeed in its 1973 report on breakfast cereals, the government's Monopolies and Mergers Commission was happy to note that the market power of the largest grocery supermarket chains was instrumental, through the growth of their own-label sales, in modifying the impact of the structural market power of the brand leader Kellogg (Monopolies Commission, 1973a: para. 97). Such a beneficent, or at least *laissez faire*, view of the influence of large-scale retailers continued into the 1980s, with the Commission responding to manufacturer concerns regarding the balance of their trading relationship with the largest grocery retailers with the view that 'Concessions made by a manufacturer to strong buyers may be said to be economically justified in the sense that, if they were not, the manufacturer would not have made them (Monopolies and Mergers Commission, 1981: para. 6.18). And the Office of Fair Trading, in following up this general inquiry by the Commission, reached the conclusion that 'despite some further increase in concentration in grocery retailing ... competition in this sector is evidently still very strong and in general lower buying prices [on the part of the largest retailers] are being passed on to the benefit of consumers' (Office of Fair Trading, 1985: para. 7.3).

The most recent investigation by the UK authorities into this area – the inquiry by the retitled Competition Commission, and published in three volumes after an estimated cost to the Commission of £3.7 million – was widely regarded as anodyne (Competition Commission, 2000; *Financial Times*, 11 October 2000). This reference to the Commission had been stimulated by the existence of significant apparent disparities between grocery supermarket prices in the United Kingdom on the one hand and those in other EU countries and the United States on the other, together with concerns regarding considerable differences between 'farmgate' food prices and those faced by consumers in UK supermarkets. But while the Commission was satisfied that 'the industry is currently broadly competitive and that, overall, excessive prices are not being charged, nor excessive profits earned' (para. 1.13), its report conveyed evidence regarding the policies and practices of the giant supermarket chains, where the largest four firms had a combined market share of more than 70 per cent, in regard to their pricing and purchasing that cannot have been reassuring to more questioning members of the public. The Commission found in particular that most of the large supermarket groups sold frequently purchased items at below cost, that they used regional 'price flexing' to maintain prices at uncompetitive levels where regional monopolies existed, and that in the majority of their product areas these supermarket groups practised little price competition. With regard to suppliers, the Commission encountered 'a climate of apprehension' among many of them in their relations with their major supermarket customers, and found that this related, for example, to non-cost-related payments or discounts being requested by these customers. The Commission was particularly concerned that such practices 'give the major buyers substantial advantages over other smaller retailers, whose competitiveness is likely to suffer as a result' (para. 1.11). The Commission's principal recommendations were that the major supermarket groups should enter into a voluntary Code of Practice covering their relations with suppliers, and that, with regard to individual-store developments, there should be some control over new store building or acquisition by the top five firms in this sector. The current situation, early in 2002 (see *Financial Times*, 27 and 28 August 2001) is that a code of practice has been drafted, but is regarded by representatives of both the farming community and by suppliers of leading branded goods as having been watered down from an original proposal, and 'worse than useless'.

It is interesting to note in the context of the UK competition policy authorities' generally relaxed approach to the structural market power of the largest distributors, particularly in the food/grocery trades, that the Monopolies Commission has twice supported manufacturers in adopting selective distribution arrangements. Such arrangements strengthen the hand of manufacturers in their relations with retailers, and may generally support the continued role of smaller, more specialist retailers. In the case of the range of exclusive perfumes etc. known as 'fine fragrances', where the manufacturers operated a system of selective distribution which prevented Tesco together with Superdrug and other cut-price distributors from obtaining normal supplies, the Monopolies and Mergers Commission, while appearing clearly to identify a number of uncompetitive results of this system, concluded that it did not operate against the public interest. In this case the Commission's decision did have the effect of offering some protection to smaller scale retailers, although this report has been subject to criticism that the Commission did not sufficiently recognize the adverse impact of the practice of a selective distribution system in a market that was highly concentrated in respect of both suppliers and distributors (see Monopolies and Mergers Commission, 1993b, paras 8.65 and 8.186; and Utton, 1996).

The Commission has twice investigated distributive arrangements in the wrapped impulse ice-cream market. In its earlier report, the Monopolies and Mergers Commission concluded that the exclusive outlet policy of the two brand leaders (each of which enjoyed a market share of 45 per cent), which prevented any individual retail outlet from selling other than one brand of ice cream, and a similar wholesale distribution policy, should both cease. The Commission did not, however, make any recommendations against the practice of freezer exclusivity: arrangements under which each of the major suppliers provided smaller retailers with freezers for the exclusive use of their own product (Monopolies and Mergers Commission, 1979: chapter 10). This matter of freezer exclusivity was returned to by the Commission in 1994. By then the Commission was able to note that, without practising freezer exclusivity, Mars had entered the market and built up its market share from less than 1 per cent in 1989 to 14 per cent in 1993. By this last year the market leader, the Unilever subsidiary Birds Eye Walls, had built up its market share to almost two-thirds, while the market share of Lyons Maid (acquired in 1992 by Nestlé) had fallen to 11 per cent (Monopolies and Mergers Commission, 1994a: paras 3.24–3.25 and 3.35). Given such competitive shifts in manufacturer market shares, the fact that many retailers had more than one freezer in their shops, and that consumers could easily choose among a number of retail outlets, together with evidence on consumer prices, product development and manufacturer profitability, the Commission concluded that freezer exclusivity as currently practised did not operate against the public interest (para. 9.55).

On the other hand, the Commission expressed reservations regarding the element of selective distribution created by government regulations in respect of contact lens solutions. In this sector there was a bilateral oligopoly of two manufacturers each having some 35 per cent of the market, and one pharmaceutical distributor alone (Boots) which had 31 per cent of the retail market. In this case, the Monopolies and Mergers Commission in 1993 criticized the Government control over the introduction of new products in this area, which it felt had restricted competitive manufacturer entry into the market. The Commission equally recognized that the restriction on retailer supply had inhibited competition at this level, resulting in the monopoly retailer earning significant profits; and in this case it recommended that all retailers should be free to sell contact lens solutions provided they met relevant quality criteria (Monopolies and Mergers Commission, 1993a: chapter 8).

Further cases in which the Monopolies and Mergers Commission considered links between manufacturers and retailers were recorded music and domestic electrical goods. In the former case, the Commission encountered a situation of market dominance or 'monopoly' at both the manufacturer and retailer level, and a market in which, on the basis of international comparisons, UK consumers appeared to be paying excessive prices, particularly in the case of compact discs. However, the Commission found that the structure of bilateral oligopoly in this market had produced considerable competition, and that it did not distort competition (Monopolies and Mergers Commission, 1994b: paras 2.182–2.187). In the case of domestic electrical goods, however, with a market structure not dissimilar to that of recorded music, the Commission judged that the system of largely observed recommended retail prices and of selective distribution operated against the public interest. It was therefore recommended that the former practice be abandoned, and that the system of selective distribution be relaxed to allow, for example, warehouse clubs to distribute these goods (Monopolies and Mergers Commission, 1997). As an example, in the case of VCRs, the Commission believed that 'in the absence of RRPs, price discounters would be both more common and bolder in promoting their offers, so that consumers would be better informed about prices', and in particular that 'supplying warehouse clubs will reinforce action against RRPs by bringing into the market more retailers who are keen to compete on price and therefore not interested in pricing their goods at or close to prices indicated or preferred by suppliers' (Monopolies and Mergers Commission, 1997: 1, vol. I, paras 3.392, 3.439).

Generally the UK competition authorities have seen few possible detriments arising from proposed horizontal mergers in the retail sector. Such mergers among smaller scale food retailers in the early 1980s were not prevented, although the Monopolies and Mergers Commission had clearly received evidence from certain food manufacturers expressing concern at the general trend towards increased buying power on the part of the largest food distributors, where 'the increased concentration of retail buying power would lead to more pressure for better [trade purchase] terms unrelated to [manufacturer] cost savings' (Monopolies and Mergers Commission, 1983: para. 6.29). In grocery wholesaling too the Commission had few reservations in agreeing to the proposed merger in 1985 between the existing second and third largest grocery cash-and-carry operators (one of which also had a large chain of supermarkets), giving them a combined market share of 21 per cent (Monopolies and Mergers Commission, 1985: chapter 8). The Commission did, however, recommend against the proposed 1990 merger of Kingfisher plc and Dixons plc, where a combined market share of 26 per cent would have resulted in the retailing of consumer electrical goods by bringing together the market shares of the market leader and the second largest retailer. Here the Commission was concerned principally about the direct reduction in competition between the two existing rivals that would have followed the merger, and the anticipated rise in prices for retail consumers. Nonetheless, evidence was also presented to the Commission by manufacturers suggesting that they might be disadvantaged in their negotiations with a combined retailer having such significant market power. As in the case of food retailer buying power, it was alleged that 'This would be difficult to resist given that the merged company would be able to turn to other manufacturers for its supplies', and that 'As the suppliers' [ie. manufacturers'] own margins were small, any improvement in the terms given to the merged company would have to be at the expense of the benefits now given to the smaller retail chains and the independents' (Monopolies and Mergers Commission, 1990: para. 4.8).

General conclusions regarding this area of UK government intervention in the retail sector are offered in the final section of this chapter.

Government land-use policy and retailing

The second area of UK government policy that affects retailing falls under the heading of land-use planning, which in Britain is embodied in successive Town and Country Planning Acts and is implemented by local government authorities (Guy, 1994: chapter 5). This is an area of government involvement in UK retailing which is responding to quite rapid changes in retail developments themselves – principally the movement of a number of retail sectors to 'out-of-town' or 'off-centre' locations – and where government control itself has accelerated over the past two decades. Thus, for example, while over the period 1971–1981 some 90 per cent of new retailing space in the UK was accounted for by 'in-town' developments, during the years 1987–1992 this proportion had fallen to less than 40 per cent (Department of the Environment, 1994: para. 2.35). The outcome of this was that between 1980 and 1990 the proportion of retail turnover accounted for by out-of-town stores rose from 13 to 38 per cent in the case of groceries, from 17 to 60 per cent in DIY, and from 4 to 26 per cent for Furniture and Carpets (Monopolies and Mergers Commission, 1990: para. 3.4). Data relating broadly to the mid-1990s show that 28.7 per cent of UK consumer retail expenditure is made in off-centre stores, that 41 per cent of food purchases are accounted for by superstores, and that 39 per cent of DIY purchases are made in retail warehouses (see Guy, 1998: 963).

Identifying grocery superstores as the archetypal out-of-town development in that sector, the UK Department of the Environment, Transport and the Regions (DETR) noted in 1998 that the proportion of grocery floorspace accounted for by such outlets had risen from 24.0 per cent in 1987 to 39.2 per cent in 1996, and that their proportion of sales had risen over this period from 29.9 to 53.7 per cent (DETR, 1998: 19–20). However, the fluidity of this situation is also recognized in the same report, which highlighted that 'the significant pressure from foodstore operators to increase their market share means that smaller centres [of population] have increasingly become the focus for new store development' (DETR, 1998: 7). Figures from the Oxford Institute of Retail Management (OXIRM), for example, show that while there were 23 food superstore (over 25,000 sq. ft. net) openings in 1983, rising fairly steadily to 90 in 1989, this figure declined almost equally steadily to 50 in 1993 (presented in Howard, 1995: 223).

The usual way in which to characterize shopping-centre developments is to envisage a size hierarchy, ranging from regional shopping centres (30,000 sq. m.+) through intermediate centres (10,000–30,000 sq. m.) to retail parks of 5,000–20,000 sq. m. This hierarchy also includes individual superstores with at least 2,500 sq. m. gross retail area and speciality centres or arcades having 1,000 sq. m.+ of space (Reynolds, 1992: 57). Three further particular spacial phenomena in UK retailing are retail 'warehouse' parks comprising at least three large-scale retail establishments, each being single-level stores specializing in household goods; factory retail outlets, some of which may be grouped together in edge-of-town locations; and individual warehouse clubs in out-of-town locations featuring reduced-price quality goods sold in unsophisticated buildings ('sheds') with significant car parking provision and extending to 15,000 sq. m.

Any discussion of retail land-use planning in the United Kingdom has to be set in the context of the various 'waves' of retail decentralization that occurred in particular over the last two decades of the twentieth century. The first of these took place from the beginning of the 1980s. It saw significant out-of-town developments in the grocery supermarket sector, but is now slowing down. The second wave occurred over a much shorter time period essentially between 1987 and 1990, and saw the emigration to out-of-town locations of 'bulky goods' comparison shopping in the form of DIY and electrical goods retail warehouses and their associated 'parks'. The third wave is often dated from the announcement by Marks & Spencer in 1984 that it would seek out-of-town locations as well as its traditional position in the High Street for further expansion. This was anticipated to herald the development of out-of-town comparison shopping in categories beyond those included in the 'second wave' and to presage the significant development of regional shopping centres. In fact, as Fernie emphasizes, this movement never took place on the forecast scale, and, for example, of the 748 UK shopping-centre completions between 1965 and 1992, only 66 were out of town (see Fernie, 1995b: 4). Nonetheless, Fernie analyses a fourth wave of out-of-town retailing commencing in 1993 and comprising a miscellaneous group of more specialist decentralized retail formats including warehouse clubs, factory shopping outlets and airport retailing, to which one could add motorway and other petrol forecourt shopping (Fernie, 1998). The first two of Fernie's examples are essentially US imports, while the factory shopping outlets and airport retailing may be differentiated from warehouse clubs as being relatively 'up-market', although there is some evidence that factory outlet centres are increasing their popularity – with a current (2000) total of 29 sites and space expanding currently at about 25 per cent per annum – on the basis of 'value retailing' (Retail Intelligence, 2000a: 93–134). Of the four fourth-wave decentralized retail formats, the US imports of warehouse clubs and factory shops appear to have enjoyed only limited success overall in the United Kingdom, owing perhaps to their clash with some aspects of British shopping culture and also difficulties of securing land-use planning permission. On the other hand, airport shopping (despite the more recent abolition of the privileges of EU duty-free shopping) and non-fuel petrol forecourt sales have become an established feature of British retailing.

In origin, the UK system of land-use planning as its relates to retailing was designed to regulate the use of land in this context for the benefit of the public. The system is generally seen as regulatory, or even negative, rather than developmental. It is based in the first instance upon the need for retailers to gain local-authority planning permission for developments extending over initial construction, redevelopment and change of use. On the other hand, compared with other EU countries, the UK planning system is less prescriptive and allows more discretion to local authorities (Howard, 1995: 226). Within this planning legislation local authorities are also required to produce 'development plans' – originally Structure Plans for larger areas and Local Plans at the city or town level – relating to structural and economic development and associated land use; and the 1947 Town and Country Planning Act clearly places decisions on 'permission to develop' in the context of overall local structure and economic development plans. In this respect, however, Guy's view (1994: 67) is that the British system of land-use planning is more flexible than those in the remainder of Europe because there is no strict requirement for proposed retail developments to fit precisely within an existing local authority land-use plan; because local authorities can, on the other hand, refuse a retailer planning permission on grounds that fall outwith their existing development plan considerations; and because central government can issue 'advice' to local authorities regarding land-use development (in the form of Planning Policy Guidance Notes or National Planning Guidelines) which local authorities must regard as a 'material consideration' in arriving at their decisions in this area. There is even a recognized element of bargaining with regard to land-use development between retail developers and local authority planners, referred to as 'planning gain'. Here a retail developer may, in return for permission to undertake a development which in itself is marginally unacceptable to the local authority, create some additional facility which is of general benefit to the local authority in its structure plan. This last situation, as expressed by Guy (1994: 70), 'is thought by many to represent a "price" which developers often have to pay in return for obtaining planning permission'. The result of this, again according to Guy (1994: 69), is that 'planners often find approved development plan policies of little relevance when considering applications for planning permission'.

From the perspective of local-authority land-use planners, their intervention in retail-related planning may be justified in a wider context of planning for population growth, at a broader but retail-related level to ensure adequate provision of retail services, and at a 'micro' level to ensure that individual retail developments are properly controlled in relation to 'external' benefits such as providing an incentive for further additional retail investment and the employment-generating benefits of this, or disbenefits such as increased traffic flow. A particular issue under this last heading is the consideration by local-authority planners of the impact of, say, a new supermarket upon existing food retailers – both supermarkets and traditional small-scale retailers likely to be affected. Thus, local-authority planners are involved in decisions regarding retail competition and consumer welfare. The conclusions of these planners are reached in the context of the 'model' of a hierarchy of shopping areas classified in terms of their physical size and relationship to shopping catchment areas, and the need for planners to ensure adequate retail floorspace, to plan for specific new retail developments such as shopping centres, to react to requests for new retail areas altogether (such as out-of-town shopping centres), correspondingly to 'protect' existing city-centre shopping, and generally to control the pace of retail development.

Although the impact of the government in retail planning is essentially felt at the local level, UK national or central government also exerts some influence on issues of retail planning. Indeed, in terms of guidance and standardization in this area, Guy describes the UK system of land-use planning as it affects retail development as 'probably the most centralised' among European economies (Guy, 1998: 967). This influence of central government arises from two sources. First, there is the right of planning applicants such as retail developers to appeal to the higher authority (the Secretary of State) in cases where planning permission has been refused at the local-authority level. To this extent, a number of major retail planning decisions are finally made at a level above that of the local authorities, and Guy points out that, particularly in England from about 1993 onwards, central government increasingly 'called in' planning applications for its own more restrictive consideration rather than leaving such decisions to be made at the local-authority level. This led to a success rate for proposals for new food superstore developments of under 30 per cent in some years during this period, compared with over 50 per cent for most of the 1980s (see Guy, 1998: 972). The second source of national government influence is the consideration of planning-related matters by the relevant government department and the issuing by the national government of Planning Policy Guidance (PPG) Notes, Circulars and Statutory Instruments and Regulations. The various editions of the PPG6 relating to retail developments have been an important embodiment of thinking in this area at the national level, and this is discussed below. The UK Department of the Environment had, for example, since the early 1990s begun to express some concern regarding the impact of out-of-town retail developments (see, for example, Department of the Environment, 1992, 1994). However, with regard to public policy, by the middle of that decade the UK government was, at least in the view of the House of Commons Environment Committee, further moved to 'take a critical view of retail trends and retail planning policies'; arguing that while 'there is much to welcome in the government's new, more cautious, stance on retail development, ... there is also much to rue [i.e. regret] in the *laissez faire* approach to such development over the last decade', and that 'a much more subtle and refined approach to retail development is required' (House of Commons Environment Committee, 1994: paras 3–5). In this report, the Committee particularly expressed its belief that 'there is a need for a firmer national policy framework on out-of-town retail parks' (para. 76).

It is particularly important to see the UK system of land-use planning as having been developed in the last two decades of the twentieth century in the context of studies which showed, for example, that out/edge-of-town large foodstore developments could have a significant effect upon both numbers and market shares of town-centre convenience-shopping outlets. Furthermore, because these large out-of-town retailers increasingly stocked comparison goods and also provided services such as dry cleaning, pharmacy and post-office facilities, such comparison-goods and service providers in city-centre locations also faced a loss of business. It was noted by the mid-1990s, for example, that only one-third, 22 and 8 per cent of fishmonger, butchery and traditional bakery products respectively were in fact sold through specialist retail outlets (quoted in Burke and Shackleton, 1996: 69). The UK House of Commons Environment Committee has also more recently expressed some concern that either the major grocery supermarket groups themselves or both more specifically the UK competition-policy authorities and rather more generally the current Government might wish to see some relaxation of current land-use planning legislation as a means, from their particular perspectives, of increasing competitiveness in this market by maintaining a high degree of locational competition (House of Commons Environment, Transport and Regional Affairs Committee, 1999). Certainly, the recent Competition Commission report on the grocery supermarket sector identified the application of land-use planning controls as being a dimension of the structuring of competition in this sector. That is, the Commission considered that there might be cases where, in order to introduce further local competition into a particular grocery supermarket area, planning permission for a new supermarket/superstore might have to be given where it might otherwise have been withheld on environmental grounds (Competition Commission, 2000: vol. 1 paras 2.174–2.177 and 2.598–2.618).

The most significant of the UK government's Planning Policy Guidance Notes are PPG6 and PPG13. PPG6 was originally issued in January 1988 under the title 'Major Retail Development'. A revised version was published in July 1993 under the slightly more explicit title 'Town Centres and Retail Development', and included the 'sequential test', encouraging local planning authorities to permit new out-of-town retail developments only where it was not feasible to create these in town-centre or edge-of-town locations (House of Commons Environment Committee, 1997: paras 3–21). The most recent revision of PPG6 occurred in June 1996. The original emphasis in PPG6 was a 'rebalancing of priorities which recognise the importance of town centres: economically, socially and environmentally', with the first revised version placing increased emphasis upon the role of town centres and sustaining their 'vitality and viability' (quoted in House of Commons Environment Committee, 1994: para. 20). The related PPG13, published in March 1994, deals particularly with shopping centre provision and transport, seeking to effect some control over out-of-town retail developments that would increase further reliance upon private cars for shopping.

Opinions vary somewhat as to the impact of local-authority land-use development planning upon retailer development in the UK, particularly with regard to recent retail-location developments and the emergence of large-scale retail organizations in the grocery supermarket, DIY and furniture/household appliances sectors. On the one hand, and over the longer term, it has been argued (Guy, 1994: 71) that 'the course of retail development in Britain since the 1940s has been massively influenced by the land use planning system'. Taking a much more neutral view of more recent developments, Howard, also writing in the mid-1990s, accepted that 'Retail planning has not led many of these alterations [in the commercial landscape]; often it has tried to respond belatedly' (Howard, 1995: 217). At the other extreme from Guy, Wrigley (1994: 18) contends that, as in respect of government competition policy, land-use planning legislation has in more recent decades facilitated the growth of large-scale retailer organizations. Indeed, agreeing with Howard, Wrigley suggests that such legislation in the United Kingdom has accommodated to or reflected rather than controlled the location strategies of these retailers, particularly with regard to the balance between out-of-town and city-centre retail developments. More recently, the same author (1998: 158) has even argued that 'tightened land-use planning regulation ... [has] been annexed as a weapon of [food retailer] corporate strategy; and certainly from their institutional and procedural analysis of UK land-use planning policy and the grocery retail sector Pal *et al.* were able to conclude that retailers were not passive recipients within the system of land-use planning legislation. Rather, both individually and through collective institutions, retailers took full advantage of the consultation process involved in the framing of such legislation. They were active members of a 'policy community', through which they were able to have 'a prominent role in the consultation process for retail planning policy ... [and] a favourable position in the representation ... process' (Pal *et al.*, 2001: 243–4). This matter is returned to in a later part of the Conclusions below.

Conclusions

The United Kingdom has never attempted to recover from the otherwise supposedly pejorative references to it as 'a nation of shopkeepers': an expression variously attributed to Adam Smith, the founder of classical economics, and to the Emperor Napoleon Bonaparte (Smith, 1776: vol. II, book IV, chapter VII; Oxford Dictionary of Quotations, 1992: 490).

An experienced writer of the immediate postwar period was able to observe that, after the 'straightjacket' of rationing, building restrictions and financial controls from 1939 to 1952, 'fundamental changes in the techniques and structure of British retailing are creating a more streamlined, professional and specialist form of distribution' (Fulop, 1964b: 63); and some 25 years after Fulop's assessment, a contemporary analysis concluded that 'retailing is now virtually a paradigm of the "enterprise culture"' (Bamfield, 1988: 15). Even more recently the view on the part of some writers is that 'UK retailing is a success story, with rapidly-growing productivity, considerable technical and organisational innovation and a wide range of choice available to consumers. ... [it] appears as one of our most inventive and exciting industries' (Burke and Shackleton, 1996: 11).

As we shall see in the final chapter of this study, judging the extent of competitiveness in a market is fine art. Neither the underlying economic theory nor observable market structures nor data on, for example, company profitability provide unequivocal evidence regarding consumer welfare. Within these limitations, British consumers do appear to be well served by the retail sector. Doubts, however, must remain as to how much of this consumer satisfaction is due to the UK government's involvement in the sector. Obviously, much earlier legislation regarding manufacturer resale price maintenance and refusal to supply, and curbs on retailer loss-leader selling have a clear impact upon competition. Likewise, the application of merger legislation to affect the competitive structure of retail (and manufacturer) markets is important, although as we have seen, this has experienced relatively little use. The work of the UK competition authorities in carrying out investigations of general issues, such as 'price discrimination' by manufacturers or the wider behaviour of retailers in the grocery supermarket sector, has undoubtedly had some effect in keeping the issue of the need for competitiveness in this market at the forefront of consideration. Similarly, the investigation of particular markets where there are 'monopolies' of one kind of another has focused attention either on specific market behaviours or firms, although one suspects that individual reports of the Monopolies and Mergers/Competition Commission are more read by academics than any other group. Arguably, however, such reports over the last two or three decades of the twentieth century paved the way for the reorientation of UK competition policy in the 1990s culminating in the 1998 Competition Act, the bringing of this aspect of UK legislation into line with the remainder of the European Union, and the currently proposed further developments in this area.

Nonetheless, some authors have identified a less than healthy relationship between the UK government and its competition-policy and land-use planning legislation on the one hand and those whom it is imagined are governed by it on the other. One of the principal characteristics of UK retailing during the closing decades of the twentieth century was the growth in market share of a small number of very large-scale retailers. This was particularly true in the case of the food etc. supermarket organizations, where, for example, the combined market share of the top four organizations rose from 26.6 per cent in 1982 to 46.9 per cent in 1989 (Marsden and Wrigley, 1996: 35). These authors relate this to government policy at two levels: that of the impact of government legislation upon major retailers, and the involvement of those same retailers in the implementation of government policy. Thus the starting point for these two authors is the largely statistical fact that 'The 1980s were to be characterised by a massive and sustained concentration of capital and the emergence of a small group of retail corporations whose turnover, employment levels, profitability, and sheer market and political power came to rival the largest corporations in any sector of the UK economy'. And this is accompanied by their view of this as the outcome, along with other economic forces, of 'an environment of competition regulation in the UK which was conducive to concentration of retail capital and retailer dominance of the retailer–supplier relationship'. Marsden and Wrigley place such developments in the context of a subtle set of relationships: between the major grocery supermarket organizations and their food-manufacturer suppliers, between these food retailers and farmers, between farmers and the government, and, perhaps most importantly from our perspective, between the major food manufacturers and the UK government. They then interpret this as a policy environment in which these very large-scale retailers 'had been delegated by the regulatory state key responsibilities in the management and policing of the food system and in the social structuring of consumption'. Indeed these authors' interpretation of the implementation of the 1990 Food Safety Act was that 'the major retailers were delegated key responsibilities for the management and policing of the more internationalized food system, and both political and statutory legitimacy for their new custodial role within that system', such that by the early 1990s 'the major food retailers had, in this fashion, become enlisted as agents and promoters of public policy' (Marsden and Wrigley, 1996: 33, 40). The point of considering this analysis is not to suggest that there exists any inappropriate relationship in the United Kingdom between particular government legislation and the parties likely to be affected by its implementation. The drawing up of legislation in the broad field of competition policy has often been accompanied by importance inputs from industry (see Richardson, 1969). It is, however, in the context of the significance of the role of government legislation in affecting the retail sector, important to recognize the potential influence of retail organizations themselves in the content and implementation of this legislation. With respect to the United Kingdom, therefore, 'questions about the regulation of consumption by the state and by private retail capital, and the way in which consumption relations influence the operation of the state either directly or through the mediative role of the retailers' are likely to remain a central part of this analysis even within an increasingly uniform framework for the making of such decisions across the European Union (Marsden and Wrigley, 1995: 1900).

References

Alexander, D. (1970) *Retailing in England During the Industrial Revolution*, Athlone Press, London.

Bamfield, J. (1987) 'Rationalization and the problems of re-positioning: UK co-operatives caught in the middle', in Johnson, G. (ed.) *Business Strategy and Retailing*, John Wiley, Chichester.

Bamfield J. (1988) 'Competition and change in British retailing', *National Westminster Bank Review*, February, pp. 15–29.

Baron, S., Harris, K., Leaver, D. and Oldfield, B. M. (2001) 'Beyond convenience: the future for independent food and grocery retailers in the UK', *The International Review of Retail, Distribution and Consumer Research*, 11(4): 395–414.

Birchall, J. (1994) *Co-op: The People's Business*, Manchester University Press, Manchester.

Blois, K. J. (1972) 'Vertical quasi-integration', *Journal of Industrial Economics*, 20(4): 253–72.

Bowlby, S. R. and Foord, J. (1995) 'Relational contracting between UK retailers and manufacturers', *The International Review of Retail, Distribution and Consumer Research*, 5(4): 333–61.

Braithwaite, D. and Dobbs, S. P. (1932) *The Distribution of Consumable Goods*, George Routledge, London.

Briggs, A. (1984) *Marks & Spencer 1884–1984*, Octopus Books, London.

Burke, T. and Shackleton, J. R. (1996) *Trouble in Store? – UK Retailing in the 1990s*, The Institute of Economic Affairs, London.

Chapman, S. (1974) *Jesse Boot of Boots the Chemist*, Hodder & Stoughton, London.

Clarke, R., Davies, S. and Driffield, N. L. (1998) *Monopoly Policy in the UK: Assessing the Evidence*, Edward Elgar, Cheltenham.

Clegg, B. (1993) *The Man who made Littlewoods: The Story of John Moores*, Hodder & Stoughton, London.

Competition Commission (2000) *Supermarkets*, Cm 4842, TSO, London.

Corporate Intelligence on Retailing (1996) *UK Retailers' Cross Border Activities*, Corporate Intelligence Group, London.

Corstjens, J. and M. (1995) *Store Wars: The Battle for Minspace and Shelfspace*, John Wiley, Chichester.

Davidson, F. P. and Ervine, W. C. H. (1992) 'Legal issues in retailing', in Howe, W. S. (ed.) *Retailing Management*, Macmillan, London.

Davies, G. and Harris, K. (1990) *Small Business: The Independent Retailer*, Macmillan, London.

Davies, K. and Brooks, J. M. (1989) *Positioning Strategy in Retailing*, Paul Chapman, London.

Davies, K. *et al.* (1985) 'Structural changes in the grocery market: the implications for competition', *International Journal of Physical Distribution & Materials Management*, 15(2): 3–48.

Davis, D. (1966) *A History of Shopping*, Routledge & Kegan Paul, London.

Dawson, J. A. and Shaw, S. A. (1989) 'Horizontal competition in retailing and the structure of manufacturer–retailer relationships', in Pellegrini, L. and Reddy, S. K. (eds.) *Retail and Marketing Channels*, Routledge, London.

Department of the Environment (1992) *The Effects of Major Out-of-Town Retail Development*, HMSO, London.

Department of the Environment (1994) *Vital and Viable Town Centres: Meeting the Challenge*, HMSO, London.

Department of the Environment, Transport and the Regions (1998) *The Impact of Large Foodstores on Market Towns and District Centres*, DETR, London.

Department of Prices and Consumer Protection (1978) *A Review of Monopolies and Mergers Policy*, Cmnd. 7198, HMSO, London.

Department of Prices and Consumer Protection (1979) *A Review of Restrictive Trade Practices Policy*, Cmnd. 7512, HMSO, London.

Department of Trade and Industry (1988) *Review of Restrictive Trade Practices Policy*, Cm 331, HMSO, London.

Department of Trade and Industry (1989) *Opening Markets: New Policy on Restrictive Trade Practices*, Cm 727, HMSO, London.

Department of Trade and Industry (1992) *Abuse of Market Power*, Cm 2100, HMSO, London.

Department of Trade and Industry (1996a) *Tackling Cartels and the Abuse of Market Power: A Consultation Document*, HSO, London.

Department of Trade and Industry (1996b) *Tackling Cartels and the Abuse of Market Power: A Draft Bill*, HMSO, London.

Department of Trade and Industry (1997) *A Prohibition Approach to Anti-Competitive Agreements and Abuse of Dominant Position*, HMSO, London.

Department of Trade and Industry (2001) *A World Class Competition Regime*, Cm 5233, HMSO, London.

Fernie, J. (1994) 'Quick response: an international perspective', *International Journal of Physical Distribution & Logistics Management*, 24(6): 38–46.

Fernie, J. (1995a) 'International comparisons of supply chain management in grocery retailing', *The Service Industries Journal*, 15(4): 134–47.

Fernie, J. (1995b) 'The coming of the Fourth Wave: new forms of retail out-of-town development', *International Journal of Retail & Distribution Management*, 23(1): 4–11.

Fernie, J. (1998) 'The breaking of the Fourth Wave: recent out-of-town retail developments in Britain', *The International Journal of Retail, Distribution and Consumer Research*, 8(3): 303–17.

Fraser, W. H. (1981) *The Coming of the Mass Market 1850–1914*, Macmillan, London.

Fulop, C. (1964a) *Competition for Consumers*, Institute of Economic Affairs, London.

Fulop, C. (1964b) 'Revolution in retailing', in Harris, R. (ed.) *Ancient or Modern?*, The Institute of Economic Affairs, London.

Godley, A. (2001) 'The market share of foreign multinationals in British retailing, 1850–1960s', *11th International Conference of Research in the Distributive Trades*, Zoetermeer, Netherlands.

Godley, A. (2002) 'What was new in the 1980s? – international retailing in Britain from 1850–1991', *The International Review of Retail, Distribution and Consumer Research*, 12(1): 19–37.

Guy, C. M. (1994) *The Retail Development Process*, Routledge, London.

Guy, C. M. (1998) 'Controlling new retail spaces: the impress of planning policies in Western Europe', *Urban Studies*, 35(5–6): 953–79.

Hall, R. and Dixon, R. (1988) *Franchising*, Pitman, London.

Hay, D. (1993) 'The assessment: competition policy', *Oxford Review of Economic Policy*, 9(2): 1–26.

Hogarth-Scott, S. and Parkinson, S. T. (1993) 'Retailer–supplier relationships in the food channel', *International Journal of Retail & Distribution Management*, 21(8): 11–19.

House of Commons Environment Committee (1994) *Shopping Centres and their Future*, HCP 359-I, HMSO, London.

House of Commons Environment Committee (1997) *Shopping Centres*, HCP 210-I, HMSO, London.

House of Commons Environment, Transport and Regional Affairs Committee (1999) *Environmental Impact of Supermarket Competition*, HC 120, HMSO, London.

Howard, E. (1995) 'Retail planning policy in the UK', in Davies, R. L. (ed.) *Retail Planning Policies in Western Europe*, Routledge, London, pp. 217–41.

Howe, W. S. (1973) 'The ending of resale price maintenance: implementation of government policy', *Economics*, Summer, pp. 5–16.

Howe, W. S. (1992) *Retailing Management*, Macmillan, London.

Howe, W. S. and Dugard, P. I. (1993) 'The impact of organization size upon business development in UK retailing 1980–87', *The International Review of Retail, Distribution and Consumer Research*, 3(2): 111–32.

Jefferys, J. B. (1954) *Retail Trading in Britain 1850–1950*, CUP, Cambridge.

Jefferys, J. B. and Knee, D. (1962) *Retailing in Europe*, Macmillan, London.

Levy, H. (1948) *The Shops of Britain*, Routledge & Kegan Paul, London.

McGoldrick, P. J. (1990) *Retail Marketing*, McGraw-Hill, London.

Mackay, J. (1998) *The Man Who Invented Himself: A Life of Sir Thomas Lipton*, Mainstream Publishing, Edinburgh.

Marsden T. and Wrigley, N. (1995) 'Regulation, retailing, and consumption', *Environment and Planning A*, 27: 1899–912.

Marsden T. and Wrigley, N. (1996) 'Retailing, the food system and the regulatory state', in Wrigley, N. and Lowe, M. (eds) *Retailing, Consumption and Capital: Towards the New Retail Geography*, Longman, London.

Mathias, P. (1967) *Retailing Revolution*, Longmans, London.

Mussanif, Y. (1988) 'Store wars – the background to UK retailing', in West, A. (ed.) *Handbook of Retailing*, Gower, Aldershot.

Monopolies Commission (1969) *Recommended Resale Prices*, HCP 100, HMSO, London.

Monopolies Commission (1970) *Refusal to Supply*, Cmnd. 4372, HMSO, London.

Monopolies Commission (1973a) *Ready Cooked Breakfast Cereal Foods*, HCP 2, HMSO, London.

Monopolies Commission (1973b) *Parallel Pricing*, Cmnd. 5330, HMSO, London.

Monopolies and Mergers Commission (1976) *Frozen Foodstuffs*, HC 674, HMSO, London.
Monopolies and Mergers Commission (1979) *Ice Cream and Water Ices*, Cmnd. 7632, HMSO, London.
Monopolies and Mergers Commission (1981) *Discounts to Retailers*, HC 311, HMSO, London.
Monopolies and Mergers Commission (1983) *Linfood Holdings PLC and Fitch Lovell PLC*, Cmnd. 8874, HMSO, London.
Monopolies and Mergers Commission (1985) *The Dee Corporation PLC and Booker McConnell PLC*, Cmnd. 9429, HMSO, London.
Monopolies and Mergers Commission (1990) *Kingfisher PLC and Dixons Group PLC*, Cm 1079, HMSO, London.
Monopolies and Mergers Commission (1993a) *Contact Lens Solutions*, Cm 2242, HMSO, London.
Monopolies and Mergers Commission (1993b) *Fine Fragrances*, Cm 2380, HMSO, London.
Monopolies and Mergers Commission (1994a) *Ice Cream*, Cm 2524, HMSO, London.
Monopolies and Mergers Commission (1994b) *Recorded Music*, Cm 2599, HMSO, London.
Monopolies and Mergers Commission (1997) *Domestic Electrical Goods: I and II*, 2 vols, Cm 3675-I and II, and Cm 3676-I and II, HMSO, London.
National Board for Prices and Incomes, Report No. 151 (1970) *Bread Prices and Pay in the Baking Industry*, Cmnd. 4428, HMSO, London.
National Board for Prices and Incomes, Report No. 165 (1971) *Prices, Profits and Costs in Food Distribution*, Cmnd. 4645, HMSO, London.
National Economic Development Office (1978) *Competition Policy*, NEDO, London.
O'Brien, D. P. (1982) 'Competition policy in Britain: the silent revolution', *The Antitrust Bulletin*, 27(1): 217–39.
Office of Fair Trading (1985) *Competition and Retailing*, OFT, London.
Office of Fair Trading (1999) *The Competition Act 1998: Nine Explanatory Papers*, OFT, London.
Ogbonna, E. and Wilkinson, B. (1996) 'Inter-organizational power relationships in the UK grocery industry: contradictions and developments', *International Review of Retail, Distribution and Consumer Research*, 6(4): 395–414.
Omar, O. E. (1995) "Retail influence on food technology and innovation", *International Journal of Retail & Distribution Management*, Vol. 23 No. 3, pp. 11–16.
Oxford Dictionary of Quotations, 4th edn, 1992, OUP, Oxford.
Pal, J., Bennison, D., Clarke, I. and Byrom, J. (2001) 'Power, policy networks and planning: the involvement of major grocery retailers in the formulation of Planning Policy Guidance Note 6 since 1988', *The International Review of Retail, Consumer and Distribution* Research, 11(3): 225–46.
Pickering, J. F. (1966) *Resale Price Maintenance in Practice*, Allen & Unwin, London.
Pound, R. (1960) *Selfridge*, Heinemann, London.
Pretious, M. E. (1995) 'The development of petrol retailing at Tesco', unpublished case study, School of Management, University of Abertay Dundee, Dundee.
Randall, G. (1994) *Trade Marketing Strategies: The Partnership between Manufacturers, Brands and Retailers*, 2nd ed. Butterworth/Heinemann, Oxford.
Reddaway, W. B. (1970) *Effects of the Selective Employment Tax: First Report on the Distributive Trades*, HMSO, London.
Rees, G. (1969) *St. Michael: A History of Marks & Spencer*, Weidenfeld & Nicolson, London.
Retail Intelligence (2000a) *UK Retail Report No. 109*, Corporate Intelligence Group, London, pp. 93–134.

Retail Intelligence (2000b) *UK Retail Report No. 115*, Corporate Intelligence Group, London, pp. 96–137.

Retail Intelligence (2000c) *The UK Retail Rankings 2000*, Corporate Intelligence Group, London.

Retail Intelligence (2001) *The UK Retail Rankings 2001*, Corporate Intelligence Group, London.

Reynolds, J. (1992) 'Generic models of European shopping centre development', *European Marketing Journal*, 26(8/9): 49–60.

Richardson, J. J. (1969) *The Policy-making Process*, Routledge & Kegan Paul, London.

Ross, M. D. H. (1955) *Organisation of Retail Distribution*, Macdonald, London.

Samways, A. (1995) *Private Label in Europe: Prospects and Opportunities for FMCG Retailers,* Financial Times, London.

Senker, J. (1988) *A Taste for Innovation: British Supermarkets' Influence on Food Manufacturers*, Horton Publishing, Bradford.

Sieff, M. (1990) *Management the Marks & Spencer Way*, Weidenfeld & Nicolson, London.

Sigsworth, E. M. (1990) *Montague Burton – The Tailor of Taste*, Manchester University Press, Manchester.

Smith, A. (1776) in Campbell, R. H. and Skinner, A. S. (eds,) *An Inquiry into the Nature and Causes of the Wealth of Nations*, Clarendon Press, Oxford, 1976.

Smith, P. and Swann, D. (1979) *Protecting the Consumer: An Economic and Legal Analysis*, Martin Robertson, Oxford.

Stacey, N. A. H. and Wilson A. (1965) *The Changing Pattern of Distribution*, 2nd edn, Pergamon Press, London.

Stern, P. and Stanworth, J. (1988) 'The development of franchising in Britain', *National Westminster Bank Quarterly Review*, May.

Swann, D, O'Brien, D. P., Maunder, W. P. J. and Howe, W. S. (1974) *Competition in British Industry*, Allen & Unwin, London.

Swann, D. (1979) *Competition and Consumer Protection*, Penguin, Harmondsworth.

Swann, D., O'Brien, D. P., Maunder, W. P. J. and Howe, W. S. (1974) *Competition in British Industry*, Allen & Unwin, London.

UK Home Department (1993) *Reforming the Law on Sunday Trading: A Guide to the Options for Reform*, Cm 2300, HMSO, London.

Utton, M. A. (1996) 'Selective distribution, refusal to sell and the monopolies and mergers commission', *International Journal of the Economics of Business*, 3(1): 43–55.

Utton, M. A. (2000) 'Fifty years of UK competition policy', *Review of Industrial Organization*, 16: 267–85.

Wilberforce, Lord, Campbell, A. and Elles, N. (1965) *The Law of Restrictive Trade Practices and Monopolies*, 2nd edn, Sweet & Maxwell, London.

Wilson, C. (1985) *First with the News: The History of W. H. Smith 1792–1972*, Guild Publishing, London.

Wrigley, N. (1994) 'After the store wars: towards a new era of competition in UK food retailing?', *Journal of Retailing and Consumer Services*, 1(1): 5–20.

Wrigley, N. (1998) 'PPG6 and food stores', *British Food Journal*, 100(3): 154–61.

8 Overview and conclusions

Stewart Howe

Introduction

The individual country chapters in this volume have provided the reader with a historical and contemporary view of retail structures and key associated developments in a range of European economies, together with some attempt to analyse the important question of whether consumers in these individual economies are well served by such retail market structures and retailer behaviour. A very significant component in all cases has been the role of national governments in looking after the interests of retail consumers.

The purpose of this final chapter is to consider more broadly what we might expect to be able to conclude from such analyses, and to draw upon the material in the individual preceding chapters to provide examples of the value of such analysis.

A framework of analysis

A number of difficulties, however, stand in the way of arriving at firm conclusions in this area of analysis. Dawson (2000a: 6), for example, concluded even in the last year of the twentieth century that 'economics, to a considerable extent, still finds the analysis of retailer functions to be difficult', and we shall see that arriving at firm conclusions in this area is not straightforward. It may be helpful if we break down these difficulties into the categories of conceptual, interpretative and practical (e.g. see Howe, 1998). That is, if we are to arrive at firm conclusions regarding the economic welfare implications of particular retailer structures etc, we require to have a clear idea of what constitutes that welfare, we have to be able to interpret unambiguously the information that we have relating to the relevant variables, and the data themselves have to be both valid and reliable in this respect.

The concept of retailer performance and efficiency

In assessing retailer competitiveness and efficiency, the question that we want to be able to ask is 'are goods being supplied to consumers in the economy at the lowest possible resource cost consistent with the quality of service that shoppers want?'. However, despite the optimistic conclusion from one analysis that 'consumers' behaviour is the main determinant of channel structure in convenience goods markets' (Pellegrini, 1989: 18), the matter of 'what shoppers want' is an unclear one in a number of respects. Not least are the issues which it raises for the measurement of retailer productivity, where, for example, a small number of retail transactions per employee may, confusingly, either reflect shoppers' desire for a high level of customer service or the inefficient use of labour in retailing. As Fulop (1966: 5–8) points out, wartime reductions in retailing employment and in the availability and choice of merchandise give rise to a purely specious improvement in a range of retailing efficiencies as consumers are obliged to shop around for supplies and queue for a limited selection of goods. The opposite of this situation of retail consumers being 'underprovided' with retail services may occur within a system of resale price maintenance (r.p.m.) when, as a result of manufacturers dictating retailer selling prices and widening gross retail margins, retail competition takes the form of service provision. One obvious consumer welfare loss here is that shoppers in general are 'forced' to consume a higher overall level of retail services than they want, and that individual consumers are deprived of the opportunities to select from a range of retailer price/service combinations (see Yamey, 1966: chapter 1). The point being emphasized is not whether a system of r.p.m. is beneficial or otherwise to retail consumers, but that consumer welfare in the whole context of retailing is extremely difficult to determine. Thus one of the issues in the measurement of the performance of the retail sector is not so much 'that by neglecting variations in the service element in retail output the value of sales may be an imperfect measure of output', but that the net retail sales value (i.e. retailer value added) *is*, in a tautological sense, the measure of retail output, dependent though this may be recognized to be upon, for example, consumer standards of living in general, population density, retail services provided, *and* retailer productivity (see Smith and Hitchens, 1985: 16).

This has led to a situation where there has been little reliance upon formal economic analysis in seeking to arrive at welfare conclusions regarding the performance of the retail sector. Thus, despite the quite extensive literature in this field summarized in the United Kingdom by Dobson and Waterson (1996: v) concerning, for example, manufacturer and retailer 'double marginalisation' (each adding a profit margin to their output, leading to prices that are higher and suboptimal from the point of manufacturer–retailer joint profit maximization), manufacturer and retailer free-riding, and both manufacturer and retailer competition effects, these two authors admit that such analysis 'does not lead to straightforward conclusions for public policy'. Not surprisingly, therefore, national government and international policy in matters relating to retailer and manufacturer behaviour and its impact upon consumers has been characterized by an element of *ad hoc* reaction. Thus, the UK government of the time, in a consultation document dealing with the effects of market power, concluded that 'Despite experience of EC laws the identification of abuses of market power in many cases remains a matter for fine judgement. It can be very difficult to assess in advance what will be regarded as anti-competitive and what as acceptable business behaviour' (UK Department of Trade and Industry, 1996: para. 9.5). Echoing this sentiment, the Commission of the European Communities *Green Paper on Vertical Restraints in EC Competition Policy*, while speaking of a consensus emerging among economists in this area after an earlier 'heated debate', nonetheless emphasized that even such analysts are 'less willing to make sweeping statements' but rather to 'rely more on the analysis of the facts of the case in question' (Commission of the European Communities, 1997: iii).

The interpretation of movements in retail structures and behaviour

The second set of issues involved in the consideration of developments in the retail sector of the economy – and which is particularly important in analysing the impact of government policies in this area – covers the interpretation of events. The first set of difficulties under this issue arises from indulging in simple *post hoc* analysis. Turning again to r.p.m. as an individual example, it is in practice extremely difficult to trace the medium and longer term impact of the abolition of the practice in one particular country, or indeed equally to judge the impact of the practice by comparing two economies, in one of which r.p.m. is operated and in another of which it is absent. The problem in the latter situation is that so many of the economist's *ceteris* are not *paribus*. In the former, while there may be significant but essentially publicity-seeking price reductions in the immediate aftermath of the abolition of r.p.m. in any one trade, in the longer term any such price changes have to be seen in the context of general price increases, cost changes affecting the particular product, changes in the level of particular retail services, location etc., together with changing product characteristics (see Yamey, 1966: chapter 1). Burt (1984) provides a further example of the pitfalls of this type of analysis in his examination of the impact of the French Loi Royer of 1973 and its impact upon hypermarket developments. As we saw in Chapter 2, the intention of this legislation was to restrict the expansion of hypermarkets in order to preserve the position of the traditional smaller scale French retailer. But as Burt points out, a simple measurement of hypermarket openings following this legislation is not sufficient to allow one to arrive at conclusions regarding its effectiveness when there are underlying social and economic changes at work, the impact of the 1973 oil crisis, and assumptions to be made in terms of the length of the planning period for new hypermarkets regarding when one would expect the impact of such legislation to be discernible.

It would not be entirely sensible in the context of the above analysis to turn to company profitability data in order to judge the outcome of events. Quite apart from a number of purely practical but not unimportant aspects (dealt with below), the interpretation of changes in retailer (or manufacturer) return on investment (ROI) or sales-margin profitability data requires to be undertaken with considerable care. With regard to sales-margin data, it can be argued (see Howe, 1998: 486–7) that analysis of neither gross margin nor net sales margin data alone will yield unequivocal results. Gross margin data – total sales revenue less the basic cost of goods sold – ignores a significant range of retail expenses, including labour and occupancy costs, and is therefore an insufficiently fine measure of retailer profitability. On the other hand, net sales margins, particularly in less than competitive markets, may include significant promotional expenditures on the part of established organizations which act as barriers to new competition, and unnecessarily high occupancy costs incurred as oligopoly retailers scramble for relatively scarce sites. The incurring of these essentially uncompetitive costs by incumbent retailers, both of which will create barriers to competitive entry into the market, will, of course, have the misleading effect of reducing these retailers' otherwise excessive sales margins to 'normal' levels while bolstering their protected market position. Furthermore, as with all such analyses, retailer strategic behaviour may at one time involve a sacrificing of net margins – and therefore again the creation of the appearance of a more competitive market – in order to build up a more dominant position in the market in the expectation of increased future returns. A current example of this is the behaviour of the UK grocery supermarket sector leader Tesco, whose growth strategy of 'reinvesting incremental profits in improved services has been responsible for remarkable sales growth ... [that] has more than compensated for Tesco's decision not to widen operating margins' (*Sunday Times*, 23 September 2001). This particular market is one that has been characterized by a variety of interpretations as to its competitiveness. On the one hand, as we saw in Chapter 7, the market has been the subject of a number of government inquiries, which have at least cast some doubt on the degree of competition among the grocery supermarket organizations. On the other hand, one group of consultants characterized the same market as a 'vibrant oligopoly, with up to half a dozen major food stores competing with each other in many areas' and 'competition from other major multiples keep[ing] their margins down. *The consumer therefore reaps the benefit both of enhanced competition and of economies of scale*' [emphasis added] (London Economics, 1995: 10). Tesco's chief executive indeed sought to reassure readers in the context of the most recent UK government inquiry that 'In our sector, the reality is that competition is intense and dynamic and our customers are most definitely not being ripped off' (*Sunday Times*, 7 November 1999). And in the context of an earlier government inquiry into the power of grocery retailers *vis-à-vis* their food manufacturer suppliers, one academic author confounded the more usual analysis in this area by pointing out that manufacturer price discrimination among retailer customers is a characteristic of oligopoly rather than more competitive producer markets, and that 'the key to understanding discriminatory retail discounts [on the part of manufacturers] is not the *market power of the buyers* but *that of the sellers*' [original emphasis] (Grant, 1987: 46).

For all of these reasons, we should exercise considerable caution in interpreting the measurable or other outcomes of retailer behaviour and performance in seeking to arrive at conclusions on consumer welfare.

Practical issues

In addition to the conceptual and interpretative issues relating to the use, for example, of company profitability data, there are significant practical measurement issues that reduce the value of the resulting data. These not only apply to profit comparisons over time but also cast doubt on the reliability of cross-sectional inter-firm and international comparisons. As an example, despite the role of the accounting profession and auditors, considerable and significant latitude in profit calculation is apparent from the decision by the major UK food retailers in the early 1990s to commence depreciating their store and land assets to reflect the falling value of these (see Burt and Sparks, 1997). In one case, during this period, the additional charge amounted to 12 per cent of pre-tax profits (Wrigley, 1994). The introduction of these charges, and the associated ending of the capitalization of interest on borrowings to fund new stores, not only destroys the time-series comparability of profit and profit-margin data; but because different store groups reacted in different ways and at different times to the same underlying issues, it also makes relevant inter-firm comparisons difficult, and, in practice invalid. Indeed, the *Financial Times* (16 March 1996) reported that such contrasts in accounting treatment of business variables could result in a difference of 9 per cent in reported earnings per share of the companies. Fortunately, however, a more recent and circumspect analysis of this aspect of retailer accounting data was able to conclude that these retailers who adopted particular legitimate 'creative accounting' techniques did not in the process mislead the professional investment community. The conclusion of this study was that despite these retailers in some sense 'overestimating' their profits, 'it is unlikely that retailers have received unwarranted support from the financial markets' or that these markets have 'been misled by [the retail sector's] creative accounting techniques' (Cotter and Hutchinson, 1999: 158–9).

The difficulty of inter-company but intra-economy profit calculation comparisons is magnified as we move across national boundaries of accounting rules and requirements, standards of compliance and tax law. Corrections for such circumstances, one group of authors has argued, reduce considerably, for example, the very large apparent differences between UK and French supermarket group sales margins (Corstjens *et al.*, 1995). Perhaps more worryingly, there appears to be a body of literature that suggests that, where such latitude in accounting conventions exists, the adoption by firms of particular accounting practices, and changes in these over time, may be related to variables such as the interest shown in these companies by competition-policy or other authorities (Ball and Smith, 1992).

All of the above conceptual, interpretative and practical issues relating to both economic and accounting variables have to be taken into consideration in arriving at firm conclusions regarding retail market behaviour and performance and the contribution of these to consumer welfare.

Differences and determinants in European retailing development

One of the most obvious features of the material in the preceding individual-country chapters covering the major economies of the European Union is that there are significant differences in both the current and recent past developments in retailing across the continent. There are, for example, contrasts in the present shape of retailing among EU economies which stem, quite simply, from their geographies and recent histories. As part of this, there are quite different periods from which one can date the emergence of 'modern' retailing; there are significant differences in the major determinants of the rate of development of the retail sector; more particularly, there are different degrees and directions of government involvement and intervention in the retail sector of the economy; and there are contrasting extents of international influences on domestic retailing. These are the principal themes that are adopted in the remainder of this chapter in order to draw out some of the lessons of the earlier individual-country analysis.

The background to retailing

As one would expect, a variety of background conditions is likely to contribute to the structure of retailing in individual countries across the European Union. In the United Kingdom, the population is relatively concentrated, the geography of the country and their early development have led to clear road and rail links between major centres of population, economic growth has been steady if not spectacular, capital formation in retailing as in other sectors has been straightforward, and the government has not obviously stood in the way of the formation of large-scale retailing organizations. In other economies such as Greece very different conditions exist. There, while there is a significant concentration of the population in the capital Athens and in Thessaloniki (accounting together for more than half of the total), the remainder of the population is more scattered, and levels of income and capital accumulation are lower. There is, moreover, a tradition of retailing as a marginal or secondary source of family income, combined with a strong entrepreneurial attachment to the small-scale family business; and until 1991 there were government restrictions on shop opening hours, specialist merchandise distribution, price levels and employment. These conditions have led, amongst other characteristics, to an average retail outlet size in terms of employment that remained almost unchanged at 1.8 persons from 1958 to 1988. In Denmark too the structure of retailing is influenced by the very large metropolitan concentration of population, the fact that the country is broken down into three islands, a very high proportion of working women in the economy, and, of particular interest, the comparatively low level of car ownership, despite a high economic standard of living. The chapter on German retailing also draws attention to ongoing changes in the pattern of retailing arising from the increasing desire for convenience on the part of consumers – both in terms of retail formats and particular products, to the increased health consciousness of modern consumers, and to the unpredictable purchasing behaviour of 'smart' and 'hybrid' consumers. The 1998 European Commission noted interestingly that the relative importance for shoppers of retail location in their choice of outlets varied from 14 per cent in Germany to 27 per cent in Italy (European Commission, 1998: 8).

The establishment of modern retailing

Quite naturally, the extent to which a particular economy exhibits today the characteristics of modern retailing depends to a significant extent upon when it began this development. Seen from a UK perspective, we would expect this to have occurred within a reasonable period following the Second World War, and thus we tend to look to the late 1950s and early 1960s to find evidence of increased market concentration among retail organizations, together with phenomena such as self-service supermarkets and shopping centres. In France, the timing of such developments lagged only slightly behind the United Kingdom. Supermarkets and self-service were becoming more common throughout the 1960s, although even by 1970 supermarkets accounted for less than 14 per cent of the market. Perhaps a little surprisingly, modern retailing in Germany can also be broadly dated from this period, which saw the beginning of the demise of the smaller scale retailer component of the *Mittelstandbewegung*. And the 1960s in Germany saw a rise in their food market share of multiple-shop retailers from 5.3 to 12 per cent, accompanied by a significant expansion of self-service and supermarket grocery retailing.

By contrast, the 1950s is regarded as a decade of consolidation of traditional retailing in Spain, and it was not until the 1970s that aspects of modern retailing began to appear in the Spanish economy, at which time only 29 per cent of food sales were through self-service outlets. In Italy, while there were some moves towards a modern retail economy in the 1970s, such developments did not occur significantly until the 1980s and 1990s. Supermarket openings did not occur in Italy on any significant scale until the early 1980s, and the major period of the development of hypermarkets, which had been virtually non-existent until the early 1980s, occurred in the last few years of that decade. More obvious numerical measures of this development are the increase in the combined market share of supermarkets, hypermarkets and department stores (including variety chains) from 10 per cent in 1989 to 22.3 per cent in 1999, and the loss over the 1990s of some 10,000 non-food retailers each year. Such developments took place even later in Greece. Here, the emergence of modern retailing was held back not only by the aftermath of the Second World War but also by a subsequent Civil War 1946–1949 and also a period of military dictatorship 1967–1974; and it was not until the last decade of the twentieth century that many significant retail developments occurred. Then, as expressed in Chapter 4, 'Within ten years a system of traditional retailing based on small, independently owned and operated outlets ... had a modern system of multiple-shop retail enterprises operating a wide range of formats superimposed upon it'.

Differences and similarities

Not surprisingly, contemporary retailing across the various economies of the European Union is characterized by both differences and similarities. The European Commission study *Retailing in the European Economic Area 1997* pointed to the fact that 'The trends in socio-demographic and economic variables, commercial policies and economic policies tend to be uniform at the overall European level' to substantiate its rather ambivalent conclusion that '[European] national distribution systems tend to resemble each other more and more, although they still display some fundamental differences' (European Commission, 1998: 8). Other analyses, however, have arrived at a different emphasis. As one mid-1990s survey expressed it in the context of a generally assumed trend towards some uniformity in European retailing, 'substantial differences continue to survive, each country preserving the fruits of its history and culture. The single European market is not therefore uniform and, compared with manufacturing industry, remains localized' (Tordjman, 1994: 3). And at this time McGoldrick too (1995: 13), while acknowledging the convergence of consumer tastes and global markets, emphasized that 'the retail markets of, for example, ... France, Spain and Greece are enormously different'. Such reservations regarding any assumed uniformity across the European Union in retailing structures and policies continue to be expressed, as in Dawson's turn-of-the-century reflection that 'retailing in Europe remains ... a response to local European culture. ... Many aspects of retailing show features of divergence rather than convergence' (Dawson, 2000b: 120). There still exist, for example, quite considerable differences in the proportion of economic activity accounted for by distribution (wholesaling and retailing) among the EU countries. For the period 1987–1991, for example, the proportionate contribution of these trades to national gross added value ranged from 10.1 per cent in Germany to 17.3 per cent in Portugal, with an EU average of 12.9 per cent (Commission of the European Communities, 1993: 5). Within this average, there is a general north–south contrast, although both Belgium and Denmark have higher-than-average figures, perhaps stemming from the relatively small size of their total economies. Analysis of gross value added figures for the mid-1990s reveals a similar situation, with Germany and France having generally lower proportions accounted for by the distributive trades as a whole (8.7 and 10.8 per cent, respectively) and more southerly or smaller economies, such as Italy or Austria or Belgium, having larger proportions (13.7, 13.8 and 15.0 per cent, respectively). Denmark stands out with a figure of 32.0 per cent (see data in European Commission, 1998).

A more complete set of data is presented in Table 8.1, and the figures there allow us to see both differences that are in some sense systematic, and to note that some individual-economy variables are more unique.

Thus, the data show a fairly regular negative correlation between shop density as measured by the number of retail establishments per 1,000 inhabitants, and the employment scale of retail outlets. In other words, economies either have larger numbers of smaller individual shops or something of a concentration of retail sales within larger retail outlets. Greece, Italy, Portugal and Spain all have particularly high shop densities combined with essentially small-scale retailing, suggesting something of a 'north/south' divide in this respect within the European Union. Intuitively one might have also associated this pattern of shop density with national income per head: that is, that less developed countries would be characterized by a population of small-scale retail outlets. This has been found to be the case in larger scale studies (see Davies and Whitehead, 1995: 125–6), and there is some evidence from the data in Table 8.1 to support this hypothesis. Within this type of data, differences may also be found in the density of 'modern' forms of

Table 8.1 Retail sector variables for 15 EU economies

	Population ('million)	GDP per head of population (€ '000)	Distributive value added/ total (%)	Retail establishments per '000 population	Employment per retail establishment (No.)	Retailing self-employment (%)
Austria	8.0	18.8	13.8	3.82	8.3	14.5
Belgium	10.1	18.8	15.1	11.04	2.5	33.8
Denmark	5.2	19.1	32.0	7.36	4.8	14.5
Finland	5.1	15.1	11.8	4.52	4.0	21.7
France	58.0	17.9	10.8	5.93	4.7	21.1
Germany	81.5	18.3	8.7	5.01	7.0	15.6
Greece	10.4	10.6	n.a.	17.4	1.9	n.a.
Ireland	3.6	14.2	n.a.	8.2	5.4	24.2
Italy	57.3	17.1	13.7	15.6	2.2	66.4
Luxemburg	0.4	27.0	13.3	7.14	4.8	n.a.
Netherlands	15.4	17.3	12.2	6.55	5.9	18.4
Portugal	9.9	11.4	n.a.	12.44	2.5	12.2
Spain	39.2	12.7	n.a.	14.18	2.3	49.3
Sweden	8.8	16.2	13.5	6.21	4.0	14.5
UK	58.5	16.4	n.a.	3.36	12.1	14.1

Source: European Commission (1998) *Retailing in the European Economic Area 1997*, European Commission, Brussels.

Note: n.a. = data not available.

shopping such as hypermarkets/supermarkets, where Tordjman found food retail market shares ranging from 18 per cent in Germany to 60 per cent in Spain round an EU average of 30 per cent (Tordjman, 1995: 29). On the other hand there are patterns of retailing among EU countries that reflect national differences in both market demand and supply. There still remain, for example, quite significant differences in consumer preferences for department store, variety store and non-store retailing across the European Union (see Tordjman, 1995: 35–9), and the data above on retailing self-employment suggest that this may be a cultural phenomenon slightly separate from other more measurable variables. Such self-employment tends to be greatest in those small-shop economies, but it also stands out in Belgium, Finland, France and Ireland where average shop size in employment terms is quite high.

Within these macro-level statistical similarities and differences, however, some writers have pointed to a number of common general trends within European retailing. These include, for example, the general loss of retail market share on the part of department stores and variety store chains, the increased scale of food-grocery retailing and also a rising component of discount retailing within this sector, and the growth of non-food specialist stores. Such analysis also points to a growing trend of international retailing in the sense of large-scale retailer groups building up a portfolio of international activities (see Tordjman, 1994). In the current environment of the United Kingdom, as an illustration, for every

Marks & Spencer withdrawing from European operations there is a Dixons, a Kingfisher or a Tesco expanding into Italy, Germany or Malaysia, respectively (see *Financial Times*, 28 and 29 November 2001).

This last point does not, however, imply that at the individual-country level retailing is becoming an international commodity; and among the EU economies many interesting differences remain. Not only is there a general tendency for retailing to be more 'developed' in northern European economies than in the Mediterranean area in terms of organization ownership and scale, but some differences among these countries may be regarded as a product of the local economic or cultural environment, such as the attachment to small-scale retailing, including franchising, in Greece. The continuing importance of retail municipal markets in Spain is due partly to history and geography and also to government support of these structures; and the French associations of independent retailers, such as Leclerc and Intermarché in the hypermarket sector, are a quite unique retailing organization phenomenon. In Germany there continues to be a disproportionate attraction to mail-order retailing, which continued to account for 5.5 per cent of total retail sales up to the early 1990s (Commission of the European Communities, 1993: 72); and the same is true with regard to department stores with their almost 6 per cent of total retail sales, although these also have significant food sales compared with their UK counterparts. By contrast, in France, which saw the introduction of department stores in the 1820s, this form of retail outlet now accounts for only 1.4 per cent of retail sales.

One interesting example of both similarities and differences in the national patterns of retailing is the limited-line or 'hard' discount grocery segment, described by two authors in the mid-1990s as 'stand[ing] out as one where some of the fastest and most vigorous internationalisation activity of any type of retailing is taking place' (Bennison and Gardner, 1995: 192). A further characteristic of this internationalization is that it is based upon organic growth by those companies involved, rather than cross-border acquisitions or franchising. Thus, as examples, from the early 1980s, the German discounters Aldi and Lidl, the French Carrefour subsidiary Ed and the Danish Netto (a subsidiary of Denmark's second-largest retailer Dansk Supermarked) embarked upon a policy of internationalization, attempting to take into a range of EU economies their particular retail formula. But while one would obviously have accepted that the strategies of individual internationalizing hard-discount grocery retailers would be more or less successful, one might have expected this retailing phenomenon to display broad similarities among EU economies. Yet this turns out not to be the case in terms of its popularity among consumers; and while in affluent Norway the grocery market share of discounters in the mid-1990s was 32 per cent, and in Germany and Belgium it was 26 and 20 per cent respectively, in the United Kingdom, Finland and the Netherlands it was 11 per cent, and in both France and Italy it was only 3 per cent (Guy, 1998: 958). Obviously the relative national market shares achieved by this form of retailing are going to be influenced by the strategies of entering firms and those of existing grocery retailers. But a range of national economic variables and patterns of consumer preferences is also clearly going to be of considerable importance. Thus, the willingness of even relatively affluent German consumers to 'cross over' to discount retailing has surely played an important role in the considerable success of, for example, Aldi in its native country, resulting in such stores having 26 per cent of grocery sales in Germany, compared with 28 per cent for supermarkets, and 20 per cent for superstores. This compares particularly with the much lower combined market share of the discounters in the United Kingdom, including the history of the domestic Kwik Save (see Sparks, 1990; Burt and Sparks, 1994), and with the general performance of hard-discount stores in France. This experience suggests that although the internationalizing of their retail formulae may be an attractive strategy for retailers, and although there may be degrees of similarity among EU economies in retailing, the differences among European retail consumers in their shopping preferences are sufficient to create quite significant contrasts in the patterns of retailing from one European economy to another (see Robertet, 1997).

Retail internationalization and sources of innovation

Despite recent high-profile setbacks in this respect, such as the withdrawal of Marks & Spencer from mainland Europe at the end of the year 2001, retailer internationalization remains a popular strategy. By the end of the 1980s, Luciano Benetton was able to declare that 'Europe must become our domestic market'; and certainly in many instances within the Continent 'the Benetton name travelled seamlessly across cultural frontiers' (Mantle, 1999: 90, 161). Beyond the level of individual retail organizations, Dawson (1993) highlights three dimensions of the internationalization of retailing: international sourcing, international operations and 'the internationalisation of management ideas'. And a mixture of the second and third of these dimensions has been of some differential significance among the retail economies included in this study. The former of these two particular dimensions – international retail operations – may come into play as the growth of the retail sector slows down in more mature home economies relative to the growth of attractive host retail sectors. There is some evidence of this in the form of a north-to-south expansion of retailing developments. Burt, for example, noted in the early 1990s that among the European economies, France, (West) Germany and the United Kingdom accounted for 75 per cent of the internationalization of retailing in the important grocery sector, and that Spain and Italy were major recipients of inward retailer investment (Burt, 1991). Particular examples in this study are, for example, the internationalization activities of British, French or German retailers in Greece and Spain. Exceptions do, however, occur, as in the case of the Italian Gruppo Coin's acquisition of the German Kaufhalle.

Linked to the above, there is also the 'diffusion of retail innovation', and here again there are significant contrasts among EU member economies in the sources of resulting advances. In the United Kingdom, such innovations in the form of grocery self-service and supermarket retailing, associated out-of-town locations, and innovations in food processing itself belong very much to large-scale domestic retailers, although many would admit that they borrowed significantly from the United States in the 1950s and even earlier (see Powell, 1991: 65; Bevan, 2001: 25–6). By contrast, the much smaller scale domestic Greek retailers were significantly less responsible for their turn-of-the-twentieth-century retailing revolution, and here the role of incoming international retailers was 'pivotal'. Examples include the influence of the Italian Benetton in the clothing sector in the 1980s, the introduction of hypermarkets by the French Promodès in the early 1990s, and a range of international links in the department-store developments and in the important franchise sector. These advances were, however, accompanied by a very significant relaxation in a whole range of controls over the retailing sector that was itself the outcome of a change of domestic government and the environment of the creation of the Single European Market in 1993. One cannot, surely, discount the impact of these relaxations and the coming of the Single European Market in encouraging the entry of international retailers into this particular national market. Among other southern European economies, Spain too has experienced considerable importing of retailing formulae. The French Carrefour was responsible for the introduction of hypermarkets into Spain in the 1980s, and has remained a dominant force in Spanish retailing. It is, for example, the market leader in Spanish food retailing, where 5 out of the top 10 retail organizations in Spain are foreign companies, accounting for 39.5 per cent of total sales. Correspondingly, Carrefour, the second largest retailer in the world, derives 47.5 per cent of its sales outwith France. On the other hand, the rapidly growing discount store market in Spain has been dominated by the indigenous Dia group that has 80 per cent of the outlets, although this dominance is threatened by the deep discount operations in Spain of the German Lidl. Similarly, and in contrast to the situation in Greece, the rapidly growing retail franchise sector in Spain is dominated by Spanish organizations. By contrast, there appears to be no history of Germany importing new retailing formats from other countries. In general, there is a much greater balance there between 'importing' and 'exporting' retail organizations, with companies such as Aldi, Metro and Tengelmann deriving 29, 37 and 49 per cent, respectively of their sales from abroad. However, even here the arrival of Wal-Mart in 1997 through the acquisition of the Wertkauf hypermarket chain was regarded as a source of significant potential increased competition in this market.

Not surprisingly, large-scale retailers based in smaller economies have high proportions of their sales turnover accounted for by international sales; and in the mid-1990s, such EU league tables were led by Ikea of Sweden, Makro and Ahold of the Netherlands and Delhaize-le-Lion of Belgium with 88.9, 85.3, 48.3 and 76 per cent respectively of their sales accounted for by international operations. The group of the top-five European retailers in this respect is completed by Tengelmann of Germany with half of its sales turnover coming from international operations (European Commission, 1998: Table 20). In addition to the above individual examples, this same study showed both the concentration of EU countries characterized by international food retail operations and the economies into which their individual retail organizations had diversified, and this is set out in Table 8.2.

Table 8.2 European food retailer internationalization (1996)

Destination	Origin				
	Germany	France	UK	Belgium	Netherlands
Germany		Promodès, Intermarché			
France	Aldi, Lidl, Norma, Rewe, Edeka		Tesco	Delhaize, Colruyt	
UK	Aldi, Lidl, Rewe				
Belgium	Aldi, Lidl	Promodès, Cora, Intermarché			Vendex
Netherlands	Aldi, Tengelmann				
Spain	Tengelmann, Lidl, Rewe	Carrefour, Promodès, Auchan, Docks France, Compt Mod, Leclerc, Intermarche			
Italy	Rewe, Lidl, Tengelmann, Aldi	Carrefour, Auchan, Intermarché, Promodès			
Portugal		Carrefour, Promodès, Intermarché, Leclerc, Auchan			Ahold
Greece		Promodès		Delhaize	
Turkey		Carrefour, Promodès			
Czech Republic	Tengelmann, Aldi, Rewe Norma, Lidl Edeka		Tesco	Delhaize	Ahold
Hungary	Tengelmann, Aldi		Tesco		
Poland	Aldi, Rewe, Dohle	Leclerc, Auchan	Tesco		
Austria	Tengelmann				
Denmark	Aldi				

Source: European Commission (1998) *Retailing in the European Economic Area 1997*, European Commission, Brussels, Table 18.

Observation of the directions of the flow of international retailing, together with the relative acceptance of these retailing immigrants by their host-country customers, and also the varying management or financial success of such multinational ventures, suggest that we need to take analyses of such matters beyond the more conventional business or economic 'push' and 'pull' models of the internationalization of retailing. Briefly, such traditional models (see Treadgold and Davies, 1988; Salmon and Tordjman, 1989) see the internationalizing of retail organizations in terms of such businesses being pulled to new geographical ventures by the attraction of these business environments or as a result of particular exportable competences possessed by individual retailers. Alternatively, internationalizing retailers may be pushed from their native countries by adverse business factors (including market saturation) or a desire to enjoy the benefits of geographical diversification. Beyond this analysis, what the institutionalist literature teaches us is that retailing systems, patterns of consumption and particular institutions, amongst other variables, reflect their national histories and cultures. Some of the important variables in this context are financial markets, relationships between retailers and their suppliers, the structure of the state and its policies, and 'a society's idiosyncratic customs and traditions' (Hollingsworth and Boyer, 1997, quoted in Ferner); and these features not only determine the present but also shape the future. Internationalizing retailers, who are themselves part of their own national systems, will only to a greater or lesser extent be compatible with host-country retailing systems; and such compatibility may relate not only to the customer interface but also to the wider issue of the management of internationally-acquired retailing subsidiaries. Thus, while incoming franchise operators have generally been successful in a Greek economy which is receptive to such a retail system, the relative lack of success of the hard discounters Aldi and Lidl in the United Kingdom or Wal-Mart in Germany suggest that particular cultural or systems variables have a considerable impact upon the 'acceptability' or otherwise of international retail ventures and thus on their financial performance (see Ferner, 2000).

Channel relationships

Not surprisingly, one of the significant adjustments in retailing within EU economies over the last thirty years in particular has been structural changes in distribution channels. This was brought out particularly in Chapter 4 in relation to the Greek economy. Here, during the 1970s, large-scale retailers, particularly in the food sector, displaced traditional wholesalers, whose role in the distribution system was also reduced by the advent of cash-and-carry operators focused upon serving the remaining smaller scale food retailers. These cash-and-carry operators were often large, international organizations attracted to these developments in the Greek economy. A further organizational reaction to these changes was the formation by some of the more enterprising small and medium-sized retailers of buying groups, whose immediate function was to obtain for these smaller retailers the buying-power advantages of their large-scale competitors.

In addition to these more obvious changes in the retail organization structure, one of the virtually ubiquitous changes in retailing relationships across the European Union has been the increased power of retailers within the market channel. This has flowed from the structural changes in retailing that have seen the emergence of not only large-format retailers but also retail organizations themselves that are of very significant size, and some of which are partners in buying alliances. Correspondingly, the role of wholesalers in this sector has diminished considerably, and the largest retail organizations now enjoy considerable bargaining power *vis-à-vis* their suppliers. This changing relationship has, as we have seen in Chapter 7, been the topic of considerable but indeterminate inquiry in the United Kingdom. It has also been a noted phenomenon in Spain where it has been accompanied by the virtual disappearance of independent wholesalers, and has emerged more recently in Greece as a result of the significant changes there in the 1990s. One interesting feature of the impact of French legislation relating to retailer–supplier relations is that, although the largest retail groups possess considerable power in the market, with the three largest grocery retailers having a combined 60 per cent market share, strict controls over trade discounts to retailers have prevented these largest retailers from fully exercising their market power. However, in the case of Spain, legislation regarding credit periods taken by large organizations appears to have had very little impact.

The implementation and impact of particular government policies

Two particular areas of government policy relating to retailing have been common themes within this study, namely, competition policy and legislation relating to land-use planning.

Competition policy

With regard to competition policy, national governments across Europe have intervened in a number of ways in the retail sectors of their individual economies. The case for this has been variously made in terms of efficiency of the distribution system as a whole; 'protection' of the consumer; and some concept of 'fairness' in competition within the retail market, especially between different forms or types of retailer. Underlying all of these objectives is the desire by governments to improve the overall efficiency of retailing: an approach that is perhaps most explicit in the case of Spain, where government intervention in the retail sector is designed not only to provide 'the most effective means of preserving the interest of the consumer' but also assisting businesses in the sector to improve their efficiency.

Competition policy across a number of EU economies has recently, it is argued, displayed 'a remarkable convergence' (Neumann, 2001: 30) and a ' "quiet harmonization" [that is, without the employment of the traditional tool of a Community directive] of substantive law' in this respect (Laudati, 1998: 381). Historically, this tendency appears to have come from the adoption by a number of European countries, particularly Germany, of the US antitrust approach originating in the late nineteenth century. This development led one noted American competition or antitrust writer to comment that 'antitrust became one of America's most popular exports' (Scherer, 2000: 1). And the subsequent incorporation of the resulting individual European economy approaches into European Community law (particularly and most recently Articles 81 and 82 of the EC Treaty of Amsterdam), and the influence of the latter in turn in eliminating from the competition-policy legislation of individual EU members remaining particular exceptions or exemptions, has created a fairly high degree of uniformity among the EU economies in this respect. Even here, however, there is scope for an exception in the form of the Danish approach to antitrust which, currently embodied in the Danish Competition Act of 1990, is based upon the so-called 'transparency principle'. This principle is based in turn upon an acceptance that cartels etc. are not unnatural phenomena, and that the 'contestability' and efficiency of markets are best served not by an approach which automatically assumes that such arrangements are undesirable but one which provides for their publicity and investigation (see Albæk *et al.*, 1998). Specific EU control of mergers dates only from 1990, and individual EU member states' approaches to merger control vary quite considerably, with the United Kingdom regarded as having a particularly permissive attitude (Mussati, 1995).

The system of government regulation of retailing in Germany illustrates the application of the themes of (a) creating a 'level playing field' for competition among retailers and particularly different categories of retailer, (b) protecting consumers, (c) preventing socially adverse spatial development of retailing, (d) protecting retailing employees, and (e) protecting the environment. Thus, smaller scale, and possibly more specialist, retailers are protected from loss-leader selling by their larger, diversified rivals; and land-use planning restrictions together with legislation on shop opening hours also offer some protection to smaller German retailers. This protection is further advanced by strict controls on pricing of purchases of larger quantities of retail goods, which would probably be a feature of larger scale retailers. German retail consumers are offered specific protection in purchases through the Internet, and are also protected from misleading advertising. The German *Baunutzungsverordnung* (Regulations on the use of buildings) has operated strictly to control the emergence of large-scale retail businesses outwith city centres; legislation on shop opening, or rather closing, hours is designed in part to protect retail employees; and the *Verpackungsverordnung* (packaging regulation) is designed to achieve an environmentally friendly reuse of such retail materials.

The more explicitly interventionist approach in Spain – itself the product in part of a later 'catching up' in retail development that is perceived as being required in that economy – dates nonetheless from the establishment of the Transport and Supply Bureau (CAT) in 1936; Operation Supermarket in 1959; the MERCASA central markets for perishable food distribution which are responsible for the retail municipal markets, more than four-fifths of which are conducted by the local municipality; the establishment in 1973 of the Retail Reform Institute (IRESCO) and the transfer a decade later of its functions to the Autonomous Regions; and the range of General and Specific Programmes undertaken respectively by the Department of Interior Commerce and the Spanish Autonomous Regions for the benefit of retail organizations (see Table 6.16).

Italy and Greece have certainly in the past been characterized by perhaps the most comprehensive systems of government control over retailing activities in terms of both retail structures and competitive behaviour. In the case of the former economy, it was, interestingly, not until 1971 that it was considered necessary to introduce any legislation of this type; for until then the essentially small-scale and local Italian retailers existed unthreatened by competition from larger scale organizations, domestic or international. In summary, the 1971 legislation controlled entry into the sector, set down planned retail space requirements both in total and with respect to particular merchandise categories, and established a requirement for permission for either the enlargement of stores or changes of retail merchandise category of operation. Experience of the operation of this system provides evidence of a fine mixture of flexibility and arbitrariness. The implementation of the 1971 law was flexible in that, for example, in different geographical areas the legislation could be more or less strictly implemented having regard to the local economic and social circumstances and the extent of such adverse impacts of the introduction of large-scale retailing. However, one senses a degree of arbitrariness in the differential impact of the legislation in the area of store development as between local entrepreneurs and retail buying groups and voluntary chains on the one hand and large-scale, national multiple-shop food retailers on the other. Much more so than is the case with other EU economies, Italian legislation on retailing from 1971 had a socio-political dimension to it that went far beyond that of, say, the influence of the retailer *Mittelstandsbewegung* in Germany. The 1970s was a decade of considerable political and social unrest in Italy, culminating perhaps in the kidnap and assassination by the Red Brigades of the Prime Minister Sr. Aldo Moro in 1978 (Mantle, 1999: chapters 3, 4); and the legislation discussed above has to be seen in this particular context as an attempt to maintain in place the small-scale retailer stratum as an element of stability in Italian society. By the 1980s, however, this legislation became less concerned with the preservation of the role of small retailers *per se* and more with land-use planning aspects such as retail location and shopping-centre development. This whole framework of legislation was considerably relaxed in 1998, although it remains quite restrictive; but it is yet too early to judge the impact of this change.

In Greece there was in place by the 1960s a system of government control of the retail sector which limited the number of shop-opening hours to fifty per week, restricted the sale of fresh bread, meat and fish to specialist outlets, enforced price controls on food and other convenience goods, and in effect prohibited the employment of part-time workers. Again later than similar developments in other EU economies, and moreover partly as a result of changes in political leadership in the country and also the coming of the Single European

Market from 1 January 1993, Greece experienced a significant liberalization of controls over its retail sector along with other parts of the economy in 1991. Controls in each of the above four areas were largely abolished, and this coincided with an upsurge in an interest in the Greek economy by internationalizing retailers; and the result of this was the significant modernization of the Greek retailing economy in the 1990s which was highlighted in Chapter 4.

The most obvious areas of government intervention over competition are controls of market structures and in the area of behaviours such as pricing and shop opening hours. Sometimes, as in the case of the United Kingdom, the impact of the ending of price controls such as r.p.m. has been drawn out, has been brought about over a period of time essentially as a result of market forces in the sector, and has not resulted in any obvious distinguishable long-term effects. On the other hand, in the case of Greece, the lifting of retail price controls in the early 1990s had a particularly dramatic effect. This led to the 'price wars' of 1991–1992, that were especially welcomed by consumers. This increased competition stimulated retailers particularly in the food/grocery trade to seek economies of scale. Hypermarkets were introduced – often by incoming international retail organizations; and the result of these changes was a structural polarization of this sector between a handful of large-scale organizations and a reducing number of single-outlet retailers. In France, there has been a lengthy history – leading up to the Galland Law of 1997 and the New Economic Regulations of 2001 – regarding retailer competition and retailer–supplier relations. Retailer sales of goods at a loss are prohibited, and strict controls are exercised over trade terms offered by manufacturers to large retailers (what in a UK context would be referred to as price discrimination). But the combined effect of these regulations appears to have been a blunting of retail price competition, and indeed even a tendency towards increased retail prices both of national brands and private label products. French retailer profitability thus appears to have increased in the context of these regulations, and consumers have been deprived of the opportunities of experiencing lower-cost retail formulae combined with reduced prices.

Particularly interesting are government regulations relating to supplier trade terms available to large-scale retailers, retailer pricing policies and consumer prices. As we saw in Chapter 7, successive inquiries into this aspect of UK retailer behaviour have led to few firm conclusions and little practical action. In Germany, retailers are prevented from selling at below cost, and clear mechanisms are in place to determine the relevant cost data. But consumers have had to relinquish considerable potential retail price reductions as a result of this; and such regulations appear undoubtedly to have restricted the freedom of consumers to choose between a higher cost 'full retail service' shopping experience and the 'deep discount' form of retailing. As we saw above, in France, the Galland Law of 1997 was designed to introduce more transparency into manufacturer–retailer trade price relations; but the analysis suggests that, while this may have provided some protection to smaller scale manufacturers and retailers, consumers have suffered in terms of a significant reduction in retailer price competition at least on national brands.

Government land-use planning

The objectives of government intervention in the location of retailing are less easily summarized, and are also less susceptible to being based upon some underlying welfare theory than is the case with competition policy. Retail location, and government intervention in this sphere, involves issues of efficiency, of competition and consumer convenience, of equity, and of the maintenance of the environment and an overall balance of development (see Guy, 1998). Thus, there is a desire to capitalize upon more 'efficient' forms of retail provision such as scale-efficient supermarkets and retail outlets for bulky comparison goods. Furthermore, planners need to ensure that (mobile) consumers have access to a competitive range of such retailers, and this may be extended to the idea of meeting consumer convenience in providing for large-scale shopping facilities combining both food and non-food shopping and associated recreation in the form of superstores or hypermarkets and regional shopping centres. On the other hand, considerations of equity require that planners ensure access to a range of shopping for poorer, older and less affluent consumers. Environmental concerns relate both to the avoidance of undue use of 'green belt' land for retailing developments, and also the maintenance of the viability of city-centre locations for shopping and for potential social and cultural use for employers and employees, for residents and for tourists.

Land-use planning and its impact upon retailing is a common feature of EU economies. Writing in the mid-1990s, Davies' view was that while there was much that was different across Western Europe in this area, 'there are arguably more similarities in the directions of new policy formulation than at any time since the 1960s' (Davies, 1995: xv). The same author did, however, characterize land-use controls across EU economies as being of different degrees of severity, and was able to identify patterns of development of these over the last four decades of the twentieth century. Thus, while in the 1960s there was a general consensus among EU economies in the adoption of land-use planning to maintain the status quo of retail development, there were clear divergences among these countries in the 1970s. During this decade, Belgium, France and West Germany relaxed their controls in this respect in order to allow in the case of the former two economies for the development of the hypermarket, and in the case of West Germany to permit the growth of out-of-town shopping generally. However, by the 1980s, these three countries had significantly reversed their earlier relaxed polices and tightened control on large-scale, out-of-town shopping provision. At the same time, a number of smaller and Mediterranean European countries such as Austria, Ireland, Greece, Italy and Portugal and Spain were experiencing for the first time the emergence of large-scale retailing developments, often imported from those countries that had experienced rapid domestic growth of such developments in the previous decade. There was an understandable concern regarding the potential adverse effects of these; and thus the United Kingdom stood almost alone during the 1980s in its policy described by Davies as 'the virtual abandonment of any retail planning' (Davies, 1995: xvii). This author's perceived greater consensus in retail planning approaches across the individual EU economies in the 1990s is characterized by a general feeling of 'caution and restraint': a desire by national governments to play a greater role in the structural and spacial development of the retail sector of the economy, but a realization at the same time that there are ultimately limitations on what can be achieved in this respect, and a recognition that retailing provision has to be responsive to advances in technology and merchandising and to consumer wants. The result of the interaction of retail consumer preferences, the strategies of individual retailers and of investors in large-scale retail developments, and of both national and local planning authorities across the European Union is that there are some differences in the balance of city-centre and decentralized retailing. Among those countries covered in this study, France, Germany and the United Kingdom have higher levels of retail decentralization than, for example, Italy and Spain. But, as in other aspects covered by this study, it is difficult to know how much of each of these different situations to ascribe to the impact of government control and how much to the working out of consumer preferences (see Guy, 1998: 973–7).

In respect of EU economies covered in this study, in countries such as France and Germany, the systems of government intervention in the retail sector could be described as strong, and they have had a clear impact upon both the geography of retailing and its market structures and competition. In France, for example, such legislation even led to a more recent revival of city-centre department store retailing. In the United Kingdom, while the government has had some effect on the location of retailing through land-use planning legislation, the overall impact has been limited, and such controls have not held back the emergence of large-scale retailers. In other countries such as Greece, the government has evidenced little interest in the retail sector of the economy, and there is no particular tradition of government land-use planning restrictions applied to retailing other than a general requirement to keep within local government physical infrastructure planning. This *laissez-faire* attitude appears to have been at least partially abandoned in 1995 in order to afford traditional retailers some protection against the incursions of supermarket operators. However, such restrictions on supermarket development did not apply to cities of over 100,000 inhabitants, and in general edge- or out-of-town hypermarkets appear to have been able to develop in an unrestricted manner sofar as retail planning requirements are concerned. However, the small scale and fragmented pattern of land and property ownership in Greece – themselves a legacy of the aftermath of the war between Greece and Turkey 1921–1922 and also the traditional Greek attachment to family land ownership – have had some effect in holding back new, large-scale forms of retailing. These factors may be just as important in this area as the more recently introduced controls on large-scale supermarket developments in medium-sized towns intended to protect smaller-scale retailers from such competition.

The impact of these government interventions appears to have varied considerably among the EU economies. As we have seen, the opinion of some regarding the impact of land-use planning legislation in the United Kingdom has been modest, with such legislation fitting in largely with the location strategies of the major grocery supermarket retail organizations. In Germany, the land-use planning restrictions on large-scale, out-of-town retail developments have not been entirely effective sofar as the increased market share of multiple-shop retail organizations is concerned (see Howe, 1997), and the conflict between regulations on shop opening hours and the desire by consumers for convenience in this respect has led to the slightly ludicrous phenomenon of the petrol forecourt shop with no petrol sales.

However, one of the problems with legislation of this type is not simply that it may have only a limited impact in terms of its original intentions but also that it may have wider unforeseen effects, some of which may not be wholly desirable. Thus, for example, the 1973 Royer Law in France restricting large-scale store openings did not prevent the food market share of supermarkets rising from 13.6 per cent in 1970 to 21.8 in 1980. This legislation, and the Raffarin Law of 1996, had somewhat more of an impact in slowing down hypermarket openings over a shorter period in the mid-1990s, although it did not prevent their subsequent advance. However, in his detailed analysis of the impact of the Royer Law, Burt (1984) goes further and points out that there had been some decline in French hypermarket openings in 1971 *prior* to this legislation; that some part of the slowing down of such openings in 1974 and 1975 might have been due to the impact of the 1973 oil crisis; that the subsequent reduction in the average size of new hypermarkets may have been the result of the maturing of the hypermarket retail format and its expansion into smaller towns; that there was in any case a continued growth of hypermarket openings in the years following the Royer Law, particularly on the part of those 'grandes surface' retail organizations which traded primarily through hypermarkets and against whom the Law had been primarily directed; and that underlying economic and social factors were at work, all of which may have contributed to the share of total French retail sales accounted for by hypermarkets doubling from 6 per cent in 1972 to 12 per cent a decade later. This particular example simply highlights how fraught *ex post* analysis of the impact of such legislation can be.

With regard to wider, and perhaps unintended, effects of such legislation, one outcome of the Royer Law and its successors was the burst of internationalization of French food retailing in the 1980s as the largest organizations in this sector experienced legislation-related frustration in expanding at home (see Burt, 1986, on the case of Carrefour), and the amalgamations of the late 1990s, such as the merger of Carrefour and Promodès in 1999, which were also encouraged by the difficulties of large-scale organic expansion. Thus, there appears in this instance to be a need to balance any protection offered by such legislation to smaller scale retailers against the market concentration effects and the adverse impact of these upon consumers. Paradoxically, however, this French legislation on large-scale store openings did have the effect of encouraging the initial entry of the German hard-discount retailers in the 1980s, operating originally through relatively small-scale outlets. These too, however, experienced subsequent difficulties in expanding through larger scale outlets as a result of the Royer and Raffarin Laws.

Conclusions

The subtitle of this study implied, perhaps too boldly, that it would be able to arrive at firm conclusions on the matters of competition and efficiency in retailing across a number of economies in the European Union. This has not been entirely possible in a formal sense. In the first instance, and at a level of detail, valid and reliable measures of, for example, retailer productivity and profitability and of consumer satisfaction are not available. Indeed, as we argued in the first part of this final chapter, the whole issue of retailer productivity and the measurement of company profitability are extremely difficult concepts on the basis of which to arrive at firm conclusions on company performance or consumer welfare. More broadly, it is not clear, for example, that any purely economic analysis would have allowed us to arrive at conclusions in this area.

Writing almost half a century ago, Jack Downie justified his meagre one and a half pages of conclusions at the end of *The Competitive Process* by a reference to Keynes' famous remark on economics being an 'apparatus of the mind', and a suggestion that 'it is because economics is as he [Keynes] described it that few books on economic subjects have a very lengthy chapter on conclusions' (Downie, 1958: 194). However, Downie's remarks would now perhaps be interpreted as belonging to a school of economics which overemphasized the significance of market structures in arriving at conclusions on likely consumer welfare (see High, 2001: Introduction). Today the emphasis among economists is upon the *process* of competition in markets; and this, it is argued, has 'led professional opinion away from ... emphasizing the role of perfect competition in achieving societal economic efficiency towards the current recognition of the greater relevance of the dynamic process of competition for an understanding of the achievements of free markets' (Kirzner, 2000: 11). Thus, even almost twenty years prior to Downie's remark, economic analysis was moving away from an insistence that only formally 'perfectly' structured markets could lead to the best possible outcomes for consumers; and the work since then on 'workable' competition has led on to the practical concept of 'contestable' markets as a means of arriving at conclusions on the extent to which markets are serving the interests of consumers (see Clark, 1940; Baumol *et al.*, 1982). Interestingly, the present Director General of the UK Office of Fair Trading appears to believe very much in the concept of competition as a process rather than a purely theoretically desirable state. Hence perhaps his earlier remark as an Oxford University academic that 'competition seems very well in practice, but it is not so clear how it works in theory' (Vickers, 1995: 1).

'Competition', as one recent author puts it, 'is the cornerstone for a market economy to achieve maximum welfare for the great majority of people' (Neumann, 2001: 189); and the developments in the economics literature emphasized above allow us to look at markets – including retail markets – in an informed but more informal manner in order to answer our question regarding consumers, 'Are they being served?'. Certainly, European retail markets present a dynamic picture. Retail structures, in terms of the balance of different categories and forms of retailer, vary quite considerably among the EU economies covered in this study in a way that suggests a responsiveness to national consumer preferences. Despite acknowledged oligopolies in retail sectors such as grocery supermarkets, retailing is still very significantly a small- to medium-sized firm part of most economies; individual, local decision-making units in the form of shops are, in terms of employment per outlet, small scale; and at the organizational level, self-employment remains a strong characteristic of retailing in many individual economies. This suggests not only low barriers to entry into such markets but also a relative lack of market power possessed by individual firms, and also opportunities to cater for the particular needs of specific groups of consumers. As the 1998 European Commission study pointed out (European Commission, 1998: 19), most retailers focus considerable energies on cost-reduction strategies; and the competitiveness of the European retailing markets has been heightened both by 'intertype' competition (Palamountain, 1955) in the form, for example, of the hard-discount groups in grocery retailing competing with more established retail formats in this sector, and the diversification of grocery supermarkets into a range of non-food merchandise, particularly clothing. Furthermore, not only are intra-economy barriers to entry low for most retail sectors, but the international mobility of large-scale retailers indicates that the same conditions operate at an inter-economy level, often in markets that are characterized at a national level by fairly high levels of market concentration.

Within this context, the retail sector in each of the economies covered by this study have been subject to a quite significant level of government intervention, particularly with regard to market structures, competitor behaviour and the geographical location of activities. Although the form, comprehensiveness and pace of change of such intervention have varied among the EU economies, it has generally been justified on the bases of maintaining 'fair' competition in retail markets, offering some 'adjustment' protection to smaller scale retailers during periods characterized by the emergence of large-scale competitors, and ensuring an appropriate geographical layout of retailing complementary to other land uses. Such intervention appears to have been largely effective, although to what extent cannot be fully judged without making some assumptions as to what would have happened in its absence. There have also occasionally been unforeseen side-effects. Ultimately, however, major changes in the structure of retail markets, in the nature of competition in these, and their geographical location have been slowed down rather than halted; and the forces of consumer choice and retailer strategies and competition, including internationalization, have proved resilient. The advantages of such interventions are, nonetheless, that they have been used to meet particular national needs with regard to the stage of development of the retail sector of each economy, they have allowed individual governments to choose the direction and pace of change in retailing, and, by being carried out in a relatively public manner, they have exposed the various retail sectors to informed debate. To these extents, intervention by national governments can be seen as a very significant and worthwhile policy area in respect of what continues to be a vitally important part of each economy.

References

Albæk, S. *et al.* (1998) 'The Danish Competition Act and barriers to entry', in Martin, S. (ed.), *Competition Policies in Europe*, Elsevier, Amsterdam, pp. 75–104.

Ball, R. and Smith, C. W. (eds) (1992) *The Economics of Accounting Policy Choice*, McGraw-Hill, New York.

Baumol, W. J., Panzar, J. C. and Willig, R. D. (1982) *Contestable Markets and the Theory of Industry Structure*, Harcourt Brace Jovanovich, New York.

Bennison, D. and Gardner, H. (1995) 'The internationalisation of limited line discount grocery operations', in McGoldrick, P. J. and Davies, G. (eds), *International Retailing: Trends and Strategies*, Pitman, London, pp. 191–206.

Bevan, J. (2001) *The Rise and Fall of Marks & Spencer*, Profile Books, London.

Burt, S. (1984) 'Hypermarkets in France: has the Loi Royer had any effect?', *Retail & Distribution Management*, January–February, pp. 16–19.

Burt, S. (1986) 'The Carrefour Group – the first 25 years', *International Journal of Retailing*, 1(3): 55–78.

Burt, S. (1991) 'Trends in the internationalization of grocery retailing: the European experience', *The International Review of Retail, Distribution and Consumer Research*, 1(4): 487–515.

Burt, S. and Sparks, L. (1994) 'Structural change in grocery retailing in Great Britain: a discount orientation?', *International Review of Retail, Distribution and Consumer Research*, 4(2): 195–217.

Burt, S. and Sparks, L. (1997) 'Performance in food retailing: a cross-national consideration and comparison on retail margins', *British Journal of Management*, 8(2): 133–50.

Clark, J. M. (1940) 'Toward a concept of workable competition', *American Economic Review*, 30(2): 241–56.

Commission of the European Communities (1993) *Retailing in the European Single Market 1993*, European Commission, Brussels.

Commission of the European Communities (1997) *Green Paper on Vertical Restraints in EC Competition Policy*, European Commission, Brussels.

Corstjens, J., Corstjens, M. and Lal, R. (1995) 'Retail competition in the fast-moving consumer goods industry: the case of France and the UK', *European Management Journal*, 13(4): 363–73.

Cotter, J. and Hutchinson, R. W. (1999) 'The impact of accounting reporting techniques on earnings enhancement in the UK retailing sector', *The International Review of Retail, Distribution and Consumer Research*, 9(2): 147–62.

Davies, R. L. (ed.) (1995) *Retail Planning Policies in Western Europe*, Routledge, London.

Davies, G. and Whitehead, M. (1995) 'The Legislative environment as a measure of attractiveness for internationalisation' in McGoldrick, P. J. and Davies, G. (eds), *International Retailing: Trends and Strategies*, Pitman, London, pp. 117–30.

Dawson, J. (1993) 'The internationalization of retailing', in Bromley, R. D. F. and Thomas, C. J. (eds), *Retail Change*, UCL Press, London.

Dawson, J. (2000a) 'Viewpoint: retailer power, manufacturer power, competition and some questions of economic analysis', *International Journal of Retail & Distribution Management*, 28(1): 5–8.

Dawson, J. (2000b) 'Retailing at century end: some challenges for management and research', *The International Review of Retail, Distribution and Consumer Research*, 10(2): 119–48.

Dobson, P. W. and Waterson, M. (1996) *Vertical Restraints and Competition Policy*, Office of Fair Trading Research Paper 12, OFT, London.

Downie, J. (1958) *The Competitive Process*, Duckworth, London.

European Commission (1998) *Retailing in the European Economic Area 1997*, European Commission, Brussels.

Ferner, A. (2000) 'The embeddedness of US multinational companies in the US business system: implications for HR/IR', *De Montfort University School of Business Occasional Paper*.

Fulop, C. (1966) *Competition for Consumers*, Allen & Unwin, London.

Grant, R. M. (1987) 'Manufacturer–retailer relations: the shifting balance of power', in Johnson, G. (ed.), *Business Strategy and Retailing*, Wiley, Chichester.

Guy, C. M. (1998) 'Controlling new retail spaces: the impress of planning policies in Western Europe', *Urban Studies*, 35(5–6): 953–79.

High, J. (ed.) (2001) *Competition*, Edward Elgar, Cheltenham, UK.

Hollingsworth, J. R. and Boyer, R. (eds) (1997) *Contemporary Capitalism: The Embeddedness of Institutions*, Cambridge University Press, Cambridge.

Howe, W. S. (1997) 'Nations of shopkeepers: the United Kingdom and Germany', in Groner, U. *et al.* (eds), *Wirtschaftswissenschaft: Anwendungsorientierte Forschug an der Schwelle des 21. Jahrunderts*, R.v. Decker, Heidelberg, pp. 251–62.

Howe, W. S. (1998) 'Conceptual, interpretative and practical issues in the use of retailer sales-margin profitability data' in Neely, A. D. and Waggoner, D. B. (eds), *Performance Measurement – Theory and Practice*, vol. II, The Judge Institute of Management Studies, Cambridge, pp. 483–90.

Kirzner, I. (2000) 'Competition and the market process: some doctrinal milestones', in Krafft, J. (ed.), *The Process of Competition*, Edward Elgar, Cheltenham, UK.

Laudati, L. L. (1998) 'Impact of Community Competition Law on Member State Competition Law', in Martin, S. (ed.), *Competition Policies in Europe*, Elsevier, Amsterdam, pp. 381–410.

London Economics (1995) *The Grocery Retailing Revolution*, London Economics, London.

Mantle, J. (1999) *Benetton: The Family, the Business and the Brand*, Little, Brown & Co., London.

McGoldrick, P. J. (1995) 'Introduction to international retailing', in McGoldrick, P. J. and Davies, G. (eds), *International Retailing: Trends and Strategies*, Pitman, London.

Mussati, G. (ed.) (1995) *Mergers, Markets and Public Policy*, Kluwer, Dordrecht.

Neumann, M. (2001) *Competition Policy: History, Theory and Practice*, Edward Elgar, Cheltenham, UK.

Palamountain, J. C. (1955) *The Politics of Distribution*, Harvard University Press, Cambridge, MA.

Pellegrini, L. (1989) 'Consumers' behaviour and producer–distributor relationships in convenience goods markets', in Pellegrini, L. and Reddy, S. K. (eds) *Retail and Marketing Channels – Economic and Marketing Perspectives on Producer–Distributor Relationships*, Routledge, London.

Powell, D. (1991) *Counter Revolution: The Tesco Story*, Grafton Books, London.

Robertet, E. (1997) 'How social change affects retail habits: a typology of the European population', *European Retail Digest*, Winter, pp. 4–14.

Salmon, W. J. and Tordjman, A. (1989) 'The internationalisation of retailing', *International Journal of Retailing*, 4(2): 3–16.

Scherer, F. M. (2000) *Competition Policy, Domestic and International*, Edward Elgar, Cheltenham, UK.

Smith, A. D. and Hitchins, D. M. W. N. (1985) *Productivity in the Distributive Trades: A Comparison of Britain, America and Germany*, Cambridge University Press, Cambridge.

Sparks, L. (1990) 'Spatial-structural relationships in retail corporate growth: a case-study of Kwik Save Group PLC', *The Service Industries Journal*, 10(1): 25–84.

Tordjman, A. (1994) 'European retailing: convergences, differences and perspectives', *International Journal of Retail and Distribution Management*, 22(5): 3–19.

Tordjman, A. (1995) 'European retailing: convergences, differences and perspectives', in McGoldrick, P. J. and Davies, G. (eds), *International Retailing: Trends and Strategies*, Pitman, London, pp. 18–50.

Treadgold, A. D. and Davies, R. L. (1988) *The Internationalisation of Retailing*, Longman/Oxford Institute of Retail Management, Harlow.

UK Department of Trade and Industry (1996) *Tackling Cartels and the Abuse of Market Power: A Consultation Document*, HMSO, London.

Vickers, J. S. (1995) 'Concepts of competition', *Oxford Economic Papers*, 47: 1–23.

Wrigley, N. (1994) 'After the store wars: towards a new era of competition in UK food retailing?', *Journal of Retail and Consumer Services*, 1: 5–20.

Yamey, B. S. (ed.) (1966) *Resale Price Maintenance*, Weidenfeld & Nicolson, London.

Index

218   *Index*

Germany (*Continued*)
format structure 62–7; store opening
hours 74; superstores 65; technological
environment 61; trade organization
committees 57; urban-entertainment
centres (UECs) 67; UWG (Law against
Unfair Competition) 72
global impact of e-commerce 53
globalization 2, 52, 129
global retailers 19
governments: competition policy 181;
control of retailing 106; intervention
203, 210; land-use planning 206–8;
legislation in retail sector 183; policies
99, 202–8; in retail planning 179;
role of 3
Greece 106, 193–5, 207; *antiparochi* 97;
Census of Commerce records 85;
channels of distribution 84, 86, 90; City
Planning Area 95; Civil War 81–2;
economy 201; EEC, accession to 82;
EPOS 91; equity financing 85, 100;
food/grocery sector since 1990 88–91;
foreign retailers 92; franchising of
specialist retailers 93; GDP 82;
geographical and historical features 81,
84; globalization and information
technology, influences of 98;
government control of retail sector,
system of 204–5; government, role of
94; 'green field' sites 95; harmonization
programme 87; hypermarket format
88–9; internationalization activities 87;
kiosk 94; land and property 96–7;
liberalization of market 88; liberalization
of regulation 99; Market Police 85;
Ministry for Planning, Settlement and
the Environment 94; modern retail
management 91; modern system of
multiple-shop retail enterprises 81;
National Statistical Service of Greece
(NSSG) 83, 88, 99; New Democracy
party 87; new large formats,
introduction of 92; political situation
100; refugees from Turkey 82, 97;
retailer–supplier relationships 89–90;
retailing 1950–1990 83–7; retail location
and planning 94–6; retail outlets 83;
retail revolution 87–93; Spata, airport at
96; specialist chains 93–4; supermarkets,
growth of 89; ties of family and kinship
82; Town Planning Service 94–5;
traditional retailing 81
'green belt' land 206

greenfield: shopping centres 74; sites 66
grey market 4
grocery: market share of discount chains
29; maturity of 89; and provisions trade
156; retail 14–15, 20; self-service 198;
supermarket 59, 173; superstores 176;
trade 10
gross domestic product (GDP) 1
gross margin data 190
Gruppo Coin 121, 198
guild structure in retailing and
wholesaling 127
Guy, C.M. 178

hard discount stores 30
Harrods 156
Harvey Nichols 156
Home & Colonial Stores 157
home delivery services 78
household consumption 103
hypermarket 28, 37, 40, 42, 50, 108–9,
114, 116, 123, 128, 196, 199;
development 12, 16–17; maturity
stage 41

Ikea 2, 199
'importing' and 'exporting' retail
organizations 199
import-wholesalers 84
independent retail organizations
158, 161
individual-country level retailing 197
individual economies and governments 4
individual entrepreneurship 85
individual retailers 1, 199
information and communication
technologies 61
inheritance practice 97
innovative fields 78
Insee 25–6
integrated commercial information
systems 77
integrated foreign groups 110
Intermarché 42, 197
international embargo 126
international food retail operations 199
internationalisation of retailing 2–3;
economic 'push' and 'pull' models 201;
waves 67
'internationality' of retailing 2; literature 2
inter-type competition 116–17
intra-type competition 116–17, 147
inventory policies 140
Ireland 196, 206